To Gordon .....

100 Scotsman Walks

also known as the Mountain Lamb

With best wishes,

Robin

September 2011.

100 Scotsman Walks

Robin Howie

Whittles Publishing

Published by
Whittles Publishing Ltd.,
Dunbeath,
Caithness, KW6 6EG,
Scotland, UK

www.whittlespublishing.com

first published in *The Scotsman*

Disclaimer

The author has made every effort to ensure that the information contained in these 100 Walks, written over some ten years, has been brought up to date. However, there is always constant change, whether to paths, forestation or places of refreshment. Accordingly the author would welcome information of any discrepancies and/or comments from readers.

ISBN 978-184995-031-2

Printed in Poland

Contents

Acknowledgements

This book would not have achieved fruition without the assistance and co-operation of so many friends and colleagues. From the very start Margaret has been of constant support. When I was first approached by *The Scotsman* over 10 years ago to write a weekly column on the joys of hillwalking, her encouragement helped to persuade me that doing and writing were not mutually exclusive. That approach came from Adrian Morgan (the then outdoors editor), and his support in those early days for this journalistic neophyte was always appreciated. I am also grateful to Morag for her earlier contributions, typing and dealing with my Gaelic queries.

I have been blessed with the number of friends who have accompanied me over decades of climbing and/or lower-level walks – frequently in bad weather. My grateful thanks go to this mostly eccentric group, bound by a love of the great outdoors. Those eccentrics identified in this book have my particular thanks. I refer to Jimbo, Rhona, Peter and Dave, as well as the nameless Mountain Maid, Mountain Hare and Mountain Lamb.

My thanks go to *The Scotsman* staff to whom nowadays I submit copy: Alison Gray and Mark Kirkham. Then there is my superb team of proof-readers: The Mountain Maid and Hare; Jimbo; and my sister, Frances. Any errors or omissions are of course solely my responsibility. And finally my thanks go to Keith Whittles for his faith in this publication. He and his staff have also been a pleasure to work with.

Introduction

For over ten years Robin Howie's popular column *Walk of the Week* has appeared in *The Scotsman* every Saturday. Though Robin is very well-known in Scottish hill-walking circles, his *100 Scotsman Walks* is a collection of those (mostly) shorter lower-level walks – from hill to glen to riverside – that will appeal to the whole family and those less sure of venturing to the high tops. Conveniently arranged within shires with a location map, each walk has a key guide to all the important facts that will maximise your enjoyment: map; start point; distance; terrain; duration of walk; height to be climbed; and the all-important recommended refreshment point. It will be a delight for active walkers, the would-be explorer or the armchair enthusiast ... a book for the whole family, young or old ... a book in fact for everyone.

The author heading for the hills

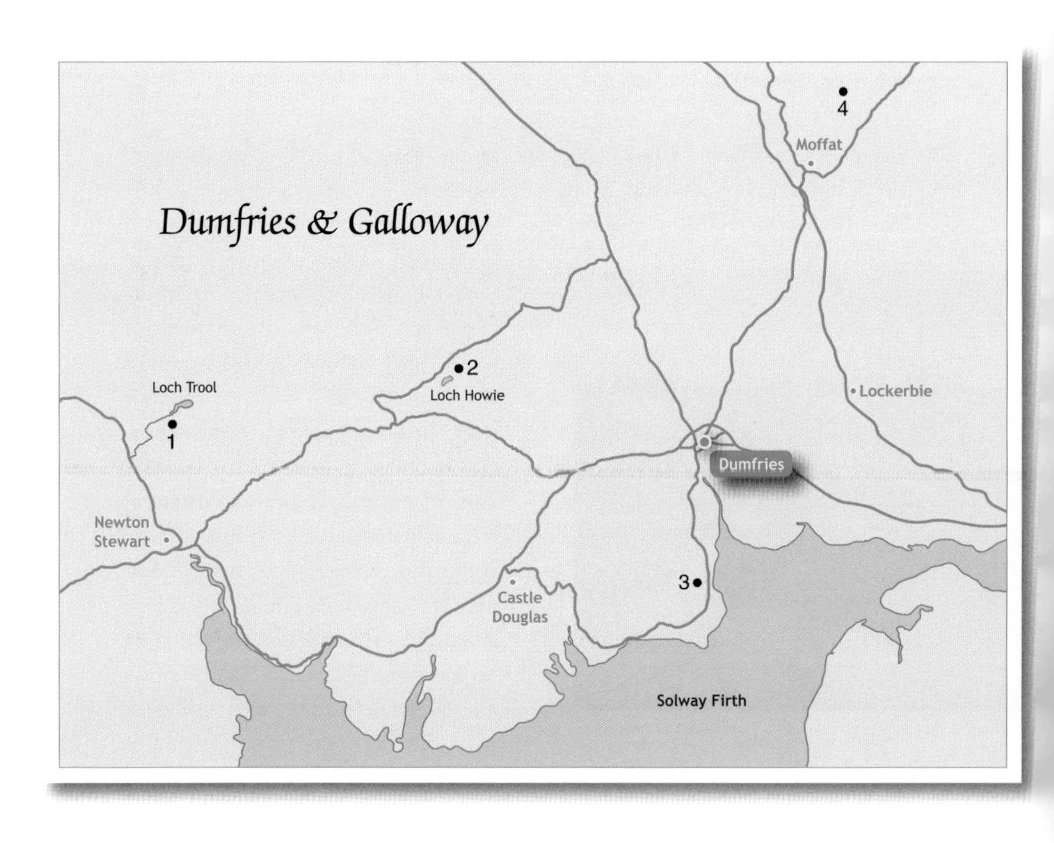
Dumfries & Galloway
4
Moffat
2
Loch Trool
Loch Howie
Lockerbie
1
Dumfries
Newton
Stewart
3
Castle
Douglas
Solway Firth

Dumfries & Galloway

01 Loch Trool – a sheltered walk for a stormy day

FACTFILE

Map Ordnance Survey map 77, Dalmellington & New Galloway
Distance 6 miles
Height 200m
Terrain well made paths and tracks, with one mile on tarmac
Start point car park at west end of loch, map ref 397791
Time 2 to 3 hours
Nearest village Glentrool
Recommended refreshment spot Glentrool Visitor Centre tearoom and shop, open from mid-March

Glen Trool – in the heart of the extensive Galloway Forest Park – has a myriad of waymarked trails, ideal for a sheltered stroll on a storm tossed day. Early in February, Margaret and I were staying at Castle Douglas for a few days. Margaret was there as part of a bird watching group, leaving me to explore the area. Alas, we were there in the mid of nasty weather: gale force winds and blizzards on the high tops, such that I had to opt for more sheltered walks. One such walk took me to Loch Howie (but more of that another time) and one led me to a circuit of Loch Trool.

The circuit of less than six miles may take longer than anticipated. The route – with apparently little height gain – is in fact gently undulating, giving an overall climb of some 200m. In addition, time will undoubtedly be spent in admiring the views and musing on the historic aspect of Robert the Bruce and the Battle of Loch Trool.

From the A714 (the Girvan to Newton Stewart road), some eight miles north of the latter, turn off for Glentrool Village (both village and Glen Trool are signposted). Continue east past the visitor centre, by the east bank of the Water of Minnoch, and almost two miles later look out for a road to the right, signposted Loch Trool Trail. Go down that road a short distance to a parking area by the concrete bridge over the Water of Trool.

Follow the green waymarkers (Loch Trool Forest Trail) and walk upstream on the west bank of the Water of Trool. At first there is no sight of the loch, then suddenly it appears: tranquil water amid a rough setting. The path enters woodland and when it heads north to the Glen Trool road, be alert to one waymarker that is not too obvious at first. The path becomes a grassy track and the road is soon reached.

The watching stag

The road continues for one mile on the north side of the loch, climbing steadily round the rhododendron-covered grounds of Glen Trool Lodge, with gradually emerging views of the loch. At the road end is Bruce's Stone – a large granite boulder and an impressive viewpoint down the length of the loch. Unveiled in June 1929 it is 'in loyal remembrance of Robert the Bruce, King of Scots, whose victory in this glen over an English force in March 1307 opened the campaign of independence which he brought to a decisive close at Bannockburn on 24 June 1314'.

At the road end a path goes north for four miles to the highest hill in Scotland's south – Merrick, a Corbett at 843m. However stay with what is now a gravel track to descend east past Buchan, heading for Glenhead. In curving round the head of the loch, the route goes past the Buchan and Glenhead Woods – stunning oak woodland claimed to be one of the least spoilt in Scotland and a Site of Special Scientific Interest with many species of birds and mammals, including deer and feral goats.

Cross the stone arched bridge over the gorge of the Buchan Burn, ignoring the sign for Gairland Burn and Loch Valley. The track goes through the open wooded flat ground at the head of the loch, crossing a wooden bridge over the tumbling waters of the Gairland Burn. Before reaching Glenhead, be alert to a green post (there is also an extra sign for the Forest Walk) where the path leaves the track on a charming stroll by the Glenhead Burn.

Cross the wooden bridge over the Glenhead Burn to join the Southern Upland Way. The path (and Way) climbs slightly then heads west by the southern shores of the loch: a lovely undulating woodland walk arguably more attractive than the north side. Pass a notice board that gives more details of the Battle of Glentrool: a successful ambush aided by an avalanche of boulders.

The final stage of the walk reaches Caldons campsite, now disused. A short distance south of the bridge over the Water of Trool is a memorial in the woods – the Martyr's Tomb, commemorating six Covenanters who were surprised at prayer and immediately shot. The Glentrool visitor centre is not open until late March, but that should not stop you from going now to Loch Trool, perhaps for a sheltered walk on a stormy day. I was lucky on my day – well clad certainly but escaping the rain and snow.

02 Loch Howie and a return to New Galloway

FACTFILE

Map Ordnance Survey map 77, Dalmellington & New Galloway
Distance 5 miles
Height 150m
Terrain well made forest tracks
Start point from the A702 at map ref 690839, on the track signposted Half Mark Forest.
Time 2 to 3 hours
Nearest town St John's Town of Dalry
Recommended refreshment spot St John's Town of Dalry or New Galloway

My 1979 Ordnance Survey map 77 (the First Series 1:50,000) was bought in the early 1980s with a view to climbing the Galloway Corbetts. I happened to be pouring over the whole of the map – reading it as others would a book or music manuscript – when my eye noticed a small stretch of water just off the A702 called Loch Howie. Understandably, my curiosity was immediately aroused. Less than one mile long the loch lies amid a forest of some three square miles. The curious thing was that the map showed only one track going from the road, well south of the loch leading towards Blackcraig Hill at the southern end of the forest. The map did show one path entering the forest from the south, running northwest from a place called Halfmark and ending at Laggan by the east end of the loch. It did not strike me at the time that there would surely be more tracks to service such a large area. I vowed to go to the loch one day, presumably with the Laggan path being the easiest approach. Well this year, some 25 years later, I made it.

Almost on a whim, I decided to buy an up-to-date map, which was just as well for otherwise I would have been thoroughly confused. I glanced at the forest surrounding Loch Howie: what a difference! The track of old and the Halfmark path were no more, swallowed up by new plantings. The forest now extends slightly north of the loch, but otherwise is much the same size, though an intricate pattern of tracks is now shown – tracks that make the way to Loch Howie both easy and obvious.

So far my investigations into the loch's name have been fruitless. On Victorian maps, prior to the forestation, the land on one side of the loch was called Wallace's Rig and on the other Ward Rig, possibly named after the people who worked those areas. Perhaps Mr Howie owned the rights on the loch, or used it a lot and so became associated with it. I wonder if any Galloway reader, walker or fisherman, can give me further information?

The forestry tracks enabled me to extend the walk to over five miles, with a fair degree of shelter on what was a windy day. You will need Ordnance Survey map 77 (Dalmellington & New Galloway), but only the most up to date one! Without such a map it would be all too easy on parts of the walk to feel disorientated, or even get lost.

From St John's Town of Dalry or New Galloway to the southwest, or Thornhill to the northeast, go along the A702 to the start of the track signposted Half Mark Forest at map ref 690839. A track end on the north side of the road also identifies the start point.

The broad gravel track heads ESE for half a mile, rising ever so slightly, then descends to give the first view of the loch, tucked away in its sylvan setting. Continue round the east end of the loch to Laggan. In an idyllic spot by a meadow, Laggan is now a ruin but, judging by the architectural style of it and its outbuildings, was obviously a fine building at one time. There is no sign of the path of old from Halfmark.

The walk to Laggan is far too short and I extended the outing by taking two large loops on the forestry tracks. The first loop goes clockwise from Laggan round another loch: the smaller and more circular Loch Skae, hidden from view until reaching its northeast side. Continue south then southwest, the track climbing high above Loch Skae. The forest is a mixture of older and newer plantings with clear fell spaces giving an airy feeling to the walk with good views, especially when descending above the southern shores of Loch Howie on the return to Laggan. Too short a walk still? Yes. Repeat the initial part of the Loch Skae circuit, but only as far as the track junction at map ref 707840. Walk anti-clockwise on the second loop, crossing the outflow of Loch Howie at map ref 702847 then walking southwest parallel to the now visible A702 and so back to the car.

03 CRIFFEL

FACTFILE

Map Ordnance Survey map 84, Dumfries
Distance 3 miles
Height 500m
Terrain track, then rough, muddy and slippery path
Start point Ardwall car park, map ref 971634, of the A710
Time 2 to 3 hours
Nearest village New Abbey
Recommended refreshment spot Criffel Inn, New Abbey

One Sunday morning in November, surrounded by keen bird watchers, I was on a bus meet organised by the RSPB, heading for Mersehead. Set between the beautiful Solway coastline and rolling, heather-clad hills, Mersehead (by Southwick, Dumfries) is an RSPB nature reserve described as a Solway gem. So what on earth was I doing there? Not to look at birds to be sure. Margaret was going bird watching. I was going hillwalking.

Viking names abound in the area, points readily identified from the sea. Southwick means 'south bay' or 'landing place'. Further east is Southerness – meaning 'salt point' – where monks worked saltpans in the 1200s.Those Viking names give a clue as to my presence on the bus. A much more dominant landmark lies just inland, a 569m/1867ft hill called Criffel.

The name means 'Crow's Hill' with 'fel' or 'fell' being names applied to many a west coast top. Like Meigle Hill of last week, Criffel is another Marilyn – a hill with a drop of at least 150m all round.

Apart from the convenience of the bus meet, I had another reason for heading to Dumfries and Galloway. I had been taken to task by one reader, Maggi Kaye, a resident of Galloway, for not having featured this lovely part of Scotland in any of my walks. Maggi kindly met me at Mersehead, and then drove to the start of the walk. Criffel hosts an annual hill race from New Abbey, going over the northern shoulder of Knockendoch – the walk described takes longer, at two to three hours.

Bothy nights

Almost two miles south of New Abbey turn west off the A710 for Ardwall. I saw no mention at this junction of it being the way to Criffel. Continue for half a mile to the now signposted and new car park – an area kindly given by the farmer. Follow the marked route: a track southeast for 100 yards, then branch right (southwest) to reach the edge of the forest that covers Criffel's northeast flanks. Leave the track for a path that follows the south side of the Craigrockall Burn that flows into Loch Kindar. The burn is well named, for both it and the path cross rough Galloway granite boulders such that the climb – crossing two forestry tracks to clear the forest – will take longer than anticipated.

Whilst the initial going is rough and slow it is of nothing compared with the final stage of 'cleared forest'. This section is very muddy, very wet and – in traversing numerous tree roots – frequently slippery. Previous improved sections of the path are in disrepair and sensible boots are essential. [See postscript]

Reach open hillside at map ref 960628. On the right take note of a large wooden bridge over the burn: a mysterious bridge that serves no purpose. One explanation given is that it was erected to serve a new path that was never built. Climb SSW on a worn grassy path, undrained and very wet, to reach the small summit dome. First approach what is known as Douglas's Cairn – a prominent large jumble of stones marking the highest spot. Despite the 'path', the effort of getting to the summit is made worthwhile by the magnificent views … or so I am told. Criffel's isolated position – an outlier of the Southern Uplands – makes it a superb viewpoint. On a clear day you can see the Isle of Man. When I was there visibility was such that I had to search for the white trig point, only a few yards distant.

The plaque on the trig point explains its well-maintained condition: 'This monument forms part of the Ordnance Survey National GPS Network. It is an offence to damage it. If damaged please ring…' Now I don't approve of hillwalkers using GPS devices, but I am pleased that this trig point is being maintained and presumably less likely to be damaged by lightning strike, as is so often the case with many a higher top.

Seeming much higher than its 1867ft, I first viewed Criffel in 1986 from Caerlaverock Castle. I did not climb the hill as I was resting for the following day's Dumfries Octocentenary marathon, but I vowed to return one day. It had taken over 20 years!

I heard complaints that relatively-remote Galloway does not appear to receive anything like the funding that goes to other areas – projects that could attract more tourists to boost the local economy. If true, that could explain the state of the Criffel path. Although I am not in favour of made-up easy approaches to hills, paths are needed to attract casual walkers and tourists to popular local hills. Road-end signposting and an improved Criffel path would help, and here's hoping that the Robert the Bruce Trail will soon materialise.

Postcript

I am delighted to report that the long-awaited improvements to the Criffel path have now been carried out. A new hard-core path, slightlt to the left of the olf route, follows the burn and up through the forestry. The felled timber of old has been removed.

04 Hart Fell

FACTFILE

Map Ordnance Survey map 78, Nithsdale and Lowther Hills
Distance 7 miles
Height 650m
Terrain path and track to the summit
Start point corrugated-iron hall by the River Annan, map ref 075104
Time 3 to 4 hours
Nearest town Moffat
Recommended refreshment spot Bank Tea Room, Broughton

Situated six miles northeast of Moffat, its southern slopes bounded by the Moffat Water and the River Annan, Hart Fell lies on the boundary between Dumfries & Galloway and the Borders. Its trig point is deemed to be on the southern side of the boundary, making it the highest hill in Dumfriesshire. According to legend it was home to the wizard Merlin, who could change into a hart. But Hart Fell is perhaps best known for its proximity to one of the most iconic landmarks of southern Scotland: the Devil's Beef Tub – a cavernous hollow at the headwaters of the Annan where the notorious Border Reivers once hid stolen cattle. Indeed from the viewpoint on the A701 overlooking the Devil's Beef Tub, Hart Fell shows up well – a mossy 750m plateau with the high point at 808m/2651ft marked by both trig point and cairn.

The Devil's Beef Tub is part of Corehead, described as a stunning area of land in the heart of the Southern Uplands with slopes once cloaked with native woodland but now grazed bare. In 2009 The Borders Forest Trust (BFT) raised £700,000 to buy 1580 acres of land to be dedicated to woodland, low intensity farming and conservation projects.

Although frequently climbed on the same day as its neighbouring Corbett, White Coomb, Hart Fell is an ideal short day pre-Christmas hill. Despite the lower starting height it is best tackled from the Annan valley rather than from above the Devil's Beef Tub (the latter a longer and undulating route that negates the 400m start). The Mountain Lamb and I ventured to Hart Fell a few weeks ago on a well-chosen blue-sky day and the following describes our route from the Annan, climbing the hill's grassy southwest ridge over Arthur's Seat. With a climb by path and track of only 650m and over nearly four miles, there is an easy overall gradient.

Go three miles north from Moffat on the minor road by the Annan and park just short of Ericstane by the small corrugated-iron hall at map ref 075104. Be careful not to block entrances to fields. Walk north on the road over the Auchencat Burn to a signpost for Hartfell Spa. At the first of five circular metal 'kissing gates', turn east into the field.

There is no immediate trace of a path, but simply follow the higher north bank and not the actual burn. After a second gate, and by now on a vague grassy track, look out for marker posts with yellow directions. More gates and posts lead to map ref 084108 at the base of the southwest ridge. Do not climb too high and then follow an excellent track that runs on the south side of the ridge but well above the burn. This gives a quick approach northeast towards the steep gully of a side stream as the valley of the Auchencat Burn curves eastwards.

At the track-end follow sheep tracks to the Spa at map ref 097115, mapped as Hartfell Spa (Chalybeate). That name means 'impregnated with iron salts' and the waters were once believed to have healing properties. Set in a much eroded gully on the far side of the stream, the Spa is a small stone-vaulted cellar, roofed with grass and heather, and surrounded by a wooden fence. The Spa was discovered in 1748 by a John Williamson, whose memorial can be found in the old Moffat cemetery. Even in nasty weather, a walk just to the Spa is a worthwhile outing.

Now for the only steep part of the outing: a northerly climb on grassy slopes to gain the southwest ridge and a well-marked track at a gate in a fence. Follow the track all the way over Arthur's Seat to reach the Hart Fell plateau and a line of fence posts, of help on a misty day. Follow the fence posts left (north) to the trig point and a grand viewpoint.

Return by the track, but this time all the way to the start of the marker signs at map ref 084108. We stopped in Broughton on our way home, at the Laurel Bank Tea Room – not the nearest but arguably the best.

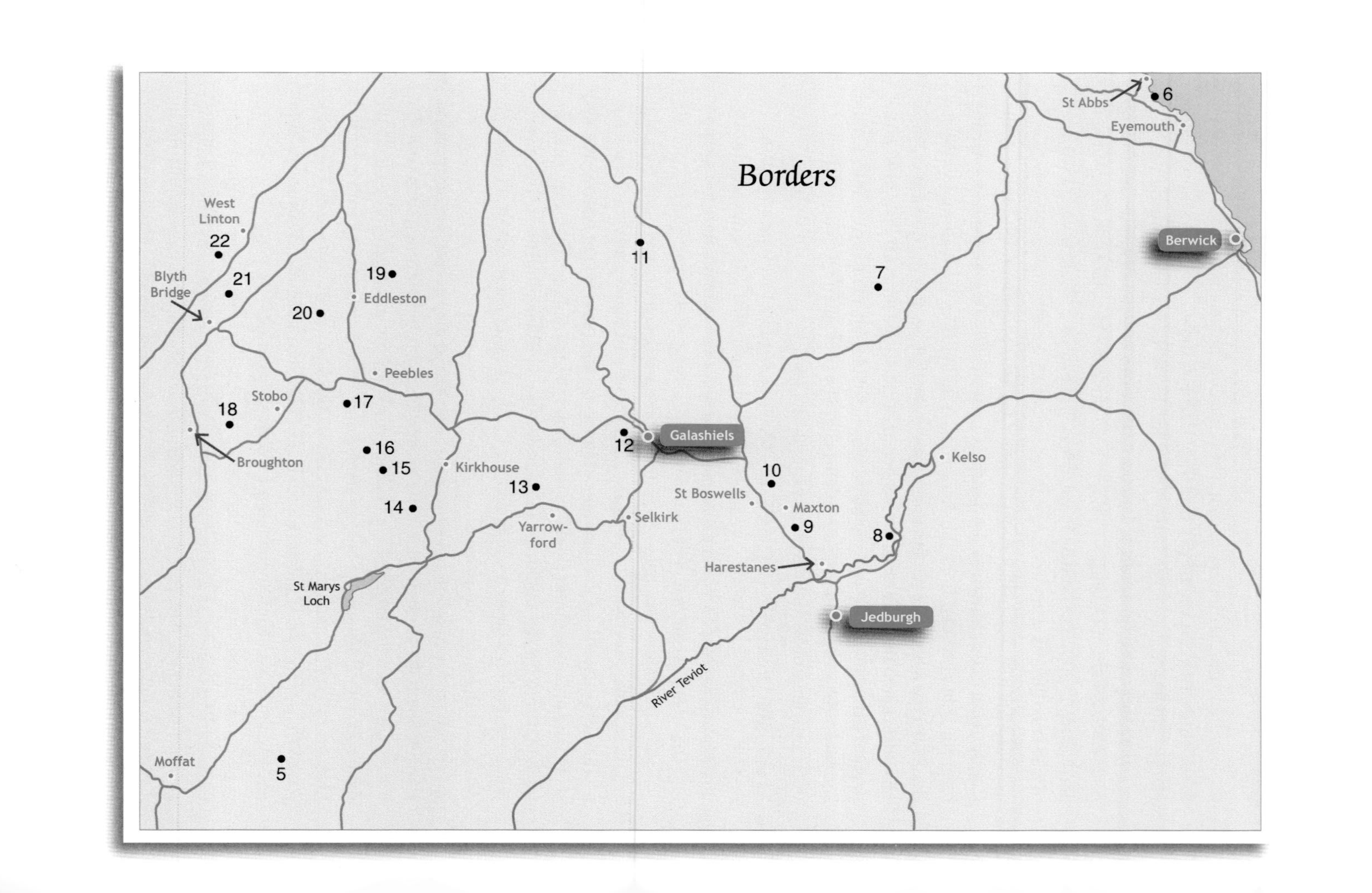
Borders
St Abbs
6
Eyemouth
Berwick
West Linton
22
21
Blyth Bridge
19
Eddleston
20
11
7
Peebles
Stobo
17
18
Broughton
Galashiels
12
16
15
Kirkhouse
13
14
10
St Boswells
Maxton
9
Kelso
8
Selkirk
Yarrow-ford
Harestanes
St Marys Loch
Jedburgh
River Teviot
Moffat
5

Borders

05 Half-way round the Ettrick Horseshoe

FACTFILE

Map Ordnance Survey map 79, Hawick & Eskdale
Distance 7 miles
Height 600m
Terrain tracks and paths by drystane dykes
Start point Ettrick road-end car park, map ref 189093
Time 3 to 4 hours
Nearest village Ettrick
Recommended refreshment spot take your own

Since 1935, Scottish hills south of the Highland boundary fault at least 2000ft/610m in height have been known as Donalds, named after the compiler, Percy Donald, who developed a complex formula to determine the difference between such hills and their subsidiary tops. Originally 89, there are now 118 New Donalds.

The Ettrick Horseshoe is the name given to the round of hills in the upper Ettrick valley. Ettrick Head at 530m separates the two arms. The western arm has two Donalds: Bodesbeck Law (though strictly speaking just outside the Horseshoe) and Capel Fell. The eastern arm has another three: Wind Fell, Hopetoun Craig and the highest of them all, Ettrick Pen, at 692m.

The Horseshoe makes for not too long a day, albeit with a lot of ups and downs; a day that can be extended to another two Donalds – Loch Fell and Croft Head, south of Ettrick Head. However, doing half a horseshoe (the walk described below) gives a most pleasant three to four hours outing, although with still a measure of gentle climbing of 600m – ideal exercise for an October day.

Margaret and I went to the Ettrick valley at the end of September. Quite apart from the hills, the valley is of interest. It contains a monument marking the birthplace of James Hogg, the Ettrick Shepherd; the residence of our friends Lucille and Donald Macleod; and a bothy at Over Phawhope. I enjoy reading Hogg's early 1800s *Highland Tours* with his descriptions of the mountains, though he did have a cavalier disrespect for spelling and facts. The Macleods live at Nether Phawhope, two miles short of the Ettrick road end. Some seven years ago, when I was having trouble with my hip, Donald Macleod – then a Sports Injury Specialist at St John's Hospital – was the first surgeon I saw. At that time he was also the Surgical Advisor for the Scottish Rugby Union, so was well qualified to comment on my marathon-running-damaged hip. His verdict at that time was short and to the point: a crumbly hip needing replacement in the near future.

After a long drive to Ettrick it was nearing noon before Donald, Lucille, Margaret and I started the walk, for which you will need Ordnance Survey map 79 (Hawick & Eskdale). The road end car park is at a welcoming height of 378m and the grassy track of good gradient soon took us through the forest to Bught Hill at 593m. A short walk west then led to Bodesbeck Law, with good views north over the Moffat Water to White Coomb. Just after the start of the walk look out for the mapped path at map ref 185095. This was once the old horse and cart road to Moffat and the signposted start of the Horseshoe. The road is not what it was and the bridge over the Longhope Burn is no more. When we descended south from Bodesbeck Law to cross the old road, the ladies decided to return to the Ettrick Water, leaving Donald and I to continue on the undulating high ground over a 568m spot height and on to White Shank and Capel Fell and so to Ettrick Head. A drystane dyke follows the mapped county boundary so that even on a misty day it would be almost impossible to get lost. We enjoyed good walking weather with fine views.

At Ettrick Head, the Southern Upland Way – Britain's first official coast-to-coast long distance walk (212 miles long) – crosses over, descends by the Ettrick Water then traverses more hills to reach St. Mary's Loch. At Ettrick Head we had to leave the Horseshoe circuit because a sumptuous meal awaited us at Nether Phawhope, though we did make a short diversion. We went a short distance southwest on the Way to have a look at the Selcoth Crags, and then returned to the Head.

From Ettrick Head a grassy path by the infant Ettrick Water – at that time little more than a trickle of water – quickly leads to a forestry track gently descending to the bothy at Over Phawhope. The bothy – a welcoming sight for many a weary walker on the Southern Upland Way – is maintained by the Mountain Bothies Association (MBA), and when we were there a goodly number of volunteers was busy undertaking essential maintenance. They were too busy to offer a cup of tea to us, yet – as we discovered later – not too busy earlier to offer hospitality to our womenfolk. It is then but a short walk back to the road-end and a few minutes later a car drove up: the ladies giving us a lift back to Nether Phawhope.

06 Eyemouth to St Abbs, a coastal walk

FACTFILE

Map Ordnance Survey map 67, Duns, Dunbar & Eyemouth area
Distance four and a half miles
Height climbed 100m or so
Terrain good paths and tracks by cliff edge
Start point Eyemouth Visitor Information Centre
Time three hours
Nearest villages Eyemouth and St Abbs
Recommended refreshment spot St Abb's Head Visitor Centre tearoom

If you are unsure of the area a road map is sufficient to direct you to Coldingham, from where the A1107 continues to Eyemouth (the start of the walk) and the B6438 leads back from St Abbs. The walk, which stays very close to the cliffs, consists of good paths and tracks. The way is well signed and marked so that a more detailed map is not required. However if you take along Ordnance Survey map 67 you will have a better idea and understanding of what is involved in what is one of the finest coastal walks in the country.

The spectacular scenery will be familiar to those who know the east coast railway line, specifically the five-mile section north of Berwick almost to Eyemouth, where the line hugs the cliff edge before heading inland into softer countryside to parallel the A1. The walk commences at the Eyemouth Visitor Information Centre and goes to the harbour and then along the quayside. It stays with the line of cliffs for most of the way, apart from some beaches and a few promontories such as Callercove Point and Yellow Craig. Then there are the bays to look out to and beyond – Killiedraught, Coldingham, Starney and Horsecastle – the very names of which should make you want to get out there and explore.

The four and a half mile walk (to St Abbs and back) – for which boots or 'sensible' shoes are a must – should take about three hours, what with ups and downs and soft sand, but that also depends on how often you stop to admire the views. Arguably, provided you are well wrapped up, a not-so-good day may be preferable, when the wind is coming in over the sea and the waves are crashing against the rocks.

A one-way-only walk of two and a quarter miles would mean organising two cars, although there are local buses (Perryman's Buses, service 235) that leave from above the harbour at St Abbs, passing by the St Abb's Head Visitor Centre a short distance away on the B6438. It is an hourly service (Sundays as well) with a 14-minute travel time. For a full timetable, contact Traveline Scotland (0871-2002233). I must confess that when the Mountain Maid and I were there we did avail ourselves of the bus service.

To the north of St Abbs lies the National Trust nature reserve of St Abb's Head – renowned for its bird life. Extending the walk round the head would add on another two miles. So we have a choice of distances: 2¼ miles; 4½ miles or 6½ miles – all of them a delight.

For refreshments there is a tearoom at the St Abb's Head Visitor Centre and a wide choice in Eyemouth, whilst one can debate the relative attractions of the scenic fishing village that is St Abbs and its larger neighbour.

07 The Bedshiel Kaims

FACTFILE

Map Ordnance Survey map 74, Kelso & Coldstream
Distance 7 miles
Height 100m
Terrain road, track and path
Start Point Greenlaw
Time 3 to 4 hours
Nearest village Greenlaw
Recommended refreshment spot Blackadder Hotel, Greenlaw

And now for something quite different: a brisk January Borders walk from Greenlaw to view the Bedshiel Kaims that lie southeast of the Lammermuir Hills and the Southern Upland Way.

James Hutton – considered to be the father of modern geology – wrote that the present is the key to the past and the past is the key to the future. The most obvious example I have come across recently of the present being the key to the past, is the Bedshiel Kaims. I had read an article about the Kaims in the *Scottish Geographical Journal* of March 2006 (by David Evans, Stuart Wilson and Duncan McGregor), and that had made me curious enough to want to pay them a visit.

Originally used to define a crooked and winding or steep-sided mound, 'kam' or 'kaim' is of Scottish origin and a lay term for esker. An esker is an elongated sinuous ridge marking the former position of glacial streams. At the end of the last Ice Age – only some 12,000 years ago – melt-water rivers cut large valleys and layers of sand and gravel were dumped, some in the form of these gravel ridges. An excellent example is the two and a half mile-long, single meandering ridge that stretches from Dogden Moss to Polwarth Moss and known locally as 'The Kaims'. Bedshiel is the name of the nearby farm. The Kaims have been clearly identified on Ordnance Survey map 74 (Kelso & Coldstream), probably due to their very striking appearance. This single ridge feature rises from the moorland to a height of 15m in places, with wide very steep slopes. The esker has been breached at a few places – the largest breach being at the mid-point, cut through by the Millknowe Burn, which then becomes the Fangrist Burn. The latter has gouged out quite a channel through Dogden Moss and Greenlaw

Moor; all words that graphically describe the terrain which is at odds with the gravel strips. The Fangrist Burn joins the Blackadder Water which flows round the village of Greenlaw.

The Kaims lie north of Greenlaw at map ref 700500 in a triangle of land enclosed by the A697, the A6112 and the B6456 – a boomerang-shaped feature that fully deserves its prominence on the map. When the Mountain Lamb and I went there at the end of November, we did a north/south traverse of the moor from the B6456, passing Bedshiel. We were lucky that it was a lovely day, albeit initially very wet underfoot – it is moorland after all – and the easiest way to the Kaims was following a vehicle track east to map ref 703507, the obvious eastern breach in the esker. This northern side would not be easy to traverse in foul weather, so the following walk goes north from Greenlaw then back again.

Park in Greenlaw and walk north on the A6112 for half a mile to a minor road on the left, signposted Greenlawdean. Follow this road to where it turns left. Leave the road for a somewhat muddy but pretty track that goes NNW to the right of a wooded strip and left of grazing fields. Pass a gate at map ref 707475 and turn right to leave the track, going by a path that is not very obvious at first, to reach the open moorland. Continue NNW by the edge of the trees, climbing slightly and following an excellent track. By now the line of the esker can be clearly seen and beyond that the white roof of a large shed beside Bedshiel Farm. Beyond the farm are the twin hills, Dirrington Little and Great Law.

The last section of trees on the left is but an open plantation and at its end at map ref 703488 continue with the track as it turns sharply west, then north, on approaching the small valley of the Fangrist Burn. A vague track does continue in a straight line from the corner of the wood, presumably the line of the path shown on the map, but on a misty day it would be safer to stay with the earlier track and its line of fence posts.

The track stays on the high ground above the burn. Continue to map ref 699495 and either cross the bridge or stay on the east side of the burn and meander round to the gap in the esker. The esker looks like a man-made flood protection bank or a defensive rampart from some ancient fortress. The pebbly undersoil of the esker is all too obvious and quite different from the surrounding terrain. Topped with sparse vegetation, it is a delight to walk on and makes a commanding viewpoint over the bleak surroundings. Take a pleasant stroll to the eastern breach and return the same way.

08 From Jedburgh to Kelso, by the River Teviot

FACTFILE

Map Ordnance survey map 74, Kelso and surrounding area
Distance 12 miles
Height negligible
Terrain minor road, good paths and tracks, though can be muddy in places
Start point Jedburgh bus station
Time 5 to 7 hours
Nearest towns Jedburgh and Kelso
Recommended refreshment spots a wide choice in Kelso (or Jedburgh)

This linear walk (completed in 1998) is part of the Borders Abbeys Way: a 65 mile route covering many of the main Borders towns, and linking the four great abbeys in Kelso, Jedburgh, Melrose and Dryburgh. The 12 mile walk by the River Teviot provides an excellent day's walking, mostly on riverside paths and on an old railway line.

When there in February 2010 we covered the distance in a steady five hours. A more leisurely walk on a spring or summer day, can be extended to seven hours, perhaps staying in the area for the weekend. The walk is described in the publication *Walking the Scottish Borders* and the map included is sufficient in itself. For more information phone the Scottish Borders Tourist Board at 0870 608 0404 or visit their web site at www.visitscottishborders.com. However, you may also want to have Ordnance Survey map 74 (Kelso and surrounding area) to give a more precise idea as to where you are along the way.

Boots or sensible shoes are a must, for after all it is a distance of 12 miles, and some parts can be muddy. When we did the walk there had been heavy rain and the riverbank path was slippy, muddy and wet in places, and surrounding flood debris told the story of recent high spates on the Teviot.

There is a regular bus service between the two towns (service 20) and bus times can be obtained by phoning 01835 824000. We were lucky, arriving in Kelso's cobbled square to find that a bus was just about to leave for Jedburgh. With a quick scramble we were on the bus and away. The decision as to which way to walk had been made for us. This meant of course that we would be walking downstream, after an early modest climb on a minor road past Mount Ulston. In truth, reversing the route would make little difference. The bus fare was £1.70 by Munro's Buses, a name that gave rise to some hilarity for this outing is well away from the high tops. The bus journey takes 25 minutes and we were quickly aware that we were facing a long walk back, but we had burned our boats so to speak.

The visitor information centre in Jedburgh is open all year round (as is Kelso's) and is situated beside the bus station. Pay a visit to the centre (and toilets) for they have a most informative pamphlet about the walk, which makes it more interesting, and it is important to know where the walk goes at a few key points. Having said that, the route is well way-marked with 'Borders Abbeys Way' or just 'AW' signs.

Leaving Jedburgh, the Jed Water is only followed for a short distance by the A68 before the route climbs by Mount Ulston and on to the old Roman road, Dere Street. This section gives panoramic views along the Teviot valley. Dropping down to Jedfoot, the path then goes along the east side of the River Teviot by its flood plain, before crossing over near Nisbet for the next three-mile section, which follows the old railway line. The line makes for faster walking, as it curves away from the meandering Teviot, but is not quite so interesting. However, look out for the sudden change in direction as the way abruptly leaves the railway line, turning right to rejoin the riverbank at map ref 696289, for what is undoubtedly the most attractive part of the walk. Apart from a brief diversion by Roxburgh after the impressive railway viaduct, the path stays by the river all the way to Kelso. Bird life is active and we were lucky enough to see a host of herons, mallards and mute swans.

The final part of the walk goes by the ruins of Roxburgh Castle and the confluence with the Tweed. Kelso square is just round the corner, over Rennie's splendid 1803 bridge.

09 A Trip to the Borders – Maxton to Harestanes

FACTFILE

Map Ordnance Survey map 74, Kelso & Coldstream
Distance 7 miles
Height 150m
Terrain path, track and minor road
Start point village of Maxton, map ref 613301
Time 3 to 4 hours
Nearest town Jedburgh
Recommended refreshment spot Harestanes Countryside visitor centre tearoom

A few weeks ago Margaret and I had an important Melrose rendezvous with a couple hitherto unknown to us, but who were about to become close relations by our respective offsprings. We sat in a pre-arranged restaurant, wondering if we would instantly recognise our new friends. How easy it was, as expectant eye contact was instantly made and with the right couple. As we later reported to the relief of the soon-to-be-weds, the evening was a great success.

With dry weather forecast it would have been a shame to immediately return home. The next day Margaret needed no persuasion to spend a few hours bird-watching and I had with me the programme of the 15th Borders Walking Festival, 'In the Footsteps of the Reivers'. Taking place from the 5–13 September, the festival (part of

Homecoming Scotland 2009) boasts a wide range of over 60 led walks – something to suit all ages and abilities, as well as a host of other activities. For information, or to order a programme, phone 01835 863170 or visit www.borderswalking.com.

Two walks in the programme caught my attention. The 11 mile walk from St Mary's Loch to Traquair along the Southern Upland Way is an enjoyable and highly recommended traverse that I wrote about last year. However, a walk starting nearer Melrose was a more sensible choice and I selected a nine-mile walk from Maxton to Jedburgh that I had never done before. Not that I did it all. I excluded the final stage to Jedburgh but added a short hill climb to Peniel Heugh. The walk follows a section of the Roman road Dere Street (and of later times, part of the St Cuthbert's Way that runs from Melrose to Holy Island). Green waymarkers are evident for the latter, and though not entirely necessary, are of assistance.

Margaret dropped me off at Maxton. From the west end of the village take the minor road that heads for the A68 and look out for the marker by the strip of woodland just before the road (it is possible to take a detour via Morridgehall to this point). The nearly-four-mile stretch of Dere Street to the B6400 is mapped as a straight line, but the path weaves in and out to give a charming route. The wooded strips are larger than the map might suggest and as the busy A68 goes off at a tangent, it is a peaceful walk.

Melrose from the lower Eildons

The highest point of Dere Street as it crosses a prominent ridge (now known as Lilliards Edge) is marked by Lilliards Stone, erected 800 years ago by the monks of Melrose Abbey. Representatives of the Scottish and English crowns met there to try to resolve disputes by peaceful negotiation. Sadly these meetings were not always successful and war followed. Nearby is the site of the Battle of Ancrum Moor (1545).

On the gentle descent from the ridge it is easier to visualise what Dere Street might have looked like. Cross a minor road into woodland with a later surprising change southwest to reach the B6400 at map ref 644248. Follow that latter road northeast to a minor road at map ref 648251 and go north to reach a track (map ref 647254) that climbs to Peniel Heugh. Follow that track, then the obvious path to reach the summit.

On the summit of Peniel Heugh are the remains of a fortified settlement. In more recent times a 150ft tower was built between 1817 and 1824 to commemorate the Battle of Waterloo (1815). The monument – dedicated to the Duke of Wellington and his army – was erected by the sixth Marquis of Lothian and his tenantry. What the tenantry thought of all this I know not. In truth, from afar the monument looks more like a lighthouse. In the interests of public safety there is no access to the top of the tower, but even from its base it is a commanding viewpoint. I had met no other walker on my walk so was pleasantly surprised to come across a large number of children and their teachers from Burnfoot School in Hawick taking shelter from the strong wind and enjoying their picnic.

Return to the B6400 at map ref 644248, cross the road and then take the path that runs parallel to the road to reach the drive that goes to Harestanes. Margaret was waiting at the visitor centre. We both had enjoyed our respective mornings and after some refreshment at the tearoom we happily headed for home.

10 A Trip to St Boswells

FACTFILE

Map Ordnance Survey map 74, Kelso & Coldstream
Distance 9 miles
Height 200m
Terrain mixture of path, track and road
Start point St Boswells bus station
Time 4 hours
Nearest town St Boswells
Recommended refreshment spot Buccleuch Arms, St Boswells

Many a hillwalker may be called Craig or Ben, but the most appropriate name I knew until recently was that of my brother-in-law: Munro Dunn (and yes he has completed all the Munros). However, I have now met Hugh Munro – not he of the eponymous list of course, but a present day resident of Penicuik. Hugh had sent me some of his favourite lower-level outings suitable for winter – one of which by the banks of the Tweed starts and finishes at St Boswells. It had been a while since my last visit to that area (a walk from Maxton towards Jedburgh) so I was delighted to meet Hugh and his Munroist friend John Darling at St Boswells. By coincidence, John and I had briefly met a couple of years before on top of Beinn a'Bheithir when we were lucky enough to see a Brocken Spectre.

It was a raw blustery end of November day with the threat of rain and we were quickly on our way from the bus station.

Head northwards, then turn left down The Wynd, past the white building of the Air Training Corp, and turn right at a T-junction onto a path. Some 200 yards later take the right fork and go up some steps to a road. Continue to a track that leads downhill to the riverside golf course. The path stays by a boundary fence clear of the golf course (then with more ponds than bunkers, the driftwood tidemark showing the extent of recent floods). For the first two miles to Maxton Church, follow the waymarked St Cuthbert's Way. After recent heavy rain, the path was distinctly glutinous.

Pass the salmon ladder at Mertoun Mill (with obligatory heron) to reach Mertoun Bridge that carries the B6404 over the Tweed. The path under the bridge was flooded so we opted for the stepped path that leads to the road. Cross with some care, then another stepped path leads back to the riverside to continue on the south bank.

Less than one mile later look out for a wall on the steep bank below Benrig House: the site of the Crystal Well – a romantic name for a spring, the source of clean water for the House. In the mid 1800s a pump was built to bring the water to the house, powered by mules or donkeys obliged to trudge round the larger of two vaulted cellars.

Continue past Maxton Church. One mile further downstream a footbridge leads to the beautiful grounds of Mertoun House. Cross the footbridge and turn right (east) for the charming stroll by the southern end of the grounds. Continue to a small bridge that spans a burn. In spate when we were there, the brown silt-carrying water contrasted with the purer waters of the Tweed. Follow the burn, heading northwest to reach the B6404. Continue southwest to Mertoun Bridge (the heron was still there). Head west on the north bank of the Tweed, passing Mertoun Mill and cottages that had sandbags at the front doors (the Tweed had risen some 15ft just a few days before). Continue past the entrance to the 12th Century Dryburgh Abbey – now in ruins and the burial place of Sir Walter Scott.

For a pleasing diversion and the only short climb of the day, go north on the road to a signpost on the left hand side. Wallace's Statue is this way. It is less than 100m to climb and on a gentle gradient and the commanding stern statue (no silly Braveheart here) is an excellent viewpoint over to the Eildons.

Return to the road and head west through the hamlet of Dryburgh to a footbridge to return to the south bank and the St Cuthbert's Way path that quickly leads back to St Boswells.

We retired to the Buccleuch Arms for coffee and a good chat. Delight of delights, the heavens only opened on our way back home.

11 Soutra Hill, Soutra Aisle and Dere Street

FACTFILE

Map Ordnance Survey map 66, Edinburgh and area
Distance 6 miles
Height 250m
Terrain wet and rough Roman road, with farm track and drier moorland
Start point car park on B6368, at map ref 453583
Time 3 hours
Nearest town Dalkeith to the north, Lauder to the south
Recommended refreshment spot Goblin Ha' at Gifford

Wind turbines on Dun Law

Soutra Hill – on the edge of the Moorfoot Hills by the A68 – has commanding views down to the flat and fertile Lothians. It is claimed that you can see 60 peaks from there, over to the Pentlands, the Ochils and the Lomonds, but its location makes it a windy spot.

On one side of the hill runs Dere Street, the Roman road constructed in the late 1st Century AD to link the legionary fortress of York (Eburacum) and Inchtuthil, near Perth. Long after the Romans had withdrawn, this remained the principal north-south route, used for example by the armies of Edward I in the Wars of Independence, but more generally by travellers and pilgrims, for whom the nearby Soutra Hospital provided shelter. Soutra Aisle is all that remains of that hospital, founded by the Augustinians at the request of King Malcolm IV around 1160. It was a medieval institution, and in its heyday one of the three most important hospitals in Scotland. Midway between Edinburgh and the Border Abbeys on the Via Regia (royal road), it treated the sick and provided alms to the poor, hospitality to travellers and sanctuary to fugitives. Archaeological excavations have found traces of medicinal products from all over the world, including a mixture of the seeds of hemlock, black henbane and opium poppy (used as a general anaesthetic in the case of amputations). For 300 years the hospital continued to deliver its important service, but in the 1460s the Master of the Hospital was accused of misconduct and the hospital was stripped of its estates. Soutra Aisle was originally part of the hospital church. It later became the burial vault of a local family, and this saved it from the fate of the rest of the institution.

So how about something quite different for a winter outing? A visit to Soutra Hill and the remains of the hospital, followed by a walk down Dere Street to the remains of a Roman camp. And on the way back, take in some modest hills, including Dun Law and its wind farm.

Some may find this rapid travel through time to be incongruous, contrasting the modern with the medieval. I found it all to be fascinating, nor oddly enough did I find the lofty wind turbines to be intrusive. Walking past the wind farm to inspect the remains of the Roman camp by Kirktonhill only whetted my appetite to more closely inspect this modern intrusion on my return.

Just before the high point of the A68 on the north side of Soutra Hill, turn off to the southwest on the B6368. After half a mile the Aisle is on the left, but continue 100 yards further on to the sign-posted car park on the right amongst some trees, at map ref 453583.

Whilst the Aisle is all that is left of this Augustinian Abbey and Hospital that served travellers for centuries, it is not difficult to imagine travellers wearily climbing to over 350m (just by-passing the top of Soutra Hill) and dropping down for a welcome refuge. And after visiting the Aisle, what about a walk? It is only a mile there and back to Soutra Hill to the north-east – a raw and bleak spot on a nasty day. Wrap up well. Remember that 368m height translates to over 1200ft.

Now for a two and a half mile walk along Dere Street, southeastwards to the Roman camp. Admittedly there is little to see on the ground there, but there are good views to the south. From just south of the car park, leave the road opposite a gate appropriately marked as Dere Street Farm. Head south for King's Inch, crossing the Armet Water at a clearing in a plantation. The timber hereabouts has been felled in the thin strip and recently replanted. With the plantation on your right, follow the edge of the trees southeast then SSE. You are walking the Roman road – or rather the line of the road, for although marked on the map, it is not at all obvious in many places. The high part at the half-way stage is flat and rough, and can be very boggy. Be well shod, and hope for a hard frosty day.

Linn Dean Water

On the lower slopes of Turf Law a farm track starts, making for easier going. Look out for the Historic Buildings sign confirming that you are on part of Dere Street. It was 7 metres wide, and gravel for its construction was quarried from the pits beside the road.

On the way back from Kirktonhill, slightly firmer ground can be reached by walking over Turf Law and, after a deviation to the west, over Dun Law. This last section contains the wind farm, as if you had not noticed! It is a slightly spooky feeling walking under the humming giants, hoping that the large turbine blades are well secured.

Once back at the car, have a look at the Linn Dean Wildlife Reserve (run by the Scottish Wild Life Trust). There is a lay-by on the north side of the A68 at map ref 468594. A small steep-sided glen, formed by the Linn Dean Water, was an area of interest to the old hospital doctors as a source of natural remedies.

Soutra Aisle is open all year, and specialist party tours are available by arrangement by phoning 01875-833248.

12 A Circuit of Meigle Hill

FACTFILE

Map Ordnance Survey map 73, Peebles, Galashiels & Selkirk.
Distance 5 miles
Height 400m
Terrain good grassy tracks and paths
Start point Caddonfoot, at the junction of the A707 and the B710
Time 3 to 4 hours
Nearest town Galashiels
Recommended refreshment spot Clovenfords Hotel

When I mentioned to the Mountain Hare that I was looking for a short and easy (but interesting) December walk, he suggested that Meigle Hill would fit the bill very well: just a few miles, little in the way of climbing, and a lovely viewpoint. I was somewhat puzzled as, knowing the area well, I was unaware of a hill so named near the Perth and Kinross village of Meigle. He meant the hill that overlooks Galashiels. As neither the Mountain Maid nor I had been there, we happily fell in with his suggestion.

Meigle Hill lies southwest of Galashiels (indeed the town has spread to its lower slopes) and is the high point of a compact area closely bound by five roads: the A7; B7060; A707; B710; and the A72. The village of Clovenfords lies on the west side, just north of the hamlet of Caddonfoot. There is thus no problem in accessing the slopes of the hill and there is an abundance of paths and signposted trails scarcely hinted at in looking at the Ordnance Survey map 73 (Peebles, Galashiels & Selkirk). The Explorer map 338 shows more of these paths, but really no map is needed at all. In thick mist, descend in any direction and you will soon reach those perimeter roads.

Meigle Hill is one of many so-called Marilyns: hills of any height with a drop on all sides of at least 150m. Consequently, it is somewhat detached from the surrounding hills and that makes it a commanding viewpoint.

I had another reason for wanting to go to Meigle Hill. The southeast slopes are traversed as part of the Southern Upland Way. Though I have been on various sections, I have yet to walk the whole length of the Way. Was this the opportunity to cover another small section? No, it was not, for the Mountain Hare was keen to show us that the Meigle Circular Walk stays on the north side of the Way. The circular part is a bit of a misnomer, because while doing just that at the beginning of the walk, the route eventually climbs to the summit.

We agreed on one date, but nearer the time when I saw the weather forecast, we opted for the day before. That was a wise decision for the three of us set off on what turned out to be a cracker of a day; a cold day to be sure, but one of gentle breeze, bright sun and impressive visibility. End-of-year days do not come better than that.

We started at a height of 120m from Caddonfoot, opposite the primary school, for a quieter approach on the other side of the hill from Galashiels. There is a parking space on the west side of the B710, at its junction with the A707.

Cross the road and turn east, climbing sharply on a path to meet a broad grassy track above the hamlet and a prominent signpost indicating joining the Meigle Circular Route. The track goes north above the gorge formed by the Caddon Water. Look out for the first of many yellow arrows on signposts. After a short distance, the route leaves the grassy track climbing right (east), then starts its undulating contour round the northwest slopes of the hill, at first following a dyke.

Cross a track at around map ref 456366 – a track that could be followed direct to the summit. However, continue with the circuit. Some of the yellow arrows are not easy to see from a distance and the path can be vague at times, but keep heading for the south side of the large quarry at map ref 467373. Follow the quarry track southeast to Cheviot View at map ref 477366, overlooking Galashiels. The undulating route has added only some 100m of climb, but the serious (albeit short) work now begins: a climb of 200m going southwest on the northern rim of a plantation direct to the summit.

The grassy summit bristles with communications masts (though not as ugly as those on the summit of Cairnwell above the Glen Shee ski slopes) and has a large beehive cairn slightly lower than the trig point. Enjoy the views to the north and west.

The route descends southwest, at first by the access track and then leaving it for a grassy descent between Blakehope and Mossilee Hills to follow the north side of the burn that flows to the southern end of Caddonfoot. Rejoin the broad grassy track, climb slightly and then descend by the path back to Caddonfoot to complete a lovely five-mile circuit.

13 Broadmeadows, Yarrowford

FACTFILE

Map Ordnance Survey map 73, Peebles, Galashiels and Selkirk
Distance 6 miles
Height 400m
Terrain superb track
Start point Traquair village hall, junction of B709 and B7062, map ref 332346
Time 2½ to 3 hours
Nearest towns Innerleithen and Selkirk
Recommended refreshment spot Traquair House restaurant, or Traquair Arms, Innerleithen

This week's walk is less of a 'walk on the wild side' and more of 'a trip down Memory Lane'. I mentioned last week that I was looking forward to a visit to the Borders on

Tuesday 2 May to take part in a special celebratory anniversary walk. Seventy-five years ago to the very day, the first president, Lord Salvesen, opened the Scottish Youth Hostels Association's very first hostel at Broadmeadows. The hostel is at Yarrowford on the north side of the Yarrow Water, by the A708 some four miles west of Selkirk.

Well, Tuesday has come and gone and for the invited guests it was a wonderful day out, walking along the Minchmoor Road from Traquair to the hostel, exactly the same route as at that opening in 1931. I was delighted to be invited because Broadmeadows was my very first hostel and my personal trip down Memory Lane recalled that visit which was (subject to a few months) exactly 50 years ago. I was a very young schoolboy. I have at home a copy of a painting of Old Broadmeadows by Jim Nicholson and there was more than a touch of nostalgia in arriving at the hostel, beautifully maintained yet little changed. In those 1931 days, staying at Broadmeadows cost one shilling a night (around 5p in today's money) and in the morning each person did a chore such as bringing in coal, sweeping the floor, washing dishes, making beds etc. Now, as guests, we were royally looked after with a buffet lunch at the hostel, followed by the unveiling of the 75th Anniversary Plaque. Transport was then provided to get us back to Traquair. I am sorry, but you will have to pre-arrange your own transport! Originally a row of four cottages, Broadmeadows is still a charming and ideal base for exploration. Much of the Border country is rich in history and this area is no exception. Telephone 0870-004-1107.

The route from Traquair to Broadmeadows using the Minchmoor Road follows part of the Southern Upland Way, in turn part of an old drove road. The Minchmoor Road has been in use for centuries. In 1296 Edward I and his army used the road during his incursion into Scotland and, four centuries later, the Marquis of Montrose took the same road after his defeat at Philiphaugh by General Leslie's Covenanting army. The whole route is well way marked and on a superb dry track. The initial part is a steady but easy climb of 350m over two miles to the north side of the heathery slopes of Minch Moor, with the road going between widely-spaced walls that betray its antiquity. The area around Minch Moor is part of the Elibank and Traquair Forest, though some of it has been felled. This may cause a little confusion when studying the map. Never-

Artistic circles along the way

On the Southern Upland Way

theless, it is important to take a map – Ordnance Survey sheet 73 – as this in any case helps to identify distant views from the central part of the walk that climbs to over 500m. From the track there are good views north to Walkerburn and the Tweed Valley and the Eildon Hills show up well to the east. It is only a small diversion to the 567m trig point summit of Minch Moor.

The road goes southeast then ESE, crossing forestry tracks. Do not be diverted!

Just before Minch Moor is a spring marked by two stones, called the Cheese Well. Making an offering of cheese placates the spirits of the well and ensures protection on the Minchmoor Road. Take some food for yourself as well. It is important at map ref 369333 not to curve to the north on a forestry track towards Middle Rig. Continue southeast towards Hare Law, with a modest rise.

Though well signposted, care is required at map ref 380328 at the edge of the forest, from where the Minchmoor Road leaves the Southern Upland Way and descends on a lovely, gentle and grassy track to Yarrowford. Once there, follow the road for 400m to the bridge over the Yarrow Water and take the idyllic footpath north to the hostel.

Once back at Traquair after the walk, take time to have a look at Traquair House, visited by 27 kings and claimed to be the oldest inhabited house in Scotland. The main block dates from 1642.

14 St Mary's Loch to Kirkhouse

FACTFILE

Map Ordnance Survey map 73, Peebles, Galashiels & Selkirk
Distance 7 miles
Height 300m
Terrain waymarked track and path all the way
Start point car park off A708, east of St Mary's Loch, map ref 272244
Time 3 to 4 hours
Nearest town Innerleithen
Recommended refreshment spot Traquair Arms Hotel, Innerleithen

The Southern Upland Way (SUW) was Britain's first official coast-to-coast long distance footpath: a distance of 212 miles from Portpatrick to Cockburnspath with 80 miles crossing the Borders. I have not done the whole traverse, though sections have been walked from time to time.

In September I described a walk from Peebles to Dun Rig, the highest summit at 744m in an area of rolling hills. The eastern side of that area is traversed by part of the SUW from St Mary's Loch in the Yarrow valley to Kirkhouse (all of which is off-road), then on to Traquair. On that Dun Rig walk it occurred to me that this section of the SUW – a modest seven miles with little climbing – would be ideal for a short walk later in the year, possibly on a day of not so good weather.

And so it was on a raw late October day, in the company of the Mountain Maid and the Mountain Hare, that this stretch was tackled. We started from the south, the route described below, from the A708 just east of St Mary's Loch, going northeastwards to Kirkhouse on the B709, one mile south of Traquair. Although there is a marginally higher starting height, the main reason for the southern start was to have the prevailing wind behind us. On a squally day (wetter than forecast) that was a good decision. The walk of course can be started from the north at Kirkhouse where there is a large parking area available, unless otherwise required, beside Traquair Church and cemetery at map ref 320334. There is no off-road parking space.

Just before Dryhope a small parking space is situated off the A708 at the start of the walk at map ref 272244, less than a mile east of St Mary's Loch. The loch cannot be seen at this stage but lovely views soon emerge on the gentle ascent northwards. The start is a path used to bypass Dryhope: a rough, wet beginning going NNW but matters improve on reaching a track at map ref 268248. Thereafter the walk, going northeastwards, is mostly on track and well-signposted throughout.

Pause a while before starting on the track to look at what is left of Dryhope Tower – one of many stone tower houses built in the Borders during the 15th and 16th Centuries. On the orders of King James VI, the tower was demolished in 1592 as punishment for the participation by Walter Scott (the infamous Border reiver) in a raid lead by the Earl of Boswell against the king in his own palace at Falkland in Fife. The tower was rebuilt by 1613 and is now the property of the Philiphaugh Estate Trust. Take a short detour to climb to the top of the well-preserved remains of the tower.

The track undulates slightly on its way to Blackhouse. Look out for another tower house, now quite dilapidated though some of the walls survive to a height of five metres. Opposite the tower are the remains of three medieval cottages.

Now for the only serious climb of the day: some 150m, albeit the prettiest part. It is a steady pull up through a forest, a distance of over one mile, but the beautiful well-graded grassy track eases the effort. With larch trees on the left and Sitka spruce on the right, we had a sheltered spell on our walk. Once clear of the trees, the next mile undulates around the 470m mark to Blake Muir from where there are good views down to Innerleithen and west to the rounded top of Dun Rig. The last two miles give easy and pleasant descent to Kirkhouse.

If not retracing steps, the problem with any linear walk is how to return to the start point: a problem often solved by having two cars, but a solution less than green. We had pre-placed a bike at Kirkhouse on our way to the start point and, as the other two walked on past Traquair to Innerleithen, I cycled south on the B709. Uphill and into the strong wind, the ride was not the easiest and it was disappointing having to cycle most of the way downhill to the A708 rather than the hoped for effortless free-wheel. I was glad to get back to the car at Dryhope. After a quick drive back to Innerleithen I joined the patiently waiting other two for welcome refreshment to conclude a short but enjoyable outing.

15 Dun Rig and a Peebles weekend

FACTFILE

Map Ordnance Survey map 73, Peebles, Galashiels & Selkirk
Distance 12 miles
Height 700m
Terrain old drove road leading to hillside, then return by track
Start point car park at south end of bridge over the Tweed, map ref 251402
Time 5 to 7 hours
Nearest town Peebles
Recommended refreshment spot Simply Delicious coffee shop, Peebles

Some five miles south of Peebles lies Dun Rig: the highest summit at 744m in an area of rolling hills bounded by the Manor Water to the west and the B709 to the east. The undulating eastern side is traversed by part of the Southern Upland Way that goes from St Mary's Loch in the Yarrow valley to Traquair. The area is traversed more centrally by a right of way from Peebles to the Yarrow valley – a 12 mile section of one of the old drove roads used to take cattle from the Borders to the north of England. But what was my particular interest in this area? The Edinburgh medical graduate class of 1968 (together with their spouses and partners) hold a grand reunion every five years, and this autumn that was at Peebles Hydro. The weekend consists of lectures lasting scarcely more than two hours and (more and more) a number of gentle leisure activities, perhaps not surprising as after 40 years almost all of that class are now retired. Margaret enjoys those nostalgic moments with her fellow graduates, all of whom wonder where the past five years have gone.

I had been asked to lead one of those leisure activities – a gentle jaunt. So the week before we checked out such a walk to Dun Rig. The weather on that day was disappointingly wet and cloudy. Margaret wisely turned back, the attraction of bird-watching being more appealing, as I soldiered on to Dun Rig and then returned by Glen Sax.

The walk starts from the large free car park (with toilets) in Kingsmeadows Road at the south end of the bridge over the Tweed at map ref 251402. Opposite is Springhill Road and heading southeast this gives a gentle urban approach to the start of the path/drove road (at map ref 260392) that leads on to the line of tops undulating to Dun Rig. It is possible to park thereabouts but space is limited. The way is signposted, a tree-lined lane leading to the often-muddy Gypsy Glen and crossing the Glensax Burn, partially in spate when we were there.

Now for the initial climb of some 350m to Kirkhope Law, two miles distant. The drove road has a good surface and gradient and the steadily increasing views of Peebles and the Tweed valley distract from the efforts of the climb. The first bump – gloriously covered in purple heather – is bypassed to the east (signposted Kailzie), the drove road giving an easier line of ascent to Kailzie Hill. From there proceed by the plantation edge to Kirkhope Law.

Following the line of a new fence on the left, it is then faster walking as the drove road gently descends. Ahead is Birkscairn Hill: a climb of 150m. The road almost bypasses the hill, but do go to the top. At the dip between that hill and Stake Law the road descends southwards to the Yarrow valley. However, the way ahead to Stake Law and on to Dun Rig is southwest and another 150m to climb. By now on a less well-made (though still helpful) track, the final ascent to Dun Rig goes by the roughest part of the walk: a peat haggy area, tedious and wet when I was there, and best avoided to the north.

Eventually the summit dome is reached. The trig point on Dun Rig lies atop a grassy mound, though the highest point lies just ahead at a corner of the fence. A romp down the north ridge quickly leads past old shooting butts to an unmapped track by the Glensax Burn at map ref 261334. Glensax is soon reached and the main glen road gives an easy three-mile stroll to Haystoun, from where a tarmac road leads back to the southeast side of Peebles and Springhill Road.

So how was the actual day for the medics and spouses? The weather was glorious. The early morning cloud in the Tweed valley soon lifted and we had superb views of the Hydro. With time constraints and levels of fitness, Dun Rig was always going to be too distant, but apart from poor Ashley who missed the departure, we got as far as Kirkhope Law. More importantly, all enjoyed their short outing before the rigours of the ceilidh that evening.

16 Hundleshope Heights

FACTFILE

Map Ordnance Survey map 73, Peebles, Galashiels & Selkirk
Distance 7 miles
Height 500m
Terrain estate road, then track most of the way
Start point southeast end of Springhill Road, Peebles, map ref 259392
Time 3 to 4 hours
Nearest town Peebles
Recommended refreshment spot Osso Restaurant, Innerleithen Road, Peebles

In September I described a walk from Peebles to Dun Rig, the highest summit at 744m in an area of rolling hills bisected by Glensax Burn. The western side of that area is dominated by a moorland plateau starting with the 732m Middle Hill leading northwards to the 718m Broom Hill, from where a narrower ridge leads west to the 676m Stob Law. However, the main plateau continues to the 685m Hundleshope Heights, from where gentle slopes widen out to the 550m mark, by then giving direct views of Peebles nestling to the north.

The area around Broom Hill and Middle Hill is known as Glenrath Heights – the high ground overlooking the Glenrath Burn that flows west to join the Manor Water and so to the Tweed. It is worth mentioning that on the Ordnance Survey map Glenrath Heights is shown rather oddly as the lower ground just to the south of Middle Hill. Donalds are hills in the Scottish Lowlands over 2000ft, of which Dun Rig is one. Having a drop of 100ft on all sides, Glenrath Heights is listed as a Donald but given the map ref of Middle Hill. It's all very confusing!

Hundleshope Heights are not quite the highest area on the west side of Glen Sax, but given their advantageous position overlooking Peebles, there is no doubt that they are the most commanding. To demonstrate its surveying importance, the highest point is graced with a trig point. Well, almost the highest point. It is actually three metres lower but its position was perhaps more helpful in surveying the area to the north. 'Hope' (from the Old English *hop*) means secluded valley. The Hundleshope Burn drains the northwest slopes of the Heights, latterly through such a valley, to join the Manor Water.

Some weeks ago Jimbo and I went to Glen Sax on another two fold mission. I had suggested the good road into the glen as a possibility for another walk for his disabled ramblers group. I was keen to follow the Glensax Burn all the way to its source by Glenrath Heights, traverse north on the plateau to Hundleshope Heights, then descend on a northeast ridge over Dead Side and so return to Peebles.

We had a leisurely stroll up Glen Sax, pausing for an early lunch outside Glensax at the end of the mapped track. In fact the track continues in grassy form for over a mile, criss-crossing the burn many a time. The burn was in spate on our visit so the going was somewhat wet. At the end of the track Jimbo climbed west to Broom Hill. I headed over rougher ground, the last part of which was actually following the infant burn itself in a small ravine.

The routes we took to Hundleshope Heights may be of interest for a longer walk. However, more suitable for a shorter December day is our descent route over Dead Side – a gentle approach from the glen, climbing only 450m over two miles, mostly on a good grassy track.

Drive to the south end of the bridge over the Tweed in Peebles and turn right into Springhill Road, following that road southeast until its end at map ref 259392. There is a small lay-by on the left. Park with consideration. Continue to the entrance to Haystoun and follow the charming tree-lined private tarmac road; walkers welcome but not unauthorised vehicles.

The initial route follows the west bank of Glensax Burn and passes Haystoun on the other bank. The tarmac road then sweeps through a lovely area of grassy parkland on the right and on the left is a large pond partly hidden by a beech hedge. Continue as tarmac changes to gravel to Upper Newby at map ref 266371 and the start of Hundleshope Heights' two-mile north-east ridge.

It's good to be out in the snow

Go either side of the small plantation to reach the remains of an old settlement from where a good grassy track rises steadily over Dead Side to reach a height of 550m. The final ascent to the trig point has a less obvious track and the terrain may be wet underfoot.

Return the same way, but if it is a clear early evening linger awhile to see the lights of Peebles. Once back at Upper Newby, the return walk on the track can always be made in the dark, even without head torches.

17 Part of The John Buchan Way, starting from Peebles

FACTFILE

Map Ordnance Survey map 73, Peebles and surrounding area
Distance 6 miles
Height 200m
Terrain mixture of path, track and minor road,
Start point Peebles car park, south side of the River Tweed, map ref 252402
Time 3 to 4 hours
Nearest town Peebles
Recommended refreshment spot a multitude of choice in Peebles

A few weeks ago I mentioned The Cateran Trail: the 64 mile walk that starts and ends in Blairgowrie – one of many long-distance walks spawned by the success of The West Highland Way. Recently the Mountain Lamb and I decided on a visit to Peebles to have a look at a new Borders walking route. Yes, you've guessed it: our chosen day for a hill walk coincided with yet more bad weather, so once again the prudent decision was to opt for an easier and shorter day. Now, I did not say a drier day. Yes, it rained later on, which only confirmed that the Mountain Lamb needed a new anorak, so it was shopping in Peebles afterwards.

The new Borders route is The John Buchan Way, which goes from Peebles to Broughton – a distance of some 13 miles. It was opened in 2003 and named after the author John Buchan (1875–1940) who had many associations with the area. The cynic might say that this is just another tourist marketing ploy, trading on the back of a well-known name. Maybe so, but the walk does seem to be well devised and interesting. Not that we did the whole walk, as we had no transport pre-arranged. Instead we started out from Peebles, and later on left the Way to get back to the River Tweed upstream of the town, for an enjoyable six-mile walk, despite the rain. There were several features that caught my attention on the way, so that disappointment in not getting to the high tops was tempered, at least for the moment.

Start in Peebles at the large car park on the south side of the Tweed, just to the east of the road bridge. Go back to the bridge and head south for a lane, way-marked with one of the many small signs that say 'The John Buchan Way' with the initials 'JBW' and a book. The direction overall is southwest, but there are a number of right angle turns through the district of Kings Muir, past a school and houses. This is not as complicated as it may seem for there are more signs on the way, heading towards the west side of Tantah House, at map ref 246393.

Now it is into open country and the slopes of Cademuir Hill. When we were there, the ground was muddy, and horses had churned up the start. No matter, as the going improves, following a grassy track on the west side of Cademuir Plantation beside a drystane dyke and fence posts. Strictly speaking, the official Way goes a bit further to the west on the path shown on the map and avoids a minor climb, but you are here for exercise, so stay by the side of the wood and the partial clear fell. There are remains of a fort and settlement at the top of Cademuir Hill and it is easy to imagine what they might have looked like. Continue with the track beside the dyke for a charming descent to the minor road on the south side of the hill.

The road (and the path that parallels the road a few yards above) goes round the base of the hill and into the Manor Valley, with the charming Manor Water flowing north to the Tweed. When the road crosses the Manor Water say goodbye to the John Buchan Way and take the right-hand turn for Kirkton Manor. At the phone box turn left on a private track (walkers, no public cars) heading towards Barns Tower. Before getting to the Tower, look out for a wooden signpost (not so obvious at first) with faint lettering, pointing to the River Tweed walk.

The next mile is by the south bank of the Tweed with a few styles to cross. At the old Manor Brig cross over with caution to reach the next section of the path on the north side, before reaching the A72. This path follows an old railway line and leads to an old bridge. Staying on the north side of the Tweed gives a return to Peebles via Neidpath Castle, but I like old railway lines so we crossed to the south side. The railway line goes through a tunnel and not knowing whether it was safe to enter, we took the signposted path. The path – though slippy with wet tree roots – has the advantage of giving an impressive view of Neidpath Castle. The path regains the railway line and shortly afterwards I got talking with a local man who confirmed that the tunnel was safe to walk through. It is dry, and daylight is only briefly lost in the curving middle section. There used to be wooden doors at either end to stop such activity, but young lads over the years have removed them. My sentiments tend not to disapprove of such delinquent behaviour. Next time I will be walking through.

18 Part of the John Buchan Way from Stobo to Broughton

FACTFILE

Map Ordnance Survey map 72, Upper Clyde Valley
Distance 6½ miles
Height 400 m
Terrain mixture of gravel and grassy tracks
Start point Stobo, on the B712 by Stobo Kirk at map ref 183375
Time 2½ to 3 hours
Nearest village Broughton
Recommended refreshment spot Laurel Bank Tea Room, Broughton

It is not true to say that hill-walkers always prefer the high tops. In adverse weather or if time is short, it can be a refreshing change to be on a walk with a well-defined way. So now for something different: a lower level walk in the Borders, with minimal climbing and a shorter distance.

The new Borders 13 mile route (opened in 2003) going from Peebles to Broughton is The John Buchan Way, named after the author John Buchan (1875–1940) who had many associations with the area. The walk is well devised and interesting, and I have already covered a stretch from Peebles, over Cademuir Hill, then left the Way to return via Neidpath Castle. Two weeks ago I did the section from Stobo to Broughton – the direction determined by a tearoom at the end – and I was lucky with the weather.

The forecast was good: rain (desperately needed for our vegetable patch) to clear overnight to give a fine day. I had my doubts on the way there as I passed through a number of heavy downpours and only when starting the walk did the weather improve to give a dry but blustery day.

A leaflet about the Way is available. Contact the Scottish Borders Council Ranger Service (01835-830281) or at rangers@scotborders.gov.uk. Even without a leaflet, Ordnance Survey map 72 (Upper Clyde Valley) is not needed, but is useful to identify distant landmarks.

When looking at the map, the route may seem slightly difficult to follow, but in fact could scarcely be easier. The way is well signposted as 'The John Buchan Way' with the initials 'JBW' and a book, and best of all with bright yellow arrows. At any point when the way ahead might seem unsure there is always another marker post very near by.

The village of Stobo stretches for about a mile on the B712. The walk starts at the north end by Stobo Kirk at map ref 183375. A phone box may be a more immediate landmark, but not to be confused with another further south beyond Stobo Castle. Follow the north bank of the Easton Burn past Easterknowe farm – a lovely start that leads to the ruined cottage at Harrowhope (not named on the Landranger) at map ref 164383. Turn left there, cross the burn by a footbridge and climb gently westwards to skirt the south side of Penvalla at a height of 350m. That amounts to an easy climb of only some 150m over two miles. There is then a delightful grassy track descending to the Hopehead Burn, a gradient such that it is difficult to go slower than 3 miles per hour. Cross the burn to reach a track which in turn leads to Stobo Hopehead – one of the most remote houses in the Borders.

From there, a way-marked grassy track (not shown on the Landranger) comfortably leads west, then southwest, to a col between Hammer Head and Broomy Side. This a scarcely noticed ascent of 200m over one mile. It is then downhill all the way, passing the only small area that might be muddy, followed by an easy stroll by the Hollows Burn, crossing it to reach Shepherd's Cottage at map ref 120374. There is a parking area available to walkers at Shepherd's Cottage but I would suggest not having a car there. That would miss out a walk on the beautiful beech-lined drive from Broughton Place that then leads to the A701 at the north end of Broughton.

Continue through the village and finish at the John Buchan Centre at the south end. The Centre is open from May to mid October daily from 2pm to 5pm, and well worth the small admission charge. Giving welcoming hospitality to walkers and tourists, and good food, the Laurel Bank Tea Room (passed on the right at the junction of the Biggar Road) is strongly recommended. It is open seven days a week all year until 5.30pm, but if planning to walk in a large group do give them a phone call (01899-830462) beforehand.

Now then, if you are not prepared to walk back to Stobo and have not investigated the MacEwan number 91 bus timetable (Traveline Scotland 0871-2002233), how do you get back to Stobo? What I did was to leave my bike at Broughton and drive round to Stobo. After a rest at the tearoom I cycled on the minor road by Dreva, a slight climb at first, and then had a glorious freewheel down to the B712.

19 The Moorfoot Hills – Dundreich

FACTFILE

Map Ordnance Survey map 73, Peebles, Galashiels & Selkirk
Distance 6 miles
Height 350m
Terrain track, then moorland slopes
Start point south end of Gladhouse Reservoir (map ref 292528), off road to Moorfoot Farm
Time 3 to 4 hours
Nearest village Eddleston
Recommended refreshment spot Scots Pine Tearoom, half a mile north of Eddleston on A703

At 622m and the highest hill in the Moorfoots, Dundreich offers contrasting views of the Pentlands to the northwest and over Gladstone Reservoir to the flatter lands of East Lothian in the northeast: ample reward, particularly on a clear day. This three to four hour outing is ideal for a shorter day; a blustery day when the Mountain lamb and I were there a few weeks ago.

The walk goes from Gladhouse Reservoir through grazing land and skirts grouse moorland (so no dogs please) with a small optional detour to the remains of Hirendean Castle. Map and compass (with knowledge of how to use them) are essential for even in clear visibility the undulating moorland can be a confusing place.

Park off the road to Moorfoot Farm at the south end of Gladhouse Reservoir (map ref 292528). There is a grassy spot with an East of Scotland Water sign saying 'No Swimming' – not that you would be tempted on a cold day! Do **not** park anywhere that would block farm traffic. Walk along the road for five minutes to Moorfoot and then turn right by cottages and farm buildings to approach in a southerly direction the beautiful glen of the River South Esk.

Continue along the track to Gladhouse Cottage on the right and the ruins of Hirendean Castle in the distance to the left. Little is left of this 16th Century peel tower, with only the south wall and the west gable still standing to any height. Dundreich cannot yet be seen but is in a southwesterly direction.

Leave the track, staying on the west side of the river, to commence the ascent up the well defined ridge parallel to the river and to the left of a large stone sheep enclosure seen in the distance. There are other routes up but this one is recommended. Continue from the top of the ridge southwesterly on an easy slope to Jeffries Corse (a small rocky outcrop) then on by a fence to the trig point at Dundreich. We were lucky in having lovely views all around, though on a cold day we did not linger. Portmore Loch – another starting point for Dundreich – lies to the northwest.

Return by the same route – although in poor visibility an alternative route from Jeffries Corse is to go in a northerly direction next to a fence. Eventually leave the fence on your left, continue north on a path to meet a stone wall and then follow it northeast down to Gladhouse Cottage.

20 Eddleston and the Cloich Hills

FACTFILE

Map Ordnance Survey map 73, Peebles
Distance 8 miles in total
Height 300m
Terrain mixture of minor roads, tracks and paths; part of the track through the forest may be very muddy
Start point Eddleston
Time 4 to 5 hours
Nearest village Eddleston
Recommended refreshment spot Scots Pine Tearoom, ½ mile north of Eddleston on the A703

The walk this week is just the job for a late February day. It goes on a circular anticlockwise route west of Eddleston, skirting the lower slopes of the wooded Cloich Hills, and gives a variety of terrain ranging from minor roads and tracks to paths. The walk is not demanding and has changing scenery from open fields to plantations, with excellent views east to Dundreich and the Moorfoots. Ordnance Survey map 73 (Peebles, Galashiels & Selkirk) is essential, for although not a complicated route there are some critical points where it would be all too easy to continue in the wrong direction. Do not run the risk of being temporarily misplaced.

Eddleston is the conservation village partly bypassed by the A703 (the Edinburgh to Peebles road). Few motorists take time to stop and appreciate the tranquillity on the other side of the Eddleston Water from the main road. Quite apart from Station Road, there are traces of the dismantled railway that parallels the A703. This of course is not the Borders rail link to be resurrected: that lies further east. The outstanding building in Eddleston is undoubtedly Barony Castle – an imposing Scottish manor house, beautifully situated in the Fairy Dean, the narrow wooded valley formed by the Fairydean Burn that flows into the Eddleston Water. The castle is now the home of the Scottish Ambulance College. The immediate district is known as Black Barony.

There is a convenient bus service on the A703 but for those arriving by car, park near the side road leading to Station Road at map ref 242472. Cross the Eddleston Water and follow the road that sweeps into the grounds of the castle. Branch right before entering the immediate precincts, then continue west to overlook the castle and the Fairydean Burn. The road goes past white outbuildings used by the ambulance service, so do not be put off by the sight of ambulances. A track continues past the buildings. Take the branch that makes an 'S' bend to cross to the south side of the burn, go round Bunny Corner (signposted) and follow the way-marked route – a bypass strip to avoid the buildings ahead. When the Mountain Hare and I were there, horses had also used the strip and it was a bit churned up.

A brocken spectre

The track continues to a junction that is not immediately obvious at map ref 228472, by which time the burn is but a trickle at the head of the dean. This is the first of three must-look-out-for points. Follow the sign 'Old Road to Shiplaw'. Head northwards over a grassy meadow and open fields to join another track from Whitelaw Burn. Continue northwards for Shiplaw, with the track giving easy walking through an open plantation with good views to Dundreich, looming over the hidden A703. On the southern slopes of the hill the wind farm turbines can be seen, but they are not intrusive.

At a road junction at map ref 233495 (Shiplaw is to the east), turn west on the tarmac road signposted for Cloich and a mile later turn southwest to pass the small farm of Cloich and enter the forest that covers the Cloich Hills. Well, not quite: felling operations are underway and careful observation of the warning notices is mandatory. When we were there the lorries had churned up the track, so you have been warned. Take sensible boots!

The track goes southwards, at first through a felled area but the muddy terrain soon improves heading for Courhope. Just before reaching the white building, take the track that branches to the left at map ref 205464 and within 100 yards look out for a path that goes off to the left. This is the second must-look-out-for point. Although the path – an old drove road to Peebles – is signposted, it would be all too easy to keep on strolling up the track. The well-made path is perhaps the prettiest part of the walk. It enters the wood, then goes gently downhill to clear the forest at a white cottage, at map ref 217460.

Cross the open field, past the cottage and a pond, and follow a track a short distance southeast. Now for the third must-look-out-for point: at map ref 221459 the Eddleston path to the left can easily be missed. Do not continue walking to Stewarton. The path goes northeast, at first through open fields, then on to a more obvious track through heathery moorland to reach the initial part of the walk by the Fairydean Burn. Retrace your steps to Eddleston.

21 Blyth Bridge to West Linton

FACTFILE

Map Ordnance Survey map 72, Upper Clyde Valley
Distance 4½ miles
Height 50m
Terrain track, muddy initially, then minor road
Start point Blyth Bridge
Time 2 hours
Nearest village West Linton
Recommended refreshment spot Olde Toll Tea House, West Linton

Wanting a short outing for a not-so-good winter day, I explored part of another Borders walk suggested by Hugh Munro, who had gone with me on the excellent St Boswells walk already described. This time I was joined by the Mountain Lamb.

The four and a half mile linear walk goes from Blyth Bridge to West Linton – a walk giving varied landscape and a surprising amount of shelter despite being around the 250m mark.

Linear walks can pose logistical problems, but not this one for there is a bus service from West Linton to Blyth Bridge that also enhances one's green credentials. The MacEwan's service (number 93) passes through Blyth Bridge en route to Peebles, giving a 15 minute transfer to the start of the walk. From West Linton there are five services per day, Monday to Saturday, departing from the bus stop by the post office in Main Street. The most suitable departure times are 10.35am and 13.55pm. There is no Sunday service. For more information contact Traveline 0871-200-22-33.

From the Blyth Bridge bus stop, head north on Blyth Farm Road to the farm. A track continues on the east bank of Blyth Dene to a sheep tank at a Y-junction at map ref 131460. The main track goes NNW but the one to follow – grassy and less obvious – goes NNE. A post with a green sign 'Tweed Trails West Linton via Bogs Bank' is most reassuring because there is little trace of a track initially – the way being little more than the grassy edge to a field and a boggy one too (at least on our visit). A firmer grassy track eventually develops as it turns northeast by the infant Blyth Burn, heading between 310m Blyth Muir and 309m Blyth Bank Hill. A number of horse-rider friendly gates are passed on the way.

By now at a height of 250m, there are more open views in the direction of West Linton. At map ref 143477 where a side track comes in from Mountain Cross Steading, is another Tweed trails signpost to the right: 'Mountain Cross via New Steading'; and straight ahead northeastwards: 'West Linton'. It would be hard to get lost!

The next three-quarter mile section, to meet a minor road that links Romanno-bridge and West Linton, is arguably the most pleasant part of the walk. The road is relatively quiet, even so walking on the right hand side to face coming traffic is recommended.

On the left is White Moss, traversed by the curving line of a dismantled railway (the Leadburn, Linton & Dolphinton line) – a branch of the Peebles Railway eventually taken over by L&NER. The coming of the railway introduced an early form of tourism to the West Linton area. Linton means 'settlement by the water', in this case the Lyne Water. The line was eventually closed for passenger service in the 1930s although much of the rail track was not lifted until the 1950s.

The line parallels the road as far as Bogs Bank and then crosses where part of the old embankment is still visible on the left-hand side. Just before a cemetery the line curves northeast over the Lyne Water to the B7059 and the site of the former station, Broomlee. By a most curious coincidence, the father-in-law of my friend John McGregor bought the old Broomlee station house in 1959.

Once past the cemetery it is an easy stroll into West Linton, latterly on Bogsburn Road, to meet the B7059 Station Road on the south side of the village. The first visit had been in December. To check out an alternative return to West Linton, Margaret and I returned two weeks ago to have a look at a footbridge over the Lyne Water by the Broomlee Outdoor Education Centre. How conditions had changed between visits! Deep, soft snow – admittedly beautiful to look at, precluded that inspection, but we will be back.

The first refreshment spot is the Olde Toll Tea House, where on both visits we enjoyed refreshment before strolling on to the post office and the bus stop.

22 A circuit of Mendick Hill

FACTFILE

Map Ordnance Survey map 72, Upper Clyde Valley
Distance 7 miles
Height climbed 150m or so
Terrain superb track and path, with only a short stretch of road
Start point by West Linton golf course at map ref 140520
Time 3½ to 4 hours
Nearest village West Linton
Recommended refreshment spot Gordon Arms Hotel, West Linton

Sandwiched between the A70 and the A702, the Pentland Hills run southwest from Edinburgh for some 15 miles, before fading away to the valley of the Clyde. Over this distance no metalled roads traverse the hills.

The last Pentland hill of note is Mendick Hill, southwest of West Linton. This modest hill of 451m has a pleasing conical shape when viewed from West Linton golf course at the start of the recommended walk for this week. A circuit of the hill involves an undulating walk of some seven miles, virtually all of which is on track and path, with only a short stretch on tarmac – the minor road at Garvald at the southwest end of the hill. South of Garvald is the bigger mass of Black Mount, steeper and higher at 516m but as it is enclosed by roads, I do not regard it as one of the Pentland hills. No one can be sure of the meaning of Mendick. It certainly is an unusual name. One suggestion is that it may originate from two words: *menyie* (a group of followers or troops) and *dicht* (meaning a blow or defeat), perhaps referring to some long forgotten skirmish between native clans and Roman troops.

Mendick Hill

The hill is a traditional Ne`er Day outing for the residents of West Linton, so today's walk is an appropriate one. The walk round the hill has connections with our prehistoric past as well as the ancient Romans, and there are links with the Covenanters. Of more recent vintage, there is a dismantled railway line at Garvald. The seven miles will just glide by. A circuit of Mendick Hill fits in well with a four-hour winter outing, for any icy blast on the day will be at your back sometime and the highest point of the walk is less than 300m. Of course there is nothing stopping you making a short climb to the top of the hill and celebrating New Year with the local residents.

If driving south on the A702 through West Linton, turn right (northwest) by the Gordon Arms Hotel on a minor road that leads to the well-signposted golf course. After half a mile turn to the left for North Slipperfield and park (not by the clubhouse parking area) nearby at map ref 140520 for the track and right of way that runs on the southeast side of the hill. Shortly later you will see the right of way signposts: 'four miles to Dolphinton' on the forward route and 'three miles to Garvald' on the return route.

The track crosses the West Water and passes South Slipperfield Farm, mostly near or by a charming wooded area. You are actually walking on another road – not that you would know it – for the track follows the line of a Roman Road and there are good views south to Broughton Heights. There just may be two small irritants: horse riders also use the good track (it can thus be a bit muddy under wet conditions), and there are a number of gates to be opened and closed. The gates however, have rider-friendly attachments, which also help walkers.

At the end of the wooded stretch at map ref 125500, there is a signpost marking a path leading straight uphill for a climb of some 200m to the trig point on Mendick Hill. Time for a quick dash up?

The Roman Road continues in a straight line (as one would expect) but the track stays closer to the hillside, passes Ingraston and goes to the site of what will be a sand pit. In passing by, do not turn to the left but go straight on. Look out for red warning signs to the left: 'Private property, trespassers will be prosecuted'. The track immediately becomes quite obvious again (developed through South of Scotland trails) and descends gently to the minor Garvald road at map ref 110479. Follow the road as it goes parallel to the line of a dismantled railway, parts of which can be walked. There are two amusing road signs on this short stretch of tarmac, one saying 'Welcome to the Scottish Borders', and 200 yards later another saying 'Welcome to North Lanarkshire'. No man's land is apparently in-between.

In approaching Garvald it is possible to do a short detour by a walled garden. Look out for the small welcome sign. Pass through Garvald and continue to Ferniehaugh underneath North Muir. Keep left at the charming pond and shortly after follow the track as it goes northeast by the side of the moor, staying above a grassy ravine that holds the stream that flows to the pond.

The bleakness of the moor is relieved by the number of moorland birds and by the remnants of three pre-historic burial cairns. The Nether Cairn at ten metres in height is the best preserved of its kind in the country. The track reaches the highest point between North Muir and Mendick Hill at what is known as The Garral – an 18th Century focal point for the outlawed gatherings of Covenanters.

The track ends at the West Water reservoir road. Follow it back to the golf course.

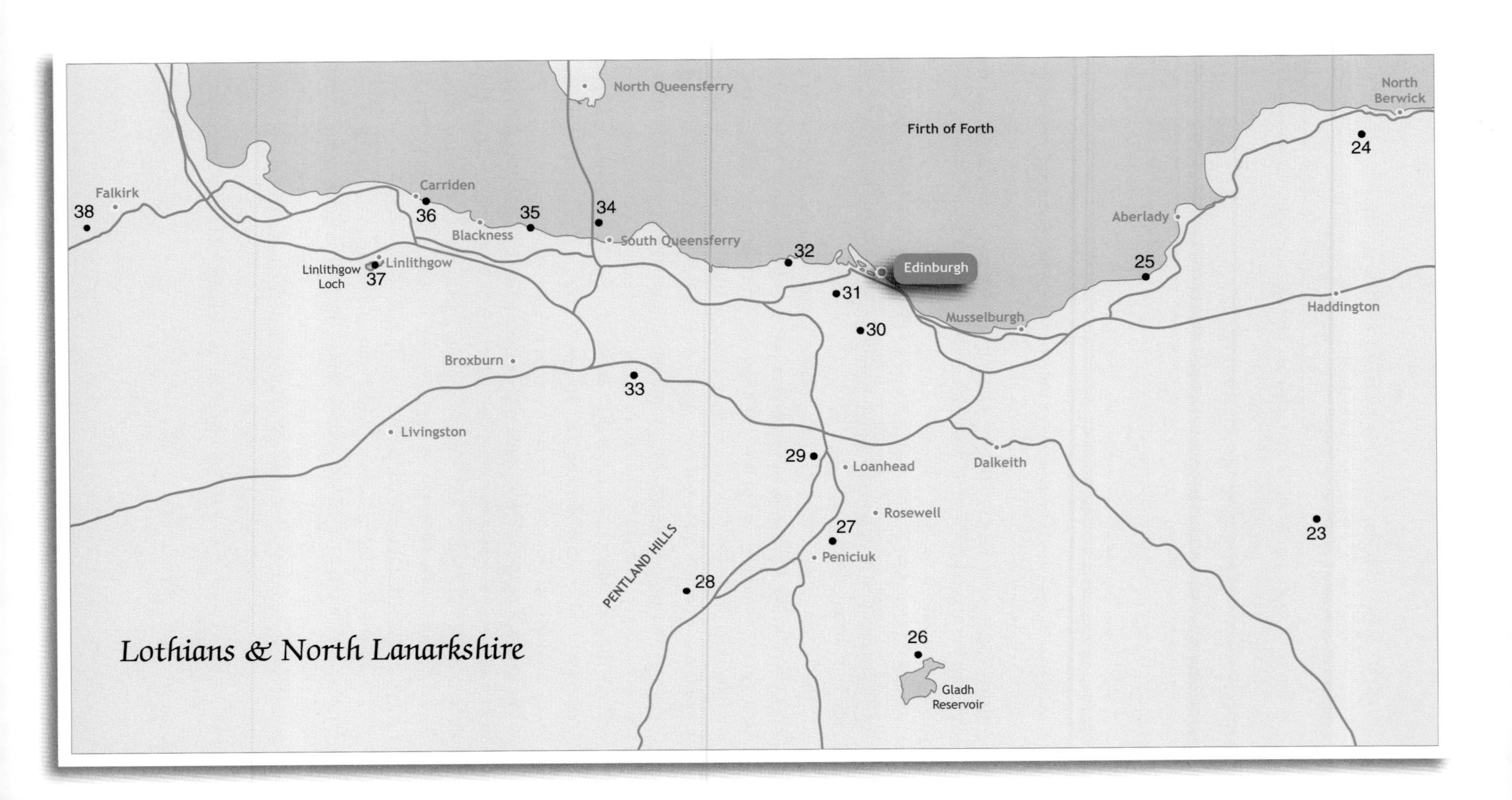
Lothians & North Lanarkshire
Firth of Forth
North Queensferry
North Berwick
24
Falkirk
38
Carriden
36
Blackness
35
34
South Queensferry
Aberlady
32
Edinburgh
25
Linlithgow Loch
Linlithgow
37
31
30
Musselburgh
Haddington
Broxburn
33
Livingston
29
Loanhead
Dalkeith
Rosewell
27
Peniciuk
23
PENTLAND HILLS
28
26
Gladh Reservoir

Lothians & North Lanarkshire

23 No snow on the Lammermuir hills

FACTFILE

Map Ordnance Survey map 66, Edinburgh and surrounding area
Distance 6 miles
Height 300 m
Terrain mixture of minor road, track and rough path
Start point Longyester, map ref 545643
Time 3 to 4 hours
Nearest village Gifford
Recommended refreshment spot Goblin Ha', Gifford

January 2005 was a difficult month for hill-walking amidst the high tops. Most days seemed to be windy and wet, and many extremely windy – up to gale force standards – with driving rain leading to extensive flooding. I am referring to conditions close to sea level. On the high tops, it was time to exercise caution and restraint – all very frustrating. Jimbo, Davie and I did have one short day on Creag Leacach (a Munro by Glen Shee) during an interlude between depressions. The wind had stripped most of the snow from the high levels, leaving the rime-covered slippery stones to be crossed with caution. Lower down on the grassy slopes, a mountain hare and a ptarmigan in their winter white stood out against the dun coloured vegetation, and nearer road level the drifting snow had accumulated.

Yet a day I enjoyed almost as much was at a different height: not as low as sea level but at the middling height to Lammer Law on the northern Lammermuir hills. It was a shorter day to be sure – one constrained by social evening events and by the weather. The forecast was for strong winds on a dry but cold day, and this proved to be so. In the event the wind, rain and above freezing temperature had whipped away any trace of snow. The Mountain Lamb, the Mountain Maid and Hare joined me.

Lammer Law stands at 527m, hence my reference to middling height. The snowless slopes made for easier walking and there was just the wind to contend with. We were all wrapped up.

Park at Longyester (map ref 545653) or further up the minor road to a cleared area by Blinkbonny Wood. The walk involves a circular walk round Hopes Reservoir, so that one half is at lower level and partly sheltered and the other is on to the rolling hills.

The first part is easy, walking northeast to reach another minor road that leads to East Hopes (at map ref 558638): a flat tarmac road, including a pleasant wooded area. It is then one mile to the reservoir on a track on the east side of the Hopes Water. Follow the track as it continues on the south side of the reservoir then take the branch that climbs south to an enclosure at map ref 543613.

At this stage I should point out that there are considerably more tracks than shown on the map so caution is required, particularly once on to the high rolling moorland. Take such a track that climbs WNW to Bleak Law; a short grassy pull up. This track curves round to the southwest. Stay with it for a while but eventually it is necessary to cut over rough tussocky ground to reach the track that is shown on the map – the right-of-way that runs from Gifford via Longyester, to Carfraemill. This route is a very old one, forming both a parish boundary and the old county boundary on the top of Lammer Law. Follow it a short distance to the north until a small rougher track heads off west for the nearby Lammer Law. Just before the top, cross yet another track not shown on the map. Even on a clear day all this can be a bit puzzling, but on a misty day strict reliance on a compass will be necessary.

The right-of-way track runs on the east side of the shoulder of Lammer Law, and on return is not immediately seen. Recross the track not shown on the map and then head northeast to reach the 'right' track a bit further north than your starting point. Confusing? Yes, so remember that compass.

It is a quick return to Longyester on this very good track (used by vehicles during the grouse season) with a gentle gradient, later passing a Scottish Rights of Way Society green signpost on the right and a quarry on the left.

The top of Lammer Law is interesting in that its cairn is shown as such on the map, indicating its antiquity. It may have seen better days – now a jumble of stones – but those stones must have been transported a long way, for the vegetation is moss and grassy, with nary an outcropping stone to be seen. There is a trig point too, this time in good state of repair. This may have been due to a triangular shaped metal cap, the likes of which I have not seen before (although the gales had blown it off). I put it back on top, in its incongruous setting. At the base of the trig point is a small and discreet memorial plaque. I fully understand the reasons beside such practices but cannot say that I agree with them.

24 Berwick Law, North Berwick

FACTFILE

Map Ordnance Survey map 66, Edinburgh, Penicuik & North Berwick
Distance 3 miles
Height 170m
Terrain urban stroll, then way-marked path to summit
Start point North Berwick railway station
Time 2 to 3 hours
Nearest town North Berwick
Recommended refreshment spot a superb choice in North Berwick

Lasting two to three hours dependent on how long spent at the summit, Berwick Law offers a short-leg stretch over the festive season: a modest climb of some 170m and an overall distance of only three miles. Throw in some items of historic interest, include the possibility for some of a short train journey and the satisfaction of leaving the car at home, and the outing will appeal to all members of the family.

Berwick Law (but shown as North Berwick Law) appears on the top right hand corner of Ordnance Survey map 66 (Edinburgh, Penicuik & North Berwick), but such is its prominence that a map is not needed. Although of modest height at 187m/615ft, this volcanic plug – formed 35 million years ago – towers above North Berwick and the flat plain of East Lothian; a plug that from a distance looks almost too steep to climb. Closer inspection of course shows that by following the obvious path there is no difficulty in reaching the top.

With an Iron Age fort on the hillside, the Law is a scheduled ancient monument with an outstanding viewpoint boasting both viewfinder and trig point. The Law, once owned by the Cistercian Convent, was used to give early warning of enemy approaches. A nun is said to have lit a beacon in 1544 when English ships sailed into the Forth. A watch house was built during the time of the Napoleonic Wars when sentries were garrisoned, ready to set fire to a beacon to signal danger of invasion. The remains of the watch house are still there as is a concrete shelter lookout post from the Second World War.

It is a crowded place on top, but that is not all. The Law is renowned for its arch made from the jawbones of an Antarctic whale, first installed in 1709 to help guide sailors safely home. There have been three successors, their presence becoming a symbol of North Berwick. Having become dangerous, the jawbones of 1935 were removed by helicopter in 2005, but after a gap of three years the latest jawbones are now in place (well not quite). Not that you would know from a distance, but the latest are made of long-lasting fibreglass. The six and a half metre high replica was winched into position by helicopter, and is now safely ensconced behind a protective fence.

The Mountain Maid and Mountain Hare came with me on a lovely early winter day. As keen cyclists their initial plan was to cycle from Edinburgh then return by rail, taking advantage of ScotRail's separate compartment racked for eight bikes. ScotRail are to be commended for this initiative. However, in the end we all travelled together by rail: a relaxing hourly service, a half-hour journey and a day return cost of £3.50 for those with a senior railcard – considerably cheaper and faster than travelling by car. However, do check on train times.

Glancing up to the Law gives a general idea of direction through the town, but before leaving the station look at the useful town map on the notice board. This gives a clearer idea of where to go.

Turn right on leaving the station and head SSE, continuing in a straight line to Trainers Brae with its gently rising tree-lined tarmac footpath. Continue to the end of the path and turn left (eastwards) into Grange Road, passing the High School and sports centre. Turn right (south), passing a black finger post for the Law and later a green John Muir Way (JMW) sign. The JMW bypasses the Law on its west side en route from North Berwick to Dunbar.

Continue due south at the end of Wishart Avenue, where a track and parallel path lead to a car park at map ref 553844, but please do not start the walk from there! Follow the path south, but a few yards after a stone stile take the side path that starts to climb the Law. With ever increasing views all round, the effort of getting to the top is soon over.

Our visit was on a day of clear blue sky and modest breeze: a day of extreme clarity. Do save the Law for such a day and spend time at the top. The viewfinder is well-worth studying and the Bass Rock will seem very close at hand.

25 From Musselburgh to Aberlady on the John Muir Way

FACTFILE

Map Ordnance Survey map 66, Edinburgh
Distance 11 miles
Height negligible
Terrain good coastal path and pavements, but beware of seaweed
Start point Fisherrow Harbour, Musselburgh
Time 4 to 6 hours
Nearest village Aberlady
Recommended refreshment spot Kilspindie House Hotel, Aberlady

Contrary to what others might think, hill-walkers can walk on flat ground! More than that, they are capable of enjoying such a walk, away from the high tops. Over the festive season (did someone mention the dreaded word 'shopping'?) with a myriad of

Robin heading for the hills

things to do, a whole day spent hill-walking may soak up too much time. Yet exercise calls, and a compromise of a low level walk taking up less time may suit – even one at sea level all the way.

East Lothian Council is developing a coastal path to provide a continuous route linking East Lothian with the City of Edinburgh and the Scottish Borders: 'the route offers magnificent views of the East Lothian coastline and a chance to see the natural history and historic sites of this unique landscape' – an accurate comment. Currently the path extends only from Fisherrow Harbour in Musselburgh (the west boundary of East Lothian) to the delightful village of Aberlady, and after a gap continues from Dunbar to the boundary with the Borders. Leaflets describing the coastal path are available from libraries, tourist information or directly from East Lothian Council.

The coastal path is called The John Muir Way, named after the father of world conservation, who was born in Dunbar.

So how about a level eleven-mile walk from Musselburgh to Aberlady, passing the villages of Prestonpans, Cockenzie and Port Seton? With so much to look at, estimating a time for the walk is almost impossible. Actual walking time could be just four hours, but with many stops of interest on the way it may be quite a bit later when you reach Aberlady.

There may be problems though: how to get back home, and how to cope with younger members of the family? Public transport goes through Aberlady, but getting a bus timetable is essential. Taking two cars to Aberlady and leaving one there can be arranged but is not ideal.

Younger members of the family do not like long walks – boring and tiring – so why not travel by bike, cycling there and back? The 22 miles can be easily covered in three hours, yet even youngsters may find the time out extending to five hours with those places of interest (and there are lots of refreshments spots). Visit the Prestongrange Museum and Visitor Centre (which has free admission, a café and toilets). Near Fisherrow harbour – an old boyhood haunt of mine – is the quayside: a good refreshment spot from which to start the day, or to return to if cycling both ways. The way is well signposted and if in doubt at any time, keep to the coastline. There is a loop back to cross the River Esk in Musselburgh, but then the path continues past the end of Musselburgh racecourse and so to Levenhall Links – a magnet for ornithologists. The expanse of sand and mudflats attracts flocks of wading birds and wildfowl, and pools have been created to encourage bird life. There were many birdwatchers when we passed by.

Afterwards you may wish to make a brief diversion to the seaside road (the B1348) to avoid one of the Scottish Power 'ponds', but children will prefer the direct muddy route. Some of the old ash lagoons have been incorporated into Levenhall Links. After a short road walk, it is back to the coast again, and a section that should only be missed if it is high-tide. This is a concrete pathway that stays close to the water's edge and is a must for children. But beware – apart from the dangers of high tide and crashing waves, footing can be very slippery with seaweed. Some short sections of the concrete have been covered in pebbles – testament to the power of the sea – and there are interesting murals on the sea walls, sponsored by the Prestongrange Arts Festival.

At Prestongrange Yacht Club, keep to the grassy slopes heading for a gate that leads to the perimeter track around Cockenzie Power Station, where the promenade attracts sea anglers. Later, after another short detour, it is on to the charming small harbours of Cockenzie and Port Seton.

Port Seton was once a very popular holiday resort. There are now more open seascapes over Seton Sands and Gosford Bay. After a short section on the cycle way, the coastal path resumes beside the road along to Gosford Sands. It is quite narrow in places and indeed you will want to walk along the beach at times. Note that this section is not for bikes – stay with care on what is now the A198. The junction with the B1348 is another of many escape-routes, this one being a short walk to Longniddry railway station.

I have always felt sorry for the poor trees sheltering behind the wall opposite Gosford Bay – all twisted and gnarled, for it can be a windy spot (of more concern if cycling).

The last mile of the walk is by the main road going into Aberlady with the path staying in the thin strip of woodland on the left side of the road.

After some refreshment, now it is time to get home, and if you are walking or cycling back to Fisherrow, I hope the prevailing wind is not in your face.

26 A winter walk around Gladhouse Reservoir

FACTFILE

Map Ordnance Survey map 66, Edinburgh or map 73, Peebles.
Distance 5 miles
Height climbed 50m at most
Terrain quiet minor roads, farm tracks and path
Start point northeast side of reservoir, map ref 308542
Time 2 to 3 hours
Nearest towns Penicuik and Peebles
Recommended refreshment spot a good choice in both towns

For a two to three hour's brisk walk on a raw January day, a five mile circuit of Gladhouse reservoir may offer sufficient exercise. The reservoir lies in the shadow of the Moorfoot hills – some five miles southeast of Penicuik and seven miles north of Peebles – and the proximity of the Moorfoots may give the frustrated hillwalker the temporary illusion of being near to the high tops. However, the minor roads that cover most of the perimeter are fairly quiet, and on the circuit it is difficult to imagine 'climbing' more than 50m.

Gladhouse reservoir is fed by the River South Esk, which has its source to the south in the Moorfoots very close to the 651m top of Blackhope Scar. The (depleted) outflow from the reservoir continues as the river, later to be joined by the River North Esk north of Dalkeith and continues to Musselburgh. Incidentally, the Esk Valley Trust – which promotes rural paths along both tributaries of the River Esk in the Lothians – is working on the creation of a continuous 27-mile route between the Pentland Hills and the sea at Musselburgh: The Esk Valley Way. At the time of writing, and with some missing links, this long term objective has still to bear fruition.

The reservoir is on two Ordnance Survey maps: map 66 (Edinburgh) and map 73 (Peebles). Although a road map may be required to get there and an OS map is more informative, strictly speaking such a map is not needed for the majority of the circuit is by the water's edge. However on the southeast side, a path/track links Mauldslie and Moorfoot farms, and whilst the way is signposted, you may prefer to have map to hand. When we were there in late December, conditions underfoot on that latter section were quite muddy, and the usual advice of sensible footwear (and winter clothing) applies.

Gladhouse is the most southerly of the Midlothian reservoirs and one of a network supplying Edinburgh with water. The depth of the water however, is only 10m and this betrays the history of the reservoir, for unusually expanding an existing loch did not create it. Old maps show that the River South Esk did not even flow through a lochan, yet the construction of a small embankment at the (now) north side was sufficient to store and spread out the waters over a large area, thus creating the largest body of freshwater in the Lothians, covering an area of 460 acres with a number of small islands. Surrounded by coniferous and mixed woodland, the reservoir is popular with anglers, being well stocked with brown trout. It is also of interest to birdwatchers, and designated as a Site of Special Scientific Interest for it is internationally significant as an important winter roosting area for thousands of pink-footed geese that feed in surrounding areas of agricultural land. The shallow waters have a small area of marginal fen. In spring, direct access to the shoreline is not promoted, so stay with the circuit road and waymarked track/path.

The walk features in a recently published booklet *Explore Midlothian*, promoting tourism in Midlothian. Further information is available from the Midlothian Ranger Service at Gorebridge (telephone 01875-821990). There are no toilets or public transport. There are two small car parks mentioned in the booklet on the north side (around map ref 305544), but when we were there last month they were boarded off. I understand that the water authority has had problems with vandalism and unruly behaviour. There are however, other small areas where considerate parking is possible, such as at the extreme northeast side of the reservoir with space for a few cars at map ref 308542, or at the southern end by the minor road to Moorfoot at map ref 293527 (although the latter spot can be muddy).

Start from the northeast end of the reservoir at map ref 308542, east of the Scottish Water car park. We did a clockwise circuit, but either way suffices. Go south on the road for less than a mile to Maudslie farm and turn right at a junction. Continue on a track/grassy path to the south of the farm and head southwest then southeast, past Huntly Cottage and southwest again to Moorfoot farm. This section is more distant from the water's edge and goes amid farmland. You can't get lost on the remaining part of the walk. Simply follow the perimeter road to Gladhouse and the Scottish Water fisheries office, continue over the short dam, and so back to the start, passing the closed-off car park.

27 From Rosewell to Penicuik and return

FACTFILE

Map Ordnance Survey map 66, Edinburgh
Distance 8 miles
Height negligible
Terrain old railway track
Start point junction of the B7003 and Rosewell
Time 3 to 4 hours; less if cycling
Nearest town Penicuik
Recommended refreshment spot a good choice in Penicuik

Part of the Dalkeith to Penicuik cycle route that goes up Roslin Glen and the River North Esk, this eight-mile walk is most definitely not a walk on the wild side. It does however, lend itself to a gentle summer evening outing (possibly for the whole family), starting at Rosewell and returning by the same route.

It has a lot of attractions for a summer evening stroll – a gentle gradient, an interesting and varied route and the opportunity to stop at the halfway point in Penicuik for a welcome refreshment. Indeed once at Penicuik there could be a clash: who is going to walk back to Rosewell to collect the car whilst the others – after a less than demanding four-mile stroll – stay in a pleasant pub? I must confess that on a previous visit, Margaret and I cycled all the way to Penicuik and back, with a pub stop at the halfway point.

Children of all ages will be impressed with the two tunnels, the variety of bridges and an old railway station at Rosslyn Castle. Younger children may be happier to be cycling!

The start point is at the junction of the B7003 and Rosewell (map ref 285629). Ordnance Survey map 66 can be used, however try to get hold of a Midlothian Cycle Map (published by Spokes and obtainable at cycle shops). At two inches-to-the-mile, much greater detail of the route is obtained.

In arriving at Penicuik there is a short climb into the town centre where there is a choice of pubs. For this reason I suggest starting at Rosewell and hence a halfway stop, but the whole route could just as well start at Penicuik.

28 Five Pentland Hills from Nine Mile Burn

FACTFILE

Map Ordnance Survey map 66, Edinburgh
Distance 5 miles
Height 350m
Terrain mostly track and path
Time 2 to 3 hours
Start point Nine Mile Burn
Nearest village Carlops
Recommended refreshment spot Allan Ramsay Hotel, Carlops

In the summer months a two-hour evening stroll on the Pentland of five miles with minimum climbing is straightforward, but winter is another matter. The Mountain Lamb and I did a circuit above Monks Burn on the day of the first November snows and the two-hour stroll became a three-hour walk fighting the elements as if we were on the high tops. So pick a fine winter's day for a pleasant circuit over five relatively easy hills, and allow some two to three hours.

The start point is at Nine Mile Burn (map ref 178577), just north of the A702 Edinburgh to Biggar road, one and a half miles before the old staging post of Carlops, if travelling from Edinburgh.

The hills to be covered in a clockwise circuit are Patie's Hill, Spittal Hill, Green Law, Cap Law and Braid Law; mainly on grassy terrain, subject to snow. Map and compass may be needed for navigation in poor visibility, especially after Green Law, otherwise the hills to head for can be clearly seen.

Park at the left-hand bend opposite the cottages and head along the minor road for a quarter of a mile until the clearly-marked right turning for Spittal Farm. Walk between the farm buildings, passing by a solid gate and into the open countryside on a wide farm track. Gradually gain height for half a mile westwards to the col between Patie's Hill on your left and Spittal Hill in the distance on your right. Climb a gate in the left hand fence to follow a path south up Patie's Hill for a quarter of a mile to the top. The lack of cairns to denote the tops may disconcert you.

A wintry day on the Pentlands

Retrace your steps to the track to climb Spittal Hill, which forms a ridge about a mile long with the next hill, Green Law. Keeping a fence on your right, a gradual half mile ascent brings you to the top of Spittal Hill. Continue north to Green Law half a mile away.

Descend NNE and then southeast, keeping to higher ground in a wide swoop to Cap Law a mile distant. There is a wood on lower ground north of Cap Law. Continue southeast to Braid Law half a mile away.

To reach the path back to Nine Mile Burn, descend steeply westwards to Quarrel Burn. The path heads broadly south on the well-signposted path for the final mile back to Nine Mile Burn.

The nearest refreshment spot is the highly-recommended Allan Ramsay Hotel in Carlops, so named after the Edinburgh poet's links with the village.

29 A circuit of Caerketton Hill

FACTFILE

Map Ordnance Survey map 66, Edinburgh
Distance 4½ miles
Height 450m
Terrain good path for most of the way
Start point public car park by Swanston Golf Club
Time 3 to 4 hours
Nearest city Edinburgh
Recommended refreshment spot Swanston Golf Club restaurant

The best laid schemes o' mice an' hillwalkers gang aft a-gley. A couple of weeks ago I had planned to meet up with Drew and John to tackle Beinn Dearg, the hill north of Blair Atholl. However, on seeing the weather forecast those plans were scrapped. Beinn Dearg lies a long way from the road end and the plateau is not the place to be on a bitterly cold windswept February day of limited visibility.

With a last minute change of plan, I met up instead with the Mountain Maid and the Mountain Hare for a morning-only walk from Swanston over Caerketton Hill and Allermuir Hill at the north end of the Pentlands. Despite being slightly lower than Allermuir, Caerketton is the more prominent hill with the ski-centre on its lower slopes being a familiar sight.

Once on top of both hills, standing upright at times in the blustery wind posed problems. The decision to climb to only 1600ft rather than over 3000ft, proved to be most sensible. However, as we descended into the shelter of Boghall Glen, it quickly felt like another day. We then returned to Swanston by way of a circuit round the east end of Caerketton.

From the public car park, follow the path that leads south through the picturesque village of Swanston with its whitewashed cottages. Built in the 18th Century for workers on the estate, the cottages were restored in 1964 and are the only group in Lowland Scotland to be thatched with reed from the Firth of Tay. Robert Louis Stevenson spent his summers in nearby Swanston Cottage and the village provides the setting for his novel *St. Ives*.

Continue gently climbing south by the Swanston Burn, with the golf course to the west and the T wood to the east, to reach a path junction at map ref 237666. The main path goes southwest direct to Allermuir; the path to the ESE goes past the Hillend ski centre and is the return route. However, continue southwards on grassy slopes, west of the crags of Caerketton and the only serious climb of the day, to reach the ridge just west of Caerketton's summit. If not too windy, it is an easy stroll to the 478m/1568ft summit. The annual Caerketton Hill Race, starting from Hillend, involves an 800ft climb. The record time of 12 minutes 18 seconds (there and back) was set by Phil Mowbray in 2000. We were considerably slower!

On our outing those grassy slopes were snow-covered and we had the strong blustery wind to contend with. Nevertheless, with glorious black and white views from the top, the effort was well worthwhile.

The way westwards to Allermuir is obvious: a descent to the dip at the head of Boghall Glen then a short ascent to the 493m/1617ft summit – also a wonderful viewpoint and boasting both trig point and viewpoint indicator. Allermuir is one of many Marilyns (UK hills of any height but with a drop of at least 150m all round).

Return to the dip. The more detailed 1:25000 Explorer map, sheet 344 (Pentland Hills) shows this dip as Windy Door Nick – an appropriate name on our outing.

Head south into the shelter of the glen to a track (shown on the Explorer map) that descends southeast above the Boghall Burn. Before reaching two masts at map ref 241653, leave the track and go northeast round the lower slopes of Caerketton to join a path that leads NNE above Boghall Plantation. Thereafter follow the signposts for Swanston.

Return on what is called Capital View Walk above the artificial ski-slopes (claimed to be Europe's longest) to the first path junction at map ref 237666 and so back to the car park.

Once muddy boots had been changed for dry shoes, we retired to the Swanston Golf Club restaurant for welcoming refreshment – our cheeks now glowing from the effect of the wind and our satisfaction in having snatched a good few hours from the elements.

So, if the weather on your planned February outing is not of the best, you could do far worse than this short walk. However, with magnificent views from both hills looking north over Edinburgh and the Firth of Forth, do keep the walk for a day of reasonable visibility.

30 From The Age of Innocence to the top of Arthur's Seat

FACTFILE

Map Edinburgh street map
Distance 2 miles
Height 200m
Terrain pavement, road and path
Start point Commonwealth Pool by Holyrood Park Road
Time 2 to 3 hours
Nearest city Edinburgh
Recommended refreshment spot a vast choice in Edinburgh

To call this weekend's outing 'a walk on the wild side' gives completely the wrong impression, for I am suggesting a more leisurely activity, perhaps in keeping with the festive season.

Now that Christmas has just passed, some of the memories of all that shopping and wrapping presents (and the myriad of those last-minute frantic requirements that go into its preparation) are fading. Yet the January sales (although some I believe now start in December) will be upon us soon. It comes as quite a shock for hill-walkers (even for some lady hill-walkers?) to realise that on a good weather day some people prefer to go into town to do some visual shopping – just looking around, or even worse to do some actual shopping. Much worse than all of that, some of them actually seem to be enjoying themselves. Margaret has enough sense to take me shopping only on highly selected days, with very clear and short objectives in mind.

Yet it is still important (at least in my book) whether or not you are a keen hill-walker, to have a break and indulge in a restricted (but nevertheless most welcome) short period of physical exercise. So it being a new year, I suggest that you make a trip to your nearest local hill, no matter how insignificant it might seem. For a short outing, the weather is of less consequence and the hour or so spent may get you into fighting trim for those January sales.

Scotland has a variety of such appropriate hills (most of which I have climbed), but being based in Edinburgh and with limited time, we will be going to Arthur's Seat. So if you are anywhere near, why not try Arthur's Seat. Oh yes I know, you may well have been there many times before, but so what?

The shortest and easiest way up is from Dunsapie Loch, but of course from the circular road there are multiple choices. For something a bit longer (and definitely different), why not start from the age of innocence, perhaps appropriate for this time of year.

The Edinburgh and Dalkeith railway – built principally to bring coal from the pits at Dalhousie to the depot at St Leonard's – was completed in 1831. Originally horses drew the wagons and because of the slow pace people were able to get on and off with

Arthur's Seat, January 2011

few accidents, without having to have official stops – hence the name of the 'Innocent Railway'. One other explanation I have come across is that the railway opened up the innocent or clean countryside to dwellers in Auld Reekie. The line carried passengers until 1860 but the transit of goods ceased in 1968.

Start near the Commonwealth Pool by Holyrood Park Road and turn into East Parkside. The old railway line immediately starts through a tunnel, all of 556 yards long. It was completed in 1829, one of the earliest railway tunnels in the world. The tunnel is lit but I have suggested starting the walk from there. 'Out of darkness and into Holyrood park and up to the top of Arthur's Seat at 251m, all very symbolic and pagan no doubt.

At the exit turn right for access to the park area and walk back up, parallel to the tunnel to the two small roundabouts that lead on to Queen's Drive. The Drive circles Arthur's Seat. Go anti-clockwise to get to Dunsapie Loch, and so to the top. No Ordnance Survey map is needed, perhaps just a street map.

31 The Water of Leith – Balerno to Leith

FACTFILE

Map The Water of Leith Walkway guide
Distance 12 miles
Height 160m, but only if walking to Balerno
Terrain old railway line, then excellent pathway system, with some road crossings
Start point by the High School in Balerno
Time a generous 5 hours
Nearest city Edinburgh
Recommended refreshment spot a wide choice in Leith

In the days when waterpower was all-important, the Water of Leith played a vital part in the development of Edinburgh. It bisects the city, yet vast stretches of it are almost hidden and the excellent pathway system gives the opportunity for a long, secluded and pretty walk that at times could be in the countryside.

Following the Water of Leith all the way from Balerno to Leith is a distance of 12 miles. Allow a generous five hours (including plenty of stops for refreshments), but do not be surprised if it takes less time than that, for it is an easy walking route, gently downhill descending 160m to sea level. In the event of any problems there are plenty of points with public transport nearby, where the walk can be left.

Take the children along, for one of the delights is the scope for doing more or less according to family situations. But for those with no such restrictions I strongly suggest the whole walk. Even on a poor day it is a sheltered outing, so do not let the

A Monet scene on the Water of Leith

weather put you off. There is a surprising amount of wild life. Over 80 species of birds have been recorded, so look out for dippers, wagtails and swans, and you might be lucky enough to see a heron or a kingfisher.

No map is really needed and the way is well signposted, but having a guidebook will enhance the enjoyment of the walk. This can be obtained at the Water of Leith Visitor Centre in Lanark Road, or by phoning 0131-455-7367. The Centre is open in the winter months Wednesday to Sunday, 10am to 4pm but from April those hours apply seven days a week. Other information on the Water of Leith Walkway can be obtained at the Visitor Centre, which is well worth a visit in any case, and when there why not consider becoming a member of the Conservation Trust?

Starting at Balerno to take advantage of the down slope, the first stage of five miles goes past Currie, Juniper Green and Colinton, and on to the Visitor Centre at Slateford. It follows the path of the Old Balerno Branch railway line, running parallel to the river. The railway – opened in 1874 – was in use until 1968, although passenger traffic was discontinued in 1943. Later the old line veers to the left and the Water of Leith path continues into Colinton Dell. The five miles to Slateford may be far enough for the younger and less fit participants, delighted in their ability to have walked that far. Take care when crossing Lanark Road to reach the Visitor Centre.

The next stage of four miles goes as far as Canonmills – another of the many escape routes with public transport nearby. Care is needed in crossing Gorgie Road, and later when leaving Saughton Gardens and crossing Balgreen Road.

The last three miles to Leith may only present a few difficulties for those not used to walking longer distances. Passing by the Royal Botanic Gardens, some quirks (not difficulties) in this last stretch are the signposts indicating the distance to Leith. They are suspect and you may feel that you are walking backwards.

32 From Cramond to the site of the former gas works at Granton

FACTFILE

Map Ordnance Survey map 66, Edinburgh
Distance 7 miles, retracing steps
Height negligible
Terrain paths and pavements
Start point Cramond Village, Edinburgh
Time 3 to 4 hours
Nearest city Edinburgh
Recommended refreshment spot Cramond Gallery Bistro, quayside, Cramond

This week's walk by the Forth from Cramond and Silverknowes Esplanade gives a circuit of the former gas works at Granton, an area now being redeveloped by National Grid Property (formerly British Gas). The redevelopment is known as The Forthquarter: an entirely new Edinburgh district of mixed development; commercial, residential, educational and leisure and formerly opened in April 2010.

The leisure aspect – a new recreation ground known as Forthquarter Park – is a remarkable transformation of the central part of the gas works. National Grid are keen for people to start using the park, which was already quite busy on the second of two visits in December [At that time there were still a few areas under construction and most gates to the park were closed, however construction has now been completed and all gates opened].

My first exploratory visit had been on an atrocious day when I toured by car to get acquainted with the layout of the new roads. However, the Mountain Maid and Mountain Hare went with me on a second visit when we cycled round the new area. Although a good day to be out and about at sea level, it was breezy and chilly enough to remind us that it was not a day for the high tops.

Ordnance Survey map 66 (Edinburgh), covers the walk but the scale is insufficient to give enough detail and my copy at least still shows the gas works. Of considerably more help and strongly recommended is a larger scale up-to-date street map showing the new roads and park.

There is a public car park (and toilets) in Cramond village. The tide was well out and the tidal causeway and sandy flats leading to Cramond Island were tempting, but we had exploration to do.

Silverknowes Esplanade goes east for almost two miles to West Shore Road, but just before reaching the road, turn left on a cycleway path to stay by the shoreline. Continue east with the path eventually leading back to the road. Turn right, heading back west for 150 yards to what will be the northern end of Waterfront Broadway. A cycle path heads south, parallel to the road, passing Royston House and Caroline Park Avenue and leading back to the Broadway.

Sir George Mackenzie bought the Barony of Royston in 1683 and built what was originally known as Royston House. His son, Lord Royston, sold the house to the 2nd Duke of Argyll who renamed it Caroline Park after his daughter. Now in private residence, its estates of old have been lost over the years to neighbouring developments including the gas works.

This last section takes a loop around a stark reminder of what used to be the one remaining gasholder. This – the oldest of three (the other two were demolished and removed by 2004) – is currently B-listed at the request of Historic Scotland, although severe deterioration and rusting has raised safety concerns.

Cross Waterfront Broadway to reach the east gate of Forthquarter Park, where a £2 million investment has created an impressive eight-hectare landscaped open space with boardwalks and water features. The environmental impact has been fundamental in the design. Native plants and trees (many a silver birch) have been used and the water features act as a Sustainable Urban Drainage System. Do make the detour via the south gate on West Granton Road / Waterfront Park to the long-established Granton Pond – a reminder of the area's industrial heritage and now home to a wide range of local wildlife.

On the day of our visit the east gate on Waterfront Broadway and the western gates leading to West Shore Road and hence back to Silverknowes Esplanade were all closed. We were thus obliged to retrace our steps. However, all gates are now open, thus giving direct access between the waterfront promenade and Edinburgh's major walking and cycle routes.

33 A towpath walk – Edinburgh to Broxburn

FACTFILE

Map Ordnance Survey maps 65, Falkirk and Linlithgow, and 66, Edinburgh.
Distance 22 miles
Height none
Terrain towpath all the way
Start point Union Canal, Fountainbridge, Edinburgh
Time 7 hours
Nearest city Edinburgh
Recommended refreshment spot The Bridge Inn, Ratho

Hill-walkers seeking the high tops sometimes have quite a walk in just getting to the lower slopes. And contrary to what some people may think, it may well be that the best part of the day out is in such a flat early walk. This could be due to adverse weather higher up, or simply because the walk in is through a beautiful glen. A few frankly boring hills are only redeemed because of such a lowland setting. And again, contrary to what some people may think, most hill-walkers can take great pleasure in seeking out only a low level walk, leaving the high tops to another day. So this is one of those days – a low level walk, flat as well.

They don't come any flatter than a canal towpath – in this case along the side of the Union Canal. I was involved with a group in Edinburgh (Ageing Well 50 plus), who amongst other things have a regular Thursday morning walk. This comprises a walk of only three to four miles with a rest spot for some tea and a sticky bun, so it is hardly challenging, yet for some who are less able, lacking in confidence, or needing to attain some fitness, then the walk is more of a challenge. Such folk are pleasantly surprised how much easier it is to be on the level all morning, and the usual question at the end of the walk is, 'how far did we walk this morning, Robin?'. It is easy to exaggerate at first, but as the weeks go by no subterfuge is necessary!

Far from the high tops, do I find canal walks a bit tame? Not really and if you don't quite believe me then why not try walking from the start of the Union Canal at Fountainbridge in Edinburgh and see how far you can walk. You may be surprised just how easy it is and interesting too to let the miles slip by. You do not really need maps, but a better understanding of just where you are is obtained by taking with you Ordnance Survey maps 65 (Falkirk and Linlithgow) and 66 (Edinburgh).

The first four miles takes one away from the city centre as far as the city by-pass. It is a most varied stretch, only partly industrialised and mostly with that appearance that causes one to think, 'am I really out in the countryside instead of passing through a city?' The contrast is immense, what with the aqueduct over the Water of Leith (have you a head for heights?) and through the recently restored section in Wester Hailes.

It must be admitted that it is noisy crossing over the by-pass road, and the next mile runs rather too close to the M8 for pleasure, yet the contrast in noise levels in this section serves in a peculiar way to heighten the enjoyment.

Now you are into the country with five easy miles done already. Too far? Well you can escape at Hermiston and get public transport back on the A71.

Two miles further on takes you to Ratho – a sylvan setting indeed with barges moored to the side, swans gracefully going past on the water and a refreshment spot into the bargain.

It is less than four miles on to Broxburn, only slightly spoiled by the proximity at times of the M8 but there are attractions in crossing the River Almond and a perverse pleasure in going under the motorway and waving it good bye as the canal curves round to the north to Broxburn. This is eleven miles in total and, subject to that refreshment stop, comfortably walked in three and a half hours.

Now have you checked up on public transport there or have you already organised transport of you own? Or why bother with all that? Just walk back to Edinburgh – it is only a round trip of 22 miles and as I have mentioned you will be surprised just how easy it is: seven daylight hours gone by in a flash.

There is plenty of scope for more towpath walking if the weather is a bit adverse for the high tops. After all, you can go all the way to Bowling on the Clyde by linking up with the Forth and Clyde canal at the Falkirk Wheel.

34 Across the Forth

FACTFILE

Map Ordnance Survey map 65, Falkirk & Linlithgow
Distance 5 miles
Height 100m
Terrain pavement and road
Start point Hawes Pier, South Queensferry
Time 2 to 3 hours, depending on tourist stops
Nearest town South Queensferry
Recommended refreshment spot a vast choice in both North and South Queensferry

Years ago, when the plan to build a road bridge across the Forth was announced, the realisation that this would mean farewell to the much-loved ferry service spurred a group of us from Edinburgh to have another crossing of the Forth. We took a train to Dalmeny station then walked to South Queensferry, followed by a nostalgic crossing. Soon the four ferries – making over 40 crossings per year, carrying 1.5 million people and 800,000 cars and lorries – would be redundant. We returned by train, looking down from the Victorian masterpiece to the ferry and throwing the odd coin for luck. Do people still do that? This summer, a boat trip on the Forth starting from the partially seaweed-covered Hawes Pier, brought back those memories.

The road bridge has now been in operation for over 40 years and the twin bridges –road and rail – have become a tourist attraction. The cantilever rail bridge (opened in 1890) looks stunning when floodlit; yet there had been criticism about insufficient maintenance. Nevertheless, it looks as if it could last forever – a tribute to Victorian engineers and conservative over-engineering following the Tay Bridge disaster. It is ironic that the road bridge (despite its relative youth) should now be having rust problems, corrosion weakening its cables. The bridge is struggling to cope with 24 million vehicles a year – double its design capacity. Now we are facing the imminent prospect of a second road bridge with the first reduced to car-only status.

I am a member of the Friendly Walkers – an informal group of enthusiasts who meet in Edinburgh every Thursday morning for casual strolls of some two hours. In May they had a three-mile walk across the Road Bridge and back. I was unable to go that week but I did the crossing at the end of November – a chilly Sunday morning short exercise away from the high tops. Unlike hill-walking however, it is not a quiet walk (the traffic takes care of that), but the views are panoramic and different.

Tired of walking?

For something different to start the New Year, the bridge walk is ideal and I have extended it to include North and South Queensferry. Ordnance Survey map 65 (Falkirk & Linlithgow) is not needed for the route but is useful to identify distant landmarks.

The walk is described from Hawes Pier in South Queensferry, though of course it could just as well start from Fife. With a hint of superiority, the locals on the Lothians side do not use the prefix 'South' nor indeed does the Ordnance Survey. To get to Queensferry, why not be green and travel by bus, train to Dalmeny, or cycle? Take time at Hawes Pier to admire the rail bridge. At your back is the Hawes Inn – known to readers of Robert Louis Stevenson's *Kidnapped* – another sign as to the antiquity of Queensferry, once a Royal Burgh. The 'Queen' was Margaret, wife of Malcolm Canmore who commuted between royal residences in Edinburgh and Dunfermline, the ferry being operated by monks from Dunfermline.

Walk west along Edinburgh Road to the more charming cobbled High Street, making a short detour to the harbour. Continue on Hopetoun Road which then climbs to the left and passes under the concrete bridge. Go under the bridge and climb south to reach its west side, north of the toll station. There is nothing to pay!

A nine-foot cycle path and walkway separates the walker from the road traffic. It could be argued that this is a high-level walk – or may seem so – for the road level at mid-span is 208ft above the water and there is an element of exposure. The railing beside the walkway is not very high and seems even lower when cycling. There is no shelter from a crosswind, so be well wrapped up.

On the way over there are good views along the Forth over to Rosyth, and below is the marine at Port Edgar – so named after the brother of Queen Margaret.

Once at the north end of the bridge, turn left to reach the Forth Bridges Visitor Centre (located off the B981, the old ferry road) within the Queensferry Lodge Hotel, where there is a coffee shop. Follow the road east under the bridge, to North Queensferry. Take time to look at the old pier, and should you have children in tow, consider including a visit to Deep Sea World by the rail bridge.

Return to the road bridge, climbing steps to the east-side walkway this time, with a closer view of the Rail Bridge and Inch Garvie. At the Queensferry end keep on the east side and descend north to Hopetoun Road, and so back to Hawes Pier.

35 Blackness to South Queensferry

FACTFILE

Map Ordnance Survey map 65, Falkirk & Linlithgow.
Distance 5 miles
Height negligible
Terrain track and beach walk, then minor road
Start point Blackness village, east of Bo'ness
Time 2 to 3 hours
Nearest town South Queensferry
Recommended refreshment spot a vast choice in South Queensferry

Two weeks ago I wrote about a walk from South Queensferry across the Forth Road Bridge and back again – a walk triggered off by the imminent prospect of a second road bridge having to be built, with implications for the coastline on either side of the Forth.

As a Christmas walk, I described a short route from Carriden (on the east side of Bo'ness) to Blackness Castle. I have long-wanted to traverse the coastline east from Blackness to Queensferry and was propelled to do just that last month when I saw a map of the possible crossing points for the new bridge. I can see the practicality of the bridge being just west of the existing one, connecting to the current roadway systems, but that would have a non-beneficial effect on the Blackness area coastline, so better to go now before any construction does start was the thought I had. Personally, I would rather have a tunnel.

There is a good parking area in the middle of Blackness village (reached from the A904, the south coastal road), from where it is a short stroll by the Boat Club to the castle. The castle is open all year (but in winter it is closed Thursday and Friday) and the castle shop serves hot drinks – perhaps ideal for the start of the walk. For those who can get a lift in a boat, here is an intriguing thought. Following works to the pier (built in 1870 to receive supplies, following Blackness' designation as the central munitions depot for Scotland), it is now open for privately owned boats – a new era of visitor access to the castle. Well, that's a different way to start a walk!

And so it was on a gloomy day just before Christmas that Jimbo, Peter and I set off from Blackness. We didn't go to the castle first. We walked from the village southeast wards by a line of houses and at the end of the short road went by a gate to the start of a grassy track. The track crosses the Black Burn at the Baillie Bridge – no army-type construction but a simple wooden crossing of a few planks. The path goes at first on the seaward side of a long plantation (Wester Shore Wood) and then goes into the wood. The first section is somewhat muddy but then leads to a superb sylvan path that is enhanced at this time of the year by the lack of leaves on the trees, thus giving views to the beach, the Forth and across to Fife.

The good track ends at the Midhope Burn, crossed by a large stone bridge to reach the grounds of Hopetoun House. Turn left and follow a large wall, built round the grounds of the House, to reach the shoreline. Set in 150 acres of rolling parkland, the construction of what is one of Scotland's finest stately homes first started in 1699, and then having been redesigned was finally completed in 1748. I do not know when the sea wall was built, but it is in need of some renovation in a few places. Most of the grassy ground immediately below the wall is usually above tide level, but the going can be rough and tedious in places. However, it is a surprisingly easy walk lower down on the upper edges of the beach, although the contour line of seaweed and other debris tells its own story. Check with tide tables before you go. Below the seaweed line is a strip of small stones that are often slippery, but further out are large stretches of sand that give delightful walking at times of low tide and which give a more direct line. Good walking boots and a look at the tide tables are recommended.

The beach walk ends at a delightful line of houses at Easter Society and the start of the minor road (Society Road) that leads east to South Queensferry. Cars must turn at Society but there are parking spaces further east by the water's edge where the road from Hopetoun House comes in. It would however, be a pity not to continue walking along what (in the winter months when the House is closed to the public and no tour buses come by) is a quiet and pretty road by the Forth.

Relax over refreshments in Queensferry, smug in the knowledge that you have remembered to pre-plan your car arrangements. Next week however, I would hope to get back to the high tops – after all I have no more excuses. The festive season is well and truly over and daylight hours are stretching out.

36 Blackness to Carriden and back

FACTFILE

Map Ordnance Survey map 65, Falkirk & Linlithgow.
Distance 5 miles
Height negligible
Terrain track/path all the way
Start point Blackness village, east of Bo'ness
Time 2 to 3 hours
Nearest village Blackness
Recommended refreshment spot Blackness Castle

Blackness Castle juts out into the Forth at the end of a promontory – a dramatically-sited 15th Century garrison fortress and state prison. Built in the 1440s, it continued to be used as a prison for 250 years. When viewed from the shore further west, the Forth Road and Rail Bridges act as a more modern backdrop that only emphasises its antiquity. The adjacent Blackness Bay and tidal mudflats (important feeding and roosting sites for wildfowl) must have offered – in tandem with the Forth itself – difficulties for any assault against the large walls of the castle: walls giving safety for the non-jailed inhabitants and presenting difficulties for any prison escape.

The castle – situated a quarter of a mile from Blackness village – was designed to protect the port of Blackness, which served as the harbour for the nearby royal palace at Linlithgow. The tidal harbour is used nowadays by Blackness Boat Club. The castle has been described as small and dour and black is certainly the prominent colour of the area, named in castle, village, bay and burn. Pick a good day if you can! The castle (maintained by Historic Scotland) is open all year (winter: closed Thursday and Friday).

What's all this then – no walk? Not at all. The castle is a superb starting point for a delightful coastal walk going west to Carriden on the eastern outskirts of Bo'ness: a distance of just over two miles and an easy five miles there and back resulting in a gentle stroll of some three hours – just right for this time of year and a good break from the busy shops. In addition there is no climbing. You would struggle to ascend more than ten metres.

Blackness village lies three miles northeast of Linlithgow and a similar distance east of Bo'ness (or to give its full name, Borrowstounness) and is reached from the coastal road (the A904). There is a bus service from Linlithgow (First bus number 49).

Ordnance Survey map 65 (Falkirk & Linlithgow) covers the area. Although not needed for the walk, it is useful to identify features over the water in Fife. The castle lies at map ref 055803 and there is also good parking at the village beside public toilets.

The coastal path west to Carriden – a right-of-way – is sign-posted intermittently but the way is quite obvious. After leaving the short promenade, the first half is on a narrow and sometimes muddy path that hugs the shoreline by fences and walls. This is the way to go at times of high tide; otherwise the stony beach can be traversed from time to time as desired – rougher going but perhaps more interesting. Looking north, the Forth is a surprising two miles wide at this point. The busy M9 motorway to the south is unseen and unheard, leaving the beach to its seclusion.

The path or beach, then leads to a short set of steps by some ruins at the mid-point. From there it is a superb walk on the inland side of a stone dyke beneath steep wooded slopes, before the path returns to the beach side. The path crosses a stream, and then starts to veer away from the shoreline in approaching Carriden, to be replaced by a wider dirt track, then a tarmac road. This road goes through an unattractive industrial area that can be avoided to the left. A swivel gate in a metal fence leads to a narrow path that runs parallel to the road but in a wooded area. Keep right at one signposted junction and come out at the church car park at the foot of Carriden Brae.

There is another small car park on the other side of the road at map ref 019814 – suitable for a pre-placed car, but surely two miles is not enough exercise. Return the same way.

Now at this stage I must declare my hypocrisy, for when I was there a few weeks ago I only walked one way. Margaret dropped me off at Carriden and I walked east to the castle as she drove round to do a bit of bird watching by the bay – a wildlife watcher's paradise with wigeon, dunlin, godwit and sanderling, to name just a few. For some reason or other, we did not have much time and on a very cold morning it was a brisk but most satisfying walk.

Blackness Castle shop, offering an hospitable welcome, serves hot drinks.

37 Around Linlithgow Loch

FACTFILE

Map Ordnance Survey map 65, Falkirk and Linlithgow, but not really needed
Distance 2½ miles
Height 50m at most
Terrain good path around the loch
Start point car park west of Linlithgow Palace
Time 1 hour
Nearest town Linlithgow
Recommended refreshment spot The Coffee Neuk

It is the start of another year and whilst January may not be the ideal month for a long walk, there is no excuse for not getting out on a short stroll to get rid of those New Year celebration cobwebs.

So why not an easy walk around Linlithgow Loch, which appears on Ordnance Survey map 65 (Falkirk & Linlithgow), though the map is not really needed. All you have to do is get to Linlithgow and with signposts at key points, you cannot get lost.

The loch is squeezed in between the town and the M9. On the south shore are the ruins of magnificent Linlithgow Palace. The Union Canal – reached by a five-minute walk from the town centre – offers an extra walk for those who may need more exercise.

Linlithgow Peel was the name originally given to the gardens and grounds around the Palace. More and more lands bounding the loch have been passed to Historic Scotland and its predecessors over the years. The Rose Garden was added in 1946, the North Shore in 1975 and Fiddler's Croft in 1977. Whilst a circular path exists around the loch, it is necessary to detour at Fiddler's Croft, go along Blackness Road for a short way and back into the Peel by an alley.

The walk will take an hour and provides some stunning views of the Palace and St Michael's Parish Church. The loch is a Site of Special Scientific Interest because of the large numbers of wintering wildfowl, and is one of only two natural lowland lochs in the Lothians. It provides an ideal habitat for reed buntings, sedge warblers, common sand-pipers, coots, moorhens and a wide variety of very tame and extremely vocal ducks. Mute swans have nested on the banks of the loch for centuries, and are very much in evidence today. One word of warning: a brisk stroll will clash with the sporadic walk of a birdwatcher, as Margaret and I quickly found out.

Linlithgow Peel has been altered by human activity, and traces of that activity from prehistoric times to the present can still be detected. This has created a wealth of archaeological and historical interest. The loch was an important food source to the Palace, providing swan, ducks, eels and fish, as well as water for brewing and baking purposes. It also acted as a natural defence against possible attack. Two of the islands in the Loch – Rickle Island and Cormorant Island – have been identified as crannogs: types of ancient loch dwellings built some 5,000 years ago – originally timber roundhouses supported on piles driven into the loch bed.

The walk is described in a clockwise direction. At first glance it may seem difficult to imagine the walk covering as much as two and a half miles. The Peel juts out into the water and the north shore is not too far away, but once on the way it does not take long to realise that the full circuit will take up to one hour.

Use the car park just to the west of the Palace, and from where steps lead down to Town Bay. With the water almost lapping the edge of the tarmac path, the lawn and the water are absolutely hooching with birds. Beware of the swans, for it is quite clear that they regard all walkers as providers of food.

On the west side of the loch is Lady's Park, and shortly afterwards an arched bridge crosses the Mill Burn – the outflow of the loch. Given the size of the loch, the outflow is somewhat small but perhaps the less-fresh water is consequently more attractive to bird life.

Linlithgow Loch and Palace

On the north side of the loch the tarmac path changes to gravel that still gives a good walking surface. On this side – although screened from the nearby M9 by a grassy and wooded embankment – the noise of the traffic is inescapable. A small burn, the Hatchery Burn, flows in at the north-east end in approaching a road. Look out for the signpost, for the way now turns more southwards and through a gate. This leads to a grassy section than can be a bit muddy.

The path gently rises to Blackness Road as the immediate waterside has no path. The walk along the road however, is short. Look out for another sign directing you down a narrow lane (Chapel Lane) and across Bell's Burn back to the waterside and a tarmac path. Pass the small yachting area and climb to the Palace. Turn left through the palace gateway known as The Fore.

Linlithgow Palace was the popular residence of Stuart kings, and the birthplace of Mary Queen of Scots in 1542. The Palace became a ruin when it was carelessly set alight by the Duke of Cumberland's troops in 1746, following the Jacobite Rebellion. It is open all year round. For further information, phone / fax Historic Scotland Ranger Service on 01506 842065.

The Palace still exudes an air of dignified splendour. Its halls and chambers, now roofless, surround a central quadrangle with a Gothic fountain (now lavishly restored) – a wedding gift from James V to his queen, Mary of Guise. The quadrangle is used in the summer to hold what is called Scotch Hop – a mixture of ceilidh and Scottish country dancing, designed for tourists and locals alike and highly recommended.

38 The Antonine Wall

FACTFILE

Map Ordnance Survey map 64, Glasgow Motherwell & Airdrie
Distance 6 miles
Height 200m
Terrain road, track and path, the latter rough and wet in places
Start point Croy railway station
Time 3 to 4 hours
Nearest village Castlecary
Recommended refreshment spot Castlecary Hotel

Once the north-western frontier of the Roman Empire, the Antonine Wall – constructed in the AD 140s on the orders of the Emperor Antoninus Pius – straddles the Forth-Clyde isthmus from modern Bo'ness to Old Kilpatrick. Only some 25 miles of the original 37 survive. The Wall – the most important surviving Roman monument in Scotland – was approved in 2008 as a World Heritage Site (alongside Hadrian's Wall in England and the German limes, part of the Frontiers of the Roman Empire World Heritage Site). Professor David Breeze (formerly Chief Inspector of Ancient Monuments for Scotland) prepared the bid for that Heritage status and now leads the team implementing the management plan. His book *Edge of Empire, The Antonine*

Wall, Rome's Scottish Frontier tells the story of the construction, occupation and then abandonment of the Wall – recommended reading prior to this week's walk.

The Wall consists of a rampart and ditch, with the material from the ditch thrown to the north to form an upcast mound. In places the rampart survives up to 2m high and the ditch up to 4.5m deep. Ideally the best way to get to know the Wall is on a guided tour. I was extremely fortunate to have a one-to-one guided tour with Professor Breeze as my personal expert.

Distributed in various sectors, Historic Scotland look after nearly five miles of the Wall, including much of the unimpeded stretch running from Twechar to Castlecary – ideal for the casual walker. It includes two spectacular lengths over Bar Hill and Croy Hill, both sites of Roman forts. That walk took us some three hours – a gentle stroll giving lots of time during which David explained facets of the Wall that I would otherwise have missed.

Ordnance Survey map 64 (Glasgow, Motherwell & Airdrie) covers the six-mile distance from Croy to Castlecary (including a detour to Bar Hill). However, for a more detailed understanding I recommend the 1:25000 map and guide published by The Royal Commission on the Ancient and Historical Monuments of Scotland (www.rcahms.gov.uk or www.antoninewall.org). This shows the course of the Wall on a modern map base, including areas where the Wall can be visited. Elements of the archaeology of the monument are highlighted, along with additional information including reading and museums to visit.

It was pleasing to reach the start of this linear walk and return home without recourse to a car. For once, using the train was faster, cheaper and more convenient. We started from Croy railway station close to Bar Hill, and finished at Castlecary. Just outside the hotel is a bus stop from where a regular service goes to Falkirk's Grahamston station.

Now for the walk. It is a short stroll from Croy station going northwest on the B802 to map ref 721763, where a signposted lane alongside the Wall leads west to Bar Hill. It is a gentle ascent through a lovely wooded area to reach the rounded dome – a magnificent viewpoint over the watery Kelvin valley with the Kilsyth hills as a back-drop. It is easy to appreciate why Bar Hill was chosen as a site for a fort (the highest on the Wall) and why in more recent times a trig point was erected. A number of markers identify individual places of interest, such as the headquarters building and bathhouse.

Return to the B802, crossing the road carefully. Pass a disused quarry and mine workings to reach the next fort on Croy Hill – again a well-chosen site and in my opinion the most interesting part of the walk. At this stage, whimsically pretend to hear the sound of Roman legionnaires patrolling the Wall, but wonder why it takes a more direct line rather than following closer to the sharp edge above the Kelvin valley (the answer is that a more direct wall saved effort, time and money and the west brow of Croy Hill holds 'expansions' – possibly beacon-platforms giving advance warning of those coming from the north).

It should be noted that there is still a lot of work to be done by the relevant bodies concerned. The Wall is not overly provided with signposts and improvements to the pathway are required in some areas (take sensible footwear). In traversing the area north of Dullatur reference to the map may be needed.

After one short section of road, pass under the railway to regain the Wall, which continues eastwards on the north side of a golf course, then an airport. A tree-lined way with a few fences to cross then leads past an industrial estate to reach the village of Castlecary and a convenient hotel.

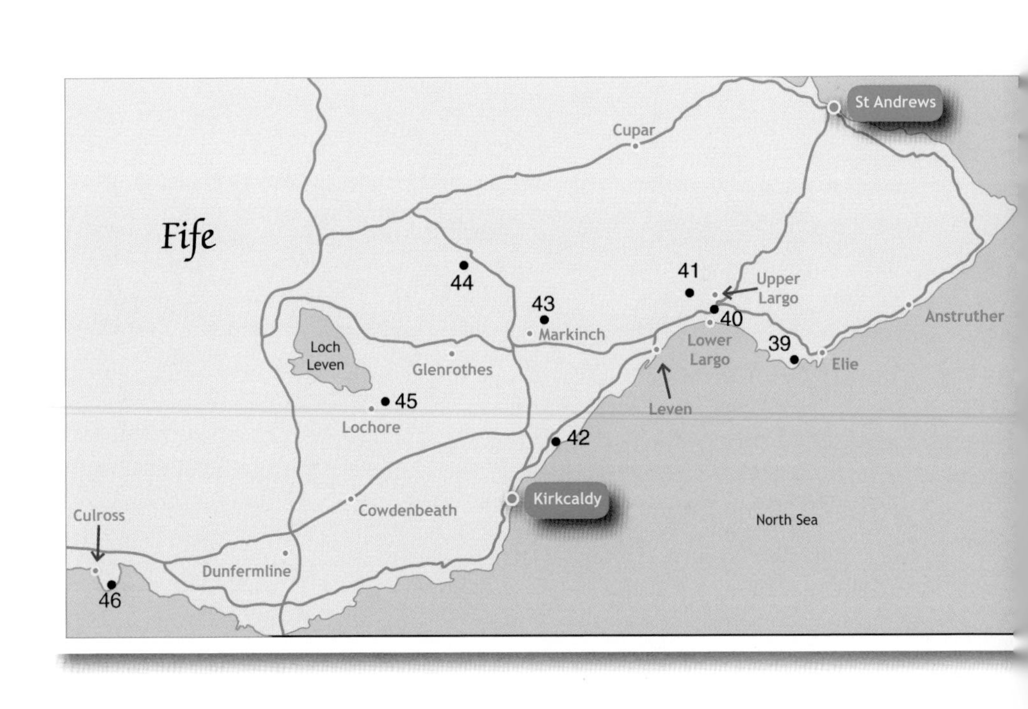
Fife
St Andrews
Cupar
44
43
41
Upper Largo
40
Markinch
Loch Leven
Glenrothes
Lower Largo
39
Elie
Anstruther
45
Lochore
Leven
42
Kirkcaldy
Cowdenbeath
North Sea
Culross
Dunfermline
46

Fife

39 Elie Chain Walk

FACTFILE

Map Ordnance Survey map 59, St Andrews
Distance 3 to 4 miles
Height 100m
Terrain quiet road, good path and beach… then the Chain Walk
Start point Elie
Time 3 to 4 hours, depending on exploration time taken
Nearest town Elie
Recommended refreshment spot Elie

Even a hillwalker enjoys a coastal walk, especially if the weather on the high tops is dreadful. The east coast of Scotland is often a dry, sunny place, so how about a scramble round a rocky headland in Fife, and a walk to see remains of wartime fortifications? Whilst only a short outing, it could be a memorable one, especially for younger members of the family.

The Fife Coastal Path – completed in 2002 – runs from North Queensferry to the Tay Bridge, yet one short unofficial section is the most challenging. It is a real 'walk on the wild side', when the more adventurous can discover Fife's best-kept secret: the Elie Chain Walk. Well, it was a secret to me until Jimbo told me about it.

The Chain Walk goes round the base of Kincraig Point amidst a jumble of volcanic rock pools and caves washed by the sea at high tide. Unlike the way-marked Fife Coastal Path, this detour has chains directing the way below dramatic cliffs and distinctive basalt columns. A modest head for heights is required on the series of carved steps, and vertical and horizontal chains – claimed to be Scotland's only *via ferrata*.

This could be the highlight of the Fife Coastal Path, yet it receives little publicity or promotion – understandably so, because the Path is advertised with access at all times, whereas a diversion to the Chain Walk is only possible at various tide times, and there is also an element of danger. There are warning signs placed comparatively recently by Fife Council. All the chains – eight in all – are of stainless steel and bolted to the rock. The old rusted chains were replaced in 2003.

There is a snag and that is why I suggest this traverse as an autumn walk. Tackling the chains with bare hands to get a better grip, could be painful or dangerous in cold weather, so pick a warmish day.

There is another snag: the tide, which would not wait for King Canute and will not wait for you. The walk should not be attempted when the tide is coming in, for it would be all too easy to get stranded. It is better to go when the tide is on the ebb, to maximise the time available. At low tide it is possible to walk some distance along the beach and rocks without needing to use all the chains, but it would seem a pity to do so. A compromise could be to do the traverse then return along the beach and coves, giving time to explore the caves and rock pools. It is essential to check tide times in *The Scotsman* and pick a calm day – unless that is you enjoy sea-spray. If in any doubt, phone the local coastguard on 01333 450666.

There is a mystery about the origins of the Chain Walk. I like to think of smugglers using it or perhaps scouring the base of the cliffs for cargo from a shipwreck. An idea that the chains were installed to help in the construction of the wartime fortifications on the headland is fanciful. It is possible that the chains and steps were built between the Wars, perhaps in the late 1920s. No one really seems to know, but maybe that is how it should be, with the mystery enhancing the enjoyment of the traverse.

For information on the Fife Coastal Path, phone their information desk at 01592 414300, or The Fife Coast & Countryside Trust at 01333 592 591.

Kincraig Point lies to the west of Elie, from where the short walk goes west to Earlsferry. From Earlsferry Links, take the path southwest through the golf course towards the coast, paying courteous attention to the golfers as requested. You will see the signpost highlighting the Fife Coastal Path, which you now join. Turn right by the side of the golf course, above the beach, for a lovely grassy walk by the sand dunes. Go towards the headland, and a good stepped path starting at map ref 473000. (A signpost at this point shows the way to the left [west] by the beach to the Chain Walk, but save that delight for the return.) The path climbs only some 50m, and with ups and downs later, the total climb for the day is no more than 100m.

Any port in a storm

Once on the headland, examine the remains of the fortifications, but also enjoy the views especially south, over the Forth to the Lothians. It may be surprising to see how wide the Forth is at this point. Continue over the headland, descending gently until around map ref 463997, looking for a grassy path that leaves the official path and goes down to a cove. This drop is short but steep, with care needed if wet.

The start of the Chain Walk is at this small rocky inlet with the sea surging towards a cave, and as the inlet is mostly under water, the rocks can be slippy. Some experience of very easy scrambling could be an advantage. All the pitches are short and the steep ones have footholds dug into the rock, some of which have been eroded over the years by the tide. The safest way of tackling the descents is to face into the rock, holding on to the chains with both hands. The first move over the edge may seem difficult, facing in and trying to find the foothold steps. Oddly enough, other chains to be climbed in near vertical ascents may be the easiest to tackle, with minimal overhangs. The last section is the most interesting, with a slanting diagonal chain and an awkward step to a raised rib of rock, leading to a cave. Then there is a horizontal chain. The rock overhangs slightly and the chain is a bit too slack, such that pressure is put on the arms in leaning outwards. Unless it is almost full tide, one can walk over the pebbles and rejoin the chain later, but you would not want to do that, would you? A short stroll along the beach leads back to the official path.

40 Largo Law and the Not So Green Hillwalker

FACTFILE

Map Ordnance Survey map 59, St Andrews, Kirkcaldy & Glenrothes
Distance 2 miles
Height 250m
Terrain farm tracks, then steep grassy hillside
Start point off-road parking area between cemetery and Kirkton of Largo primary school
Time 1 to 2 hours
Nearest village Upper Largo
Recommended refreshment spot Upper Largo Hotel

At home we pride ourselves on our responsibilities concerning green issues. The garden produces some of our fruit and vegetable needs; eight compost heaps attend to organic garden and kitchen waste; then there is the weekly ritual of sorting out glass, cans, plastic bottles, newspapers etc for collection. As a result, our dustbin need only be emptied every three weeks.

Yet we all have a weak point in matters green and mine is hillwalking, driving some 10,000 miles a year to get to the hills. Nevertheless, my friends and I share cars as far as possible and prefer to be away for a week or more in the summer rather than have daily trips from home. Yet recently I incurred a ridiculous mileage. The forecast was not exactly encouraging: severe gales with temporary blizzard conditions – when visibility would be virtually nil – wind at 900m averaging 70 to 80 miles an hour with gusts as high as 120mph, and temperature of –4°C with an extreme wind-chill effect.

Not a day for the high tops, so I spread out a few maps to see what might be possible at lower level. It may have been the subconscious memory of watching the Humphrey Bogart film *Key Largo* over New Year that led my eye to Largo Law in Fife: a 290m hill that inexplicably I had never climbed. The plan was to extend the day at lower level with a visit to nearby Keil's Den – the wooded defile of the Keil Burn. Well, I managed the former... just – but not the latter.

None of the usual gang was free that day, so I set off on my own. Being a short day, I had a leisurely start from Edinburgh, anticipating being in Upper Largo in an hour. However, on reaching Queensferry I was dismayed to see that the Forth Road Bridge had just been closed to cars after sections of a painting platform had been torn down in the gales. Oh dear, what to do? My desire to climb Largo Law over-rode common sense. A detour over the Kincardine Bridge would add an extra hour, but still give time for the complete walk and, with gales forecast to subside, the Forth Bridge would surely be re-opened by my return. Big mistake! Half the lorries and cars in Scotland seemed to converge on Kincardine – a tedious tiring travel such that I did not reach Upper Largo until 2pm, two hours later than planned.

If coming from the west, follow the A915 through Lundin Links, bypassing Lower Largo to reach Upper Largo. A minor road heads northwest from the village, skirting the southwest slopes of Largo Law. If in doubt, continue to the junction of the A915 and the A917, then return to the minor road. Go past Kirkton of Largo primary school and park on the east side of the road between the school and a cemetery.

A notice board at the start of the walk gives some details about Largo Law – the eroded remains of a volcano active between 300 and 350 million years ago. Largo Law forms part of a working farm and cattle graze much of the hill's slopes. Walkers are asked not to take their dogs and to keep to the marked route for both ascent and descent.

Walk northeast on the well-marked route: a track leading to Chesterstone Farm. On my outing, the track was very muddy – scarcely surprising considering the recent torrential downpour. The route goes through the farmyard and north, the track again signposted, to reach the base of the cone. Now for the grassy climb – short but steep – to reach the twin-topped summit. The northern bump with the trig point is the higher.

The summit offers superb views over the Forth ... or so the notice board said, but clutching the trig point all I could see was surging storm-tossed water in front of a grey curtain of cloud. The notice board also says that throughout the summer months a variety of wild plants grow on the slopes, one such being Ragged Robin – an apt description of the storm-clad solitary walker on the hillside. Buzzards are commonly seen as they soar above the slopes, but not today! Even birds have more sense.

I headed home, dismayed to learn from the car radio that the Forth Bridge was still closed. It was back to Kincardine again. The Forth Bridge re-opened at 6pm when I was still part of a five-mile tailback before Kincardine, and too late to turn back.

I got home disgusted with myself – an eight-hour day of which six hours had been wasted in the car; far too many carbon footprints just to climb a hill. Not even Largo Law is worth that.

41 Keil's Den

FACTFILE

Map Ordnance Survey map 59, St Andrews, Kirkcaldy & Glenrothes
Distance 2 miles
Height negligible
Terrain mostly unmade paths, then short road walk
Start point off the A915 by Lundin Links, on north side of Cupar Road, at map ref 410032
Time 1 hour
Nearest village Lundin Links
Recommended refreshment spot Blacketyside Farm Shop on the A915, one mile west of Lundin Links

Unsettled weather at this time of year poses problems for hillwalkers. Three weeks ago I described a less-than-green trip to Largo Law on a day definitely not made for the high tops. The Forth Road Bridge had been closed to traffic after sections of a painting platform had been torn down in the gales and I had been obliged to take a long detour via Kincardine. I got home disgusted with myself – an eight-hour day of which six hours had been wasted in the car; far too many carbon footprints just to climb a hill.

The original plan had been to extend that walk beyond Largo Law with an hour's visit to nearby Keil's Den. Well, I managed the former…just, but not the latter, so was determined to complete this unfinished business on a day of no traffic problems, but a day when again it would be prudent to avoid high ground.

Situated southwest of Largo Law, Keil's Den is a long, narrow wooded glen set in an agricultural landscape – a woodland site with a long history of management. Keil is possibly a corruption of *coille* (Gaelic for 'wood') or *cuil*, meaning a 'nook'. The Den is the steep-sided defile of the Keil Burn, or more correctly the Boghall Burn that flows only some three miles south to Lower Largo. A burn is normally a good description of this flow of water but on my visit, after another day of heavy rain, it was in muddy spate. Jimbo (plus his two dogs) and Joe came along. Quickly wet and bespattered, the dogs had a whale of a time splashing across the burn and chasing rabbits through the thick undergrowth.

The Den was bought by Woodland Trust Scotland in 1992 with a huge amount of support from the local community who in the space of only two weeks raised 75% of the purchase price. Indeed it is claimed that most of the 9000 folk per annum who visit the Den are local regular walkers.

Keil's Den has features similar to those of Maspie Den by Falkland (visited earlier in January) but the former is a wilder place with fewer made-up paths and briefly one has the illusion of being well away from civilisation. The Den offers a short summer stroll or, on our visit, a sheltered slippery walk on a day not made for the high tops. Ordnance Survey map 59 (St Andrews, Kirkcaldy & Glenrothes) may be useful if unfamiliar with the Largo area, but is not needed for the Den.

If coming from the west, follow the A915 through Lundin Links. After the A915 dips to cross the Burn, turn left (north) on a minor road marked as Cupar Road, and a short distance later park with consideration at map ref 410032 on the north side of the road. Take the obvious path between field and burn, heading northeast to soon reach the Den. The path then goes north on the west bank of the opening defile; a path that was very wet on our visit.

An old Coffin Road, now partly shown as a path on the map, traverses the Den – a short cut no doubt from Hatton to Kirkton of Largo cemetery by the lower slopes of Largo Law, but quite a pull up for those carrying the coffin.

About halfway along the Den a stepped path descends to the burn and a new wooden bridge erected in 1999, but this crossing would make for too short a walk. Continue north. The turning point of the Den walk is where a minor road crosses the burn just south of Pitcruvie Castle, whose tower is just visible through the trees. At this stage the burn can usually be stepped over. If not, use the road bridge.

Head south on the east bank of the Den, by now on a better path. Further downstream from the wooden bridge a 300m long upgraded path cuts back from the main entrance to the Den, leading to a picnic spot from where the burn can normally be forded, partially using a fallen tree. That crossing was not possible on our visit so we walked back again to the main entrance and took the minor road past the Woodland Gardens caravan site to reach the A915 within 400m. A short walk west by pavement easily got us back to the starting point.

It had been a short outing snatched from bad weather; an outing subsequently enhanced by watching the heavens open up again as we enjoyed our coffee and sticky buns.

42 A Fife Coastal Walk from Ravenscraig Castle, Kirkcaldy

FACTFILE

Map Ordnance Survey map 59, St Andrews, Kirkcaldy & Glenrothes
Distance 4 or 8 miles (more if starting from the railway station)
Height negligible
Terrain mixture of paths, mostly very good
Start point Ravenscraig Castle, Kirkcaldy
Time 2 hours for single trip
Nearest town Kirkcaldy
Recommended refreshment spot Kirkcaldy's Museum and Art Gallery café

Towards the end of December, the Mountain Lamb and I had been planning a day away, hillwalking on the high tops, but our free day was not well chosen. The weather forecast predicted gale force winds, blizzards and hence severe wind chill. We decided not to go.

Our fall back was a low level walk and they don't get much lower than a coastal walk. The east coast of Scotland was expected to experience the best of what was going, so it was an easy decision to head to Fife.

The Fife Coastal Path now extends from the Forth to the Tay, in effect from one Road Bridge to another – a distance of over 80 miles. It has a mixture of paths, all good by hillwalking standards, although parts on the Crail to St Andrews section are tidal and much rougher.

No, we did not set out to do 80 miles. Our very modest, short outing plan was to walk from Kirkcaldy to East Wemyss and back again – a total of eight miles. However, due to pressure of time and the very cold west wind, we changed our plans. We drove through Kirkcaldy to the car park beside Ravenscraig Castle at map ref 293926, just to the east of the roundabout where the A955 (the coast road) meets the A921. We could just as well have travelled to Kirkcaldy by train, and it is a pleasant one mile walk from the station to the castle, past the Museum and Art Gallery, and down to the esplanade. If you like Scottish Colourists (as I do) the Art Gallery is a must to visit. Opening hours are 10.30am to 5pm (Sunday 2pm to 5pm) and there is a café open until 4.30pm. Why not come back here after the walk?

The path to East Wemyss and beyond is well signposted, with periodic notice boards. Whilst it is not essential to take a map – in this case Ordnance Survey map 59 (St Andrews, Kirkcaldy and Glenrothes) – having one makes for a more interesting and informed day.

Ravenscraig Castle is on the west side of the park of the same name, and is well worth a visit. It is open all year. Afterwards, whilst one can walk through the park, it is better to seek out the path as it descends slightly towards the coast. The first stretch is beautifully wooded and there is time to notice the sea wall of the old estate, as it bizarrely hugs the shore's every indentation. There is a short descent to Dysart Harbour via a man-made tunnel, to reach the harbour's attractive houses, red roofed and white walled.

The next stretch to above Blair Point gives open views out east and it is possible to walk on the beach for a short while. Beware of the tide! The path climbs high above the rocky shoreline, passing the site of the Frances Colliery (now styled Frances Industrial Estate). Whilst not the prettiest part of the walk, the area has been tidied up since the days of mining, with just a solitary relic of those days: an old winding tower.

Descending past Blair Point takes one down to the shore again, with the open expanse leading to West Wemyss. With wooded slopes to the left and rocks to the right, just stay with the path. The small harbour at West Wemyss is attractive and can be crossed by a metal walkway.

The last part of the walk to East Wemyss passes Wemyss Castle on the left and is an easy stroll. Entering East Wemyss, on the right are huts belonging to the local angling club and on the left a scrap metal yard, oddly enough not at all intrusive and a welcome sign that this part of Fife is surviving the post-mining era.

By this time we had decided to get the bus back to Kirkcaldy, but that is no reason why you should. Perhaps even the party could split up. Allow a most generous two hours for the one-way walk, depending on time taken to admire the scenery and places of interest.

If not walking back, climb up to the A955 and the main bus stop called The Car Shed. We had just missed what we thought was our hourly bus, but got talking to an elderly gentleman who was also waiting at the bus stop, and he assured us that there was a regular service and that another bus would be along in five minutes. The A955 has a very good bus service, if not walking back from East Wemyss. Convenient phone numbers in any pre-planning are: Kirkcaldy Tourist Board on 01592-267-775 and Traveline Scotland on 08706-082-608. Whilst we waited he told us about the bus stop's name. It referred to the days of trams that ran to Kirkcaldy pre-war (he had been on them). He also recalled his working life as a miner at Frances Colliery. Meantime a couple of buses had gone by without stopping – express buses with limited stops. He continued to reminisce and we were almost sorry when our bus came along. It did stop, and further on the way back to Kirkcaldy it stopped again, this time because of some problem with the engine. It eventually got going again, to cheers from the passengers.

Man-made tunnel to Dysart

What an interesting and amusing end to our short walk. It was almost as good as hillwalking!

43 Markinch

FACTFILE

Map Ordnance Survey map 59, St Andrews, Kirkcaldy & Glenrothes
Distance 6 miles
Height negligible
Terrain mixture of minor roads, tracks and paths
Start point Markinch railway station
Time 2 to 3 hours
Nearest village Markinch
Recommended refreshment spot Carlton Bakeries Coffee Shop, Markinch

A few weeks ago during a spell of heavy snow, Margaret and I were looking forward to a short Italian holiday – hopefully a break to warmer climes. A couple of days before our departure and still needing to get on with holiday packing, I only had time for a part-day walk. Another constraint was that yet again my car was in the garage. Nevertheless, with commendable male efficiency, a plan was quickly devised to meet up with Jimbo, John and Bruce – all residents of Fife – at Markinch (to be honest, it was Jimbo's plan). There is a regular half-hourly train service to Markinch, with a journey time for me of less than one hour – faster, cheaper and more relaxing than travelling by car. The others were waiting for me and off we set on a circuitous route north of Markinch – a long established local walk.

From the railway station follow the B9130 northwards into the town. The road turns sharply left and shortly after we passed the Carlton Bakeries Coffee Shop on the right hand side. After the arduous journey from the station, the others needed the rest and were intent on having coffee and sticky buns. I was obliged to join them. The time was well spent, not blethering you understand but discussing matters of serious import. Eventually we got going again.

Still on the B9130 (by now going west) reach the entrance to Balbirnie Park on the right. A driveway goes past a golf course and Balbirnie House Hotel. From its end at map ref 289026, continue on a track through a lovely wooded area. Cross the Balbirnie Burn, all the while getting closer to a newish housing development on the east side of the A92 and the Balbirnie Stone Circle, excavated by Historic Scotland in the 1970s and known locally as the Druid's Circle. The site, dating from c3000BC, used to be located some 100 yards to the northwest, but had to be relocated when the A92 was widened.

After the Stones, curve right through more trees (the track avoiding the housing road), to reach a minor road at map ref 287033. Head east on that road (then track) to cross the railway line 'guarded' by a wartime concrete bunker. The track then curves northwards by open fields to Lochmuir Wood. The main way through the wood is clearly mapped, though there is a rougher track indicated by a marker post with a green arrow that parallels that track for a while. It is a choice of rough, grassy or smooth track ... the decision is yours.

At the north end of the wood, turn east on the minor road to Kirkforthar Farm. Pass the farm entrance and continue east on a track to map ref 307047, where it is a sharp turn south. Welcome to Star Moss – a Site of Special Scientific Interest; a peat bog looked after by Scottish Natural Heritage. Continue south past a lochan and skirting Broomfield Farm, reach the western side of Star Village.

Look out for the signposted path, 'Markinch ¾ mile': an ancient track and Right of Way that goes southwest for the only short climb of the walk over the 137m Cuinin Hill. The name is possibly derived from the Gaelic *coinin* meaning 'rabbit'. The leafy descent to a stone stile is a delight. Continue southwest past the Old Markinch Cemetery and under the high railway bridge to reach the northern side of Markinch. Go past the houses but look out for a blue sign on the right ('no motor or quad bikes') and climb gently by a dyke to reach a main road.

The quickest way back to the station is to head south (left), but we extended the walk by going north a short distance to the Stob Cross: an incised stone possibly marking the limit of an ancient sanctuary enclosure associated with the original early Christian church dedicated to St Drostan, a nephew of St Columba. At this point cross the road to re-enter Balbirnie Park and follow the burn with a choice of paths, to return to the driveway at map ref 289026. Return by the driveway to Markinch.

Even with soft snow underfoot, the walk was but a stroll yet once more the others insisted on a coffee break. Yes, it was a hard day.

We actually had good weather on our walk, something that kept coming back to mind when we were in Rome. There it was bitterly cold and on the streets we ate hot chestnuts rather than licking ice cream.

44 East Lomond and Maspie Den

FACTFILE

Map Ordnance Survey maps 58, Perth to Alloa, and 59, St Andrews, Kirkcaldy & Glenrothes

Distance 4 miles

Height 350m

Terrain good paths and pavements

Start point Falkland car park

Time 2 hours

Nearest village Falkland

Recommended refreshment spot an excellent choice in Falkland

What to do in January if the day is cold and blustery, but exercise is still called for? I spoke to Jimbo who suggested that an East Lomond and Maspie Den outing from Falkland (an area he knows well) could be the answer: a four-mile walk that can be shortened for younger members of the family by eliminating the hill climb. On our outing it was a cold, windy day, but once lower down we had a sheltered, easy and most interesting stroll.

Covering some 20 square miles, the Lomond Hills dominate the centre of Fife and are readily accessible. They fall away to the southeast and the rolling moorland terrain has a number of reservoirs. That area is interesting enough but on the northern flanks lie the twin volcanic peaks of East and West Lomond, both very clearly identifiable landmarks.

The route starts at the main car park in Falkland and climbs to East Lomond. It then continues west to Craigmead at the top of Maspie Den that divides the two Lomonds, then back to Falkland by the Den on a series of new paths and for which the Falkland Heritage Trust is to be congratulated.

You will need two Ordnance Survey maps: 58 (Perth to Alloa); and 59 (St Andrews, Kirkcaldy & Glenrothes). Annoyingly, East Lomond lies on the extreme west end of map 59 and Maspie Den on the other. Strictly speaking no maps are required on a good day, but on a January day of blizzards it would be folly to go ill prepared. However, Jimbo's son had shown me how to print off a self-centred map linking the requisite parts of maps 58 and 59, and that served me well.

The main car park lies just south of the centre of Falkland, but is not very obvious at first. From there continue south as the road climbs gently to the lower slopes of East Lomond, keeping west of the prominent brick building, the paper mill.

The signposted path up East Lomond climbs southwest through a lovely wooded area; a brutal start to the day maybe, but with plenty of resting spots to admire the developing views to the north. The path is well stepped, with a convenient handrail so there is no excuse for not continuing. Once on to the open hillside, try to avoid looking at the unattractive communications mast on Purin Hill and concentrate on the steep grassy cone of East Lomond. Once on top it is a grand viewpoint. Oddly enough the top has an informative plaque, yet the trig point is actually situated to the southeast below the summit. East Lomond has a height of 424m. You have climbed some 350m (or just over 1100ft) but that is the end of the climbing: it is downhill all the way now.

Once clear of the grassy summit cone it is an easy descent westwards – one mile on a broad track above an old limekiln to Craigmead. A minor road traverses the Lomonds at this point and impacts slightly on the feeling of getting away from it all, but it does give access to a popular picnic area with toilet facilities, on the west side.

The walk could start from here if transport is pre-arranged. For younger members of the family, it may be more interesting than climbing a hill, especially on a poor day.

And now for the new pathway that descends on the west side of Maspie Den, thus giving a return to Falkland that avoids the minor road.

Continuing westwards a short distance from the picnic area, go by a gate, beyond which is a path junction. The path going west leads to West Lomond; the path going north is the one to follow.

The Maspie Burn flows through a wooded area and whilst there is a choice of paths – all newly built and bridged – keep to the left (west) side on descent. As the Maspie Den starts to develop, look out for an old path that descends steeply into the Den. This path has had erosion problems and can be wet, slippery and muddy, but is most rewarding. The path cuts beneath a small cliff face and by the extraordinary undercut Yad waterfall to cross to the east bank. Further downstream the path crosses back to the west bank and goes through a short curving tunnel, then underneath an estate track. Continue gently descending by the west side of House of Falkland and on to the estate road. This road leads to the west end of the village, with a charming stroll heading to a rich choice of refreshment spots.

45 Loch Ore

FACTFILE

Map Ordnance Survey map 58, Perth to Alloa
Distance 7 miles (or 4 miles if only a circuit of the loch)
Height 300m
Terrain Tracks and path
Start Point Lochore Meadows Country Park
Time 3 to 5 hours
Nearest village Lochore
Recommended refreshment spot café at visitor centre

Loch Ore (now part of Lochore Meadows Country Park) is in Fife, south of the very much larger Loch Leven and separated by Benarty Hill. Loch Leven – a National Nature Reserve overlooked by the steep escarpments of Benarty Hill and the Lomond Hills to the east – has been in the news recently with the pending construction of a perimeter path (a path that no doubt will feature in a forthcoming walk).

The much more modest Loch Ore, nestling beneath Benarty Hill, already has a path round it, giving a pleasant four mile stroll with no climbing. Adding on a trip to Seamark – a beautiful viewpoint on the hill – extends that distance to seven miles and throws in some 300m of ascent.

The 1200 acre Country Park (open all year round) has a nine-hole golf course and facilities for boating and fishing (brown and rainbow trout) on the 260 acre loch, at the west end of which is a nature reserve. There are parking facilities, toilets and a café in the information centre.

Loch Ore lies two miles north of Cowdenbeath and less than a mile southwest of the village of Lochore. As a schoolboy it did not occur to me that the village's name came from a loch. More recently I was puzzled to learn that there actually was a Loch Ore: a flooded area on nearby reclaimed coal mining wasteland. But how could that be when I knew that Lochore had been a mining village? It was only when researching this walk that the explanation came to light.

Walk, cycle or ride?

Loch Ore existed a long, long time ago – a watery stretch of the River Ore. Of more historic times there was a castle on an island founded in the 11th Century by Duncan de Loch Orr (an interesting spelling). Later (in 1792) the bed of the loch was drained for agricultural purposes. A subsequent report stated that the land produced excellent crops of grain, but subsequently the spoil dumps from local mining and associated subsidence eliminated any potential for agriculture. Yes, as with many parts of Fife, there was coal underground.

Maps of the 1920s show the infant River Ore diverted by a channel running ENE towards Lochore Castle, the water then flowing east to join the Leven. These maps also show the flat ground of the former loch surrounded by mine workings. The ruins of the castle (no longer on an island) are near the main park entrance.

The pits closed in 1967 although some remnants of mining still remain – the old winding gear of the Mary Pit near the information centre – but the area has been landscaped and transformed over a period of nine years such that it is difficult to imagine what the former colliery looked like.

From the B920 (the Lochore/Lochgelly road) turn west, with the entrance to the Park well signposted. The centre is at the northeast corner of the loch. The area is covered by Ordnance Survey map 58 (Perth to Alloa), but a much more detailed map of the Lochore Meadows area on the pamphlet *Discovering Lochore Meadows* is available at the visitor centre.

Head west on the north side of the loch, with a good path following the water's edge round Tod Point. The path then joins a straight tarmac road (Pit Road) and leads to another parking spot at the northwest end of the loch. Immediately to the right, past a gate, is the signposted way to Harran Hill Wood: stunning mixed woodland that is a delight to walk through. Lovely leafy tracks and paths lead northeast to the summit of this rocky ridge between Loch Ore and Benarty Hill. A zigzag route of gentle descent then goes briefly west and turns east, leading to Ladath Stripe from where a good track heads west to a minor road (Hill Road) that skirts the southern side of Benarty Hill.

Cross the road to a signposted path – a series of steep steps climbing north. The path turns more gently to the east and at the end of the path cut northwest on a small worn path to clear the trees. Cross a fence and follow another worn path through the heather to reach Seamark: a large stone south of the summit of Benarty Hill. This is a superb viewpoint and a well deserved resting spot. When I was there at the end of November with the Mountain Hare it was a lovely sunny day and we lingered a while admiring the views.

Return to Loch Ore and complete its circuit. The southern side is an area of pasture. Go by the boating area to return to the visitor centre.

46 Preston Island

FACTFILE

Map Ordnance Survey map 65, Falkirk & Linlithgow
Distance 4 miles
Height negligible
Terrain tracks and paths all the way
Start point Culross
Time 2 hours
Nearest town Culross
Recommended refreshment spot The Biscuit Café, Culross

It was a blustery but dry day when five of us met in the Royal Burgh of Culross: Margaret for a spot of bird watching by the shore; Mary, Jimbo, John and I for a stroll on the Preston Island Circular Walk. Being but a two-hour outing we had plenty of time to foregather for coffee and scones at the Biscuit Café.

Preston Island has an interesting history. It never was a natural island and it most certainly is not one now. It started as an outcrop of rocks, exposed only at low-tide. Then *circa* 1800 Sir Robert Preston built a sea-wall and a levee around the edge of the rocks and the area between was infilled, with a pier located on the north side – an artificial construction to support an industrial complex for the production of salt.

Three coal mine shafts were dug using a technique little changed from medieval times, with the coal extracted being used to boil brine in the salt pans. (In earlier times the salt extraction simply used the heat of the sun. It was an industry well developed around the Firth of Forth. Indeed by 1614 salt was Scotland's 3rd largest export after wool and fish.)

Production on the island was said to have operated throughout the night, acting as a beacon to homecoming sailors. However, the coal mines were abandoned in 1811 after a firedamp explosion killed all the miners who were underground at the time. Production did continue but after the 1823 repeal of the salt duties, the works declined and were abandoned by the mid 1850s. The last salt produced around the Forth was in Prestonpans in 1959.

Several ruins remain but following a programme of restoration and consolidation undertaken in the 1990s they are now well-preserved. They include pit-head buildings, salt evaporating houses, an accommodation block, concrete slabs which seal the shafts and a cistern that once stored fresh water, piped ashore from the mainland. Interpretation boards have been provided.

Coal however, continues to play a part in the expansion of Preston Island, now no longer surrounded by water. Since 1970 the area around the island has been filled by ash from the coal-burning Longannet Power Station three miles to the west, as part of a land reclamation project. At first I mistakenly believed that a railway by the shoreline was used to transport the ash. Not so. The ash is transported in slurry form in pipelines and deposited at the artificial lagoons, hence the number of pipes and drainage points that can be seen by the perimeter fence.

The route to Preston Island only became a circular one a few years ago when new paths on the eastern side were opened (the work being funded by Scottish Power who manage the ash lagoons).

From almost any point in Culross, head to the shoreline and walk east to the Preston Island signpost. The perimeter of the island is mostly a broad gravel track, whereas the mainland side is a mixture of earth and tarmac paths (the latter part of the Kingdom of Fife Millennium Cycleways, route 76).

There are plenty of warning notices put up by Scottish Power: 'these lagoons are dangerous ... trespassers will be prosecuted.' In fact the very high wire fence would deter all but the dangerously foolhardy. The Ordnance Survey map 65 (Falkirk & Linlithgow) certainly shows lagoons but I suspect that many by now are filled in. On the west side they are well hidden by steep-banked grass-covered slopes. Only on the east side can one see the work in progress as machines mound up the banks of dry ash.

Ideal though it is for a short festive outing, be prepared for a bracing walk on a windy day. The 'island' now juts well out into the Forth, with Bo'ness less than two miles distant on the southern side. However, it is more sheltered around the ruins and on the eastern side alongside Torry Bay, whose mud flats provide an abundance of food for birds that overwinter there.

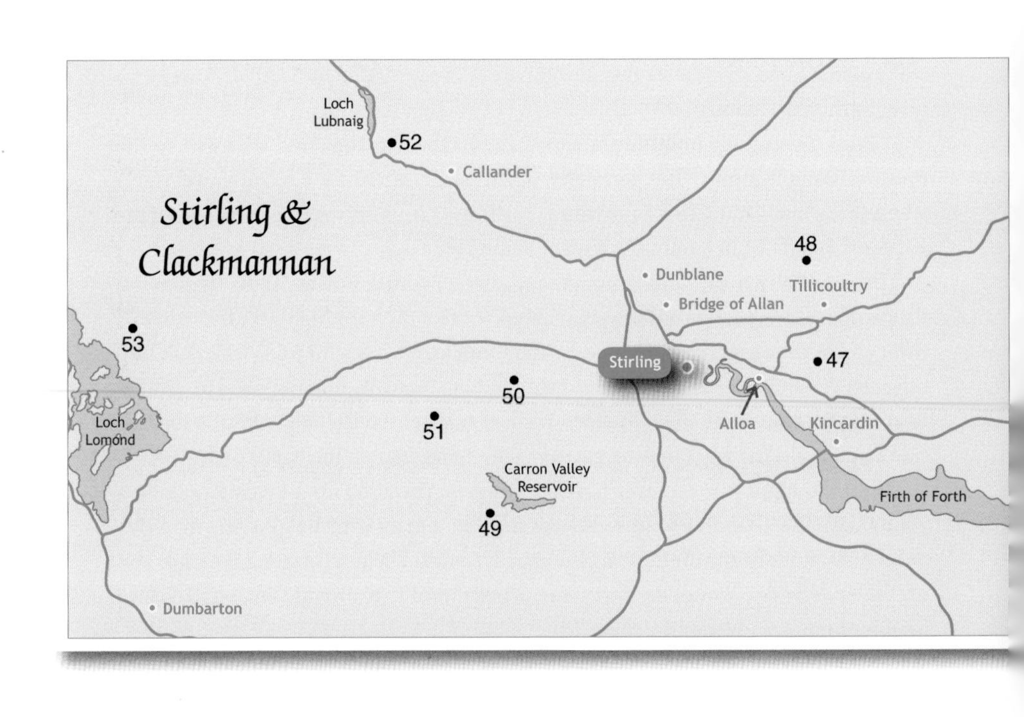
Stirling & Clackmannan
Loch Lubnaig
52
Callander
48
Dunblane
Tillicoultry
Bridge of Allan
53
Stirling
47
50
51
Alloa
Kincardin
Loch Lomond
Carron Valley Reservoir
Firth of Forth
49
Dumbarton

Stirling & Clackmannanshire

47 Gartmorn Dam Country Park and Nature Reserve

FACTFILE

Map Ordnance Survey map 58, Perth to Alloa
Distance three miles with detour
Height negligible
Terrain path and old railway line
Time one to two hours
Nearest town Alloa
Recommended refreshment spot The Royal Oak Hotel, Bedford Place, Alloa for high tea

At any busy pre-festive season time of year, shopping for presents and all that, it may be harder to work up enthusiasm for a visit to the high tops. Nevertheless hillwalkers still need to have a regular fix of physical activity. Throw in a lack of time and daylight hours, allied (say) to a spell of dreadful weather, and the hunt goes on for even a short, sheltered stroll.

Gartmorn Dam may not immediately come to mind. Tucked away behind Alloa, it is a stretch of water less than a mile long and its circuit amounts to little more than two miles, yet everything has its place in the scheme of things. Many years ago I was there on a bitterly cold winter day. Wrapped up in winter gear normally reserved for the high tops, it was a brisk walk round the water to return to the warm car. It is a different story of course in the summer – parents with young families strolling round and birdwatchers standing still with their binoculars.

The very name 'Gartmorn Dam' not 'loch', is the clue to the history of this small area of water of shallow depth and claimed to be the oldest reservoir in Scotland, dating from 1713. Signs of Clackmannanshire's mining history are to be found. The reservoir was built to power the pumps that drained the coal mines at Sauchie and this project was the catalyst for the development of Alloa as an industrial centre.

Alloa is a place of mixed memories for me. In my marathon running days, the odd half-marathon or 10k race played an important part in training. One year I went to Alloa for a 10k race yet I had scarcely gone much more than a mile from the school starting point when an Achilles tendon started to hurt. I soon ground to a halt somewhere in the district of New Sauchie. A kindly motorist gave me a lift back to the school: first runner to return but not the winner. A few years later however, I returned and this time managed to complete a half-marathon. It all comes back when I go to Gartmorn.

Head northeast from Alloa on the A908 (the road to Tillicoultry) as far as New Sauchie on the outskirts of the town. Then follow the signposted road to the east (right) towards the Dam and country park. A parking area is at the west end of the dam at map ref 911940. On a circuit of the water it is difficult to see how one could get lost, even on a pea-souper of a day!

Start from the visitor centre which gives information on the local wildlife and has toilets. It is open on weekend afternoons from October to March. In the winter months the dam is an important site for migratory wildfowl. Greylag and pink-footed geese from Greenland and Iceland spend their winter holidays there, although they also feed on the nearby mudflats and marshes of the Forth estuary.

Try an anti-clockwise circuit through this Special Site of Scientific Interest. A path keeps to the south side of the dam with gentle, grassy slopes on the right. It is a worthwhile detour to climb south to a picnic area at map ref 922935, albeit when I was last there the going was somewhat muddy and slippy. There are excellent views south over Clackmannan to the meandering Forth and north to the Ochils' escarpment.

The path then turns north by some trees at the eastern extremity. After a most gentle rise, the northeast end is reached and a small stream crossed. The way on the north side of the dam is on an old railway line, used to take coal from Sheriffyards Colliery to Alloa Harbour. Although traces of the old working can still be seen, this area beneath Gartmornhill Farm is remarkably sylvan – made by man but being reclaimed by nature. A glance at the map shows a remarkable number of dismantled railways: testimony to Alloa's industrial history of mining and brewing.

A forest watchtower

Once back at the car, I am sure you will feel all the better for your short stroll – a walk that can be extended by having a look at Alloa Tower: the last surviving keep in Scotland and managed by the National Trust for Scotland.

48 A January jaunt to Ben Cleuch

FACTFILE

Map Ordnance survey map 58, Perth to Alloa
Distance 5 miles
Height 700m
Terrain stepped paths, then short grassy slopes with easy worn paths
Time 3 to 4 hours
Start point Tillicoultry
Nearest town Tillicoultry
Recommended refreshment spots Mona's Coffee Shop, Pool of Muckhart.

The Ochils – mostly a high moorland plateau, with rounded mossy hills sloping north-west to the A9 – run from Auchtermuchty to Bridge of Allan. Ben Cleuch is the highest point. To the south of the plateau it is quite another story, for Ben Cleuch is on the edge of the most dramatic aspect of the Ochils: a sudden and dramatic escarpment. A natural break in the earth's crust – the Ochils Fault – caused the land south of the fault to be 'thrown' down into what is now the fertile flood plain of the Forth.

The word *ochil* comes from the very old Celtic word *uchil*, meaning 'the high ground'. A series of attractive glens breach the escarpment and one of them, Mill Glen, gives not only a through route from Tillicoultry to Blackford, but offers an easy and attractive start to the ascent of Ben Cleuch. *Cleuch* means 'gully' or 'defile' – a good description of the Mill Glen.

In the second week of January the plan had been for Jimbo, Alan and I to head for the very high tops. Another day not well chosen! With gale force winds it took less than a second to abandon that plan. The forecast did indicate that the gales would abate during the day, so Jimbo suggested going to the lower Ochils and Ben Cleuch.

So off we went. Not that Ben Cleuch at 721m should be underestimated for that height translates as 2365ft (just short of the 2500ft requisite height for Corbett status) and with a starting height of only 150ft or so from Tillicoultry the actual climb of 2200ft can rival that of many a Munro.

My interest in going to Ben Cleuch was that my first and only time there had been 25 years ago. A solitary visit seems absolutely pathetic when compared with the number of times others have been there. Ben Cleuch is the kind of hill that calls people to return, and for some that means very many times. It is a combination of accessibility – especially when the Highland roads are bad in winter – allied with very pleasant and easy going underfoot, and a wide variety of good ascent routes. Then of course there are fine views from the tops. The wide meandering Forth lies just below and the Kincardine Bridges and further east the Forth rail and road bridges can all be picked out. Multiple ascents of Ben Cleuch seem to be the norm. The most number of ascents I know of is by Tom Bell of Grangemouth who has climbed the hill over 1500 times. Dave Hewitt has climbed it well over 600 times. A great many ascents have been made by John Ramsay from Falkirk, who is now in his 80s and was first up Ben Cleuch in the 1930s.

With conditions forecast to improve, we had a leisurely start, meeting up with the local expert Dave Hewitt and his friend Ken, another Cleuch centurion. The popular and most direct route starts from the west end of Tillicoultry at a small car park at map ref 913974, with the entrance to Mill Glen being well signposted from the A91.

Take the path that crosses to the west bank of the burn to pass above a quarry that is still being worked. You cannot miss it! The stepped path climbs by the burn, crossing and recrossing many times, and all the while enclosed in what is a defile rather than the more open aspect we normally associate with a glen. Continue as far as the junction of two streams: the Daiglen Burn that flows into Mill Glen from the northwest; and the Gannel Burn from the northeast. This is a good turning point in atrocious weather for the stepped path ends here, and steep grassy slopes lead to the open plateau.

Climb north on the spur of land between the two burns on a good grassy path. The way is obvious. The path climbs to the Law at 638m – a route that is often sheltered from the prevailing west wind. However, the Law marks the start of the Ochils plateau and there is no shelter. The path goes northwest over gently rising ground, following a fence. The terrain is not dissimilar to the plateau walk by the fence posts on Ben Chonzie. The bleak exposed moorland stretches to the top that has both trig point and viewfinder.

A pleasant circular walk back to Tillicoultry uses the path by the Gannel Burn – part of the old trade route from Blackford to Tillicoultry. Head ESE from the summit, with a slight path to the north of the ascent path giving a more direct and sheltered route to the west of Andrew Gannel Hill. The climb to the top is easy. The highest point (just) is to the north of the point that overlooks the escarpment, but most walkers go to the edge in any case. The late afternoon lights of Tillicoultry may beckon. Gently descend east then southeast to pick up the trade route path that stays above the Gannel Burn, and gives a quick and easy return to the car park. The last section into Mill Glen has a stepped path again.

49 Meikle Bin

FACTFILE

Map Ordnance Survey map 57, Stirling & The Trossachs
Distance 5 miles
Height 400m
Terrain track, then short muddy clearing leading to open hillside
Start point B818 car park, map ref 672859, west end Carron Valley Reservoir
Time 3 hours
Nearest towns Denny and Balfron
Recommended refreshment spot Carronbridge Hotel, east of the reservoir

Rhona is bagging the mainland Marilyns (hills of any height but with a drop of at least 150m all round) and in October 2008 we went to Carleatheran – the second highest point in the Fintry, Gargunnock and Touch Hills southwest of Stirling, whose northern slopes lead to a spectacular eight-mile-long sharp basalt escarpment.

I have been amazed by the response I have had to that walk. Obviously I was not alone in having driven past on the A811 many a time and annoyed that it had taken so long to appreciate the joy of walking on the escarpment edge.

So what happened this November? We went to much the same area (but a bit further south) to climb yet another Marilyn: the 570m/1870ft Meikle Bin, the highest of the Kilsyth Hills (not the Campsie Fells as commonly stated).

The hill overlooks extensive Forestry Commission land and the Carron Valley Reservoir. Maps of the 1920s show no forestation and no reservoir; simply the upper reaches of the meandering River Carron. The valley was dammed in the 1930s to create a 1000 acre reservoir, four miles long and three quarters of a mile at its widest point – the new water supply for Falkirk and Grangemouth. As with Loch Quoich in upper Glen Garry (also located close to the east/west watershed: east to the North Sea, west to the Atlantic), not one but two dams were required. The Carron flows eastwards for 20 miles before entering the Forth at Grangemouth. However, but for the dam at the west end, the heightened water level occasioned by the east dam would have caused water to flow west to join the nearby Endrick Water (which goes west via Loch Lomond to join the Clyde at Dumbarton).

The area is a popular recreational centre for fishing, mountain biking, wildlife watching and walking. The Balfron to Denny B818 was a busy road when we were there, not with cars but with cyclists. A good parking area on the south side of the road (map ref 672859) at the west end of the reservoir is situated almost under the dam, opposite a track that leads to Todholes and the surprisingly unobtrusive wind turbines on the southern slopes of the Gargunnock Hills. From the parking area a track, that eventually leads to the tree-free northern slopes of Meikle Bin, goes south by the western end of the reservoir. Ignore two branches to the west, continuing to cross the infant Carron by a broad wooden bridge. Once over, take the right-hand track, thus leaving the shoreline and climbing southwest. At the next staggered junction continue southwest with the track eventually curving west.

Look out for a break through the trees to give access to the open slopes; not the first one (a short muddy dead-end) but the second one at 410m. Footprints show the way –a muddy morass on our visit, but thankfully not too long. It is then a steeper climb on short grass, but the views are impressive and the trig point is soon reached.

This centrally-located hill (surprisingly popular on our visit on what was a cold and blustery day) is claimed to be one of the best viewpoints in Scotland – or so we were told by an enthusiast at the summit. Views east to the Forth and the Bass Rock and west to the Clyde and Arran. A surprisingly high often cloud-covered hill, not too distant from Glasgow airport, Meikle Bin has claimed the lives of a number of pilots. A Royal Navy two-seater Fairey Firefly crashed near the summit in January 1950. The bodies of the two occupants were found nearby. Just west of the trig point can be found part of the wing section and 300ft further down the hill is part of the engine.

We took a detour to look at and reflect on the wreckage, then afterwards retired to the Carronbridge Hotel for scrumptious home-made scones.

50 Carleatheran

FACTFILE

Map Ordnance Survey map 57, Stirling & The Trossachs
Distance 10 miles
Height 400m
Terrain track (gravel, grassy, then muddy) all the way
Start point parking area southwest of Ballochleam at map ref 652922
Time 4 to 5 hours
Nearest village Kippen
Recommended refreshment spot Berits & Brown delicatessen / coffee shop, Kippen

A cold north wind (the first intimation of winter) was heading in my direction from Inverness, as was the more welcome Rhona. Bound for the Great North Run on Sunday – just one of some 50,000 runners – she wanted to conserve some energy. So a southerly hill with a short outing gave a triple benefit: a break for her on the long drive to Newcastle; a leisurely start for me and for both of us an escape from the worst of that north wind.

The downside was that we only met up at lunchtime, so a shorter day with the prospect of returning in the dark. Rhona is bagging the mainland Marilyns (hills of any height but with a drop of at least 150m all round) and on her suggestion we met at Kippen ready to tackle a hill called Carleatheran.

The Fintry, Gargunnock and Touch Hills form a compact mass southwest of Stirling. The area generally drains to the south; a gently sloping plateau of surprising complexity – challenging terrain in mist but not outstandingly scenic. The northern slopes however, can only be described as spectacular: an eight-mile-long sharp basalt escarpment giving staggering views over the flat expanse of Flanders Moss and the infant Forth meandering towards Stirling. As a backdrop further north Ben Vorlich, Stuc a'Chroin and Ben Ledi are just three peaks that dominate the skyline. The two highest points on the plateau are 511m/1677ft Stronend (part of the Fintry Hills) and 485m/1592ft Carleatheran in the Gargunnock Hills overlooking the villages of Kippen and Gargunnock. Many a time I have driven on the A811 past these two villages on my way to Ben Lomond and the Arrochar hills. Many a time I have looked up in wonder at the escarpment. Yet for my sins I had never climbed to the very edge, so I am grateful to Rhona for suggesting Carleatheran as an outing.

The escarpment is partially breached where the Boquhan Burn plunges north at the Spout of Ballochleam and on the east side of the burn is a superb gravel track. The best approach to Ballochleam farm and the start of that track is from the A811 at map ref 678954, driving southwards past Inch of Leckie on a minor road for two miles (an approach from the west on the minor road is not recommended). Do not park by the track entrance. Continue southwest for half a mile where there is a large space on the north side of the road at map ref 652922.

Walk back along the road to the track. With a starting height of 140m and a distance of almost two miles, it is an easy pull-up to the Spout of Ballochleam at 300m. Continue a very short distance on the track past a gate to the mapped track that goes northeast near the edge of the escarpment. The grassy track climbs towards Lees Hill, but look out for a junction at 350m. Take the right (east) branch to reach higher slopes and a gate where another track (this time unmapped) comes in (that track can be taken on the way back – it joins the main gravel track by Gourlay's Burn).

The grassy track weaves and undulates over what is very broken country and the odd wet and muddy spot on the way is of little significance when compared with what would otherwise be an awful slog. In any case, all the while there are fabulous views to the north – even more outstanding when the track goes close by Standmilane Craig. The track is shown on the map as stopping west of Carleatheran, but in fact it continues in wet and boggy form right to the hill. Take sensible footwear!

The dark summit cone has been described as a mere pimple. Nevertheless it is quite distinctive from afar. Do pick a good day for it would be a waste to have no views. A trig point (in good order) is surrounded by a cairn 18m in diameter and about 1.7m high – a burial chamber of some antiquity. Oddly enough, a nearby wind farm on the bleak ground to the south does not detract from that antiquity.

We had superb visibility and kept warm with a brisk walk. We did in fact include Stronend in our outing (more of that another time), which allied to the late start meant a return to the car in the gathering gloom ... but so what?

51 Stronend

FACTFILE

Map Ordnance Survey map 57, Stirling & The Trossachs
Distance 7 ½ miles
Height 400m
Terrain gravel then grassy track, the latter starting through a very wet area
Start point parking area southwest of Ballochleam at map ref 652922
Time 3 to 4 hours
Nearest village Kippen
Recommended refreshment spot Berits & Brown delicatessen / coffee shop, Kippen

In October I described a walk with Rhona to Carleatheran – at 485m/1592ft the second highest point in the Fintry, Gargunnock and Touch Hills that form a compact mass southwest of Stirling. The area generally drains to the south; a gently sloping plateau but not outstandingly scenic. The northern slopes however, can only be described as spectacular; an eight-mile-long sharp basalt escarpment. On that visit to Carleatheran, Rhona and I also included the highest point: the 511m/1677ft Stronend.

It is now Stronend that features in today's walk and despite the slightly higher climb, a shorter outing of some three to four hours, and thus more appropriate for fewer daylight hours. The escarpment is partially breached where the Boquhan Burn plunges north at the Spout of Ballochleam and on the east side of the burn is a superb gravel track. As with Carleatheran the best approach to Ballochleam farm and the start of that track is from the A811 at map ref 678954, driving southwards past Inch of Leckie on a minor road for two miles (an approach from the west on the minor road is not recommended). Do not park by the track entrance. Continue southwest for half a mile where there is a large space on the north side of the road at map ref 652922.

Walk back along the road to the track. With a starting height of 140m and a distance of almost two miles, it is an easy pull-up to the Spout of Ballochleam at 300m. Continue a very short distance on the track to a gate, turn right (west) through the gate, follow a vague grassy track and quickly reach a junction. 'Exploring' can lead to difficulties and that is where Rhona and I went wrong. We took the left fork, climbing gently southwest between the Boquhan and Shelloch Burns believing it might give us a more direct route to Stronend, rather than the longer curving way round the edge of the escarpment. The often-wet track followed a line of fence posts, but did not curve towards the summit. We ended up near a 482m spot-height at map ref 638886, from where it was an extremely rough and slow traverse over moorland to the cairn. However, on descent we did follow the escarpment and another track and that is the recommended route for ascent: just over 200m to climb over one and a half miles from the Spout of Ballochleam – eventually drier and obviously more scenic than our exploratory route.

Take the right fork of the track by the east bank of the Boquhan Burn and cross the water either at a small dam or slightly higher at a ford. Now for the wet section: a reedy traverse following a vehicle track. Admittedly we were there after heavy rain, but take sensible footwear and even better perhaps, wait for a spell of frosty weather to harden the ground. Do persevere however, for the way ahead becomes drier as the ground rises northwest towards a 437m spot-height at map ref 642903, and all the while there are those staggering views over Flanders Moss and the infant Forth. As a backdrop further north, Ben Vorlich, Stuc a'Chroin and Ben Ledi are just three peaks that dominate the skyline.

The way then goes southwest, continuing on a broad grassy terrace not quite the highest ground above the escarpment edge. In the final 50m rise the track climbs south direct to the summit that boasts a trig point surrounded by a cairn that is listed as an ancient monument – a burial chamber of some antiquity. Though smaller than that on Carleatheran, the summit is perched much closer to the edge of the escarpment.

There are fabulous views northwest to the Trossachs and possibly the setting sun. Do pick a good day for it would be a waste to have no views. Once back at the Spout of Ballochleam and the start of the gravel track, enjoy a return to the car in the gathering gloom.

52 From Callander to Strathyre, via the River Teith and Loch Lubnaig

FACTFILE

Map Ordnance survey map 57, Stirling and the Trossachs
Distance 9 miles
Height a gentle 100m that will not be noticed
Terrain on a mostly flat cycle route with a good surface with only a few muddy spots
Start point Callander
Time 3 to 5 hours
Nearest villages Callander and Strathyre
Recommended refreshment spots Callander and Strathyre

The calm waters of Loch Lubnaig

The stretch of the A84 (the Stirling to Lochearnhead trunk road) that goes north through the Pass of Leny and then on the east side of Loch Lubnaig, is well known to motorists, but not for good reasons. The road is twisty, and safe overtaking parts are few and far between, such that just one very slow-moving vehicle can cause frustration and angst. It is a busy road and despite the picnic spots by the beautiful loch side, it is not my idea of a restful area. Yet the contrast with the west side of Loch Lubnaig could hardly be more marked, for here is the track bed of a dismantled railway line that gives a delightful and peaceful nine mile walk from Callander to Strathyre.

Further north is Balquhidder at the eastern end of Loch Voil. The River Balvag flows east from the loch then curves and meanders to the south over a flat area prone to flooding, gradually picking up speed as it gently descends to Strathyre. From the village it flows quietly into the three-mile-long Loch Lubnaig. From that loch's end the water (the Garbh Uisge) gathers speed as it enters the Pass of Leny, tumbling over the Falls of Leny which are impressive when in spate. The river continues to Callander, being joined by the Eas Gobhain (the outflow from Loch Venachar). By now the River Teith, it is a lot of water flowing on the south side of the town, so it is little wonder that occasional floods occur. The water's flow only means that Strathyre is higher than Callander, yet the height difference is less than 100m and allied to the even gradient of the old railway line, walking south to north is almost as easy as walking on the flat.

The walk is also used by cyclists so keep a lookout. There is visitor centre in Callander open daily from March to December (telephone 01877 330342 if further information is required).

Head west from Callander, with the way being well signposted. The first part crosses the flood plain on an embankment and comes to the A821 (the Loch Venachar road) that should be crossed with care. Continue past the Falls of Leny to a rough car park at Stank which can be busy for to the west of the park is the popular Corbett, Ben Ledi. 'Stank' means 'foul water' so no fishing. Stank is at the southern end of Loch Lubnaig – a loch which is always a beautiful spot, but especially so when its waters are calm and reflective. It is a definite photo spot.

The woodlands on the lower slopes of Ben Ledi and at the top end of the loch are rich in bird life. Strathyre lies just ahead, crossing the river by a suspension bridge to complete a walk that will go by all too quickly.

53 Ben Lomond

FACTFILE

Map Ordnance Survey map 56, Loch Lomond
Distance 7 miles
Height 950m
Terrain excellent path all the way
Start point Rowardennan, Loch Lomond, map ref 360984
Time 4 to 5 hours
Nearest village Drymen
Recommended refreshment spot a good choice by the loch side, but try the Pottery Place, Drymen

Partly due to its proximity to the central belt, Ben Lomond is one of the most popular Scottish hills and based on the number of walkers who climb it each year, is arguably second only to Ben Nevis. And yes, Ben Lomond is the second most popular hill on which to complete a round of Munros. Nevertheless the numbers on either hill are considerably less than those climbing various 'Furth' Munros such as Helvellyn and Snowdon.

Ben Lomond is not so instantly recognisable as say Schiehallion and lacks the popular picture calendar appeal of Buachaille Etive Mor, yet it is a most scenic mountain and a wonderful isolated viewpoint. The best views are looking down on Loch Lomond and the attractive islands where the loch widens before reaching Balloch. On a good day it is difficult to imagine a better view. Its Gaelic name of *Beinn Laomainn* may well mean 'beacon hill', for its top at 974m/3192ft – although lying surprisingly back from the loch at least in terms of walking – can be seen for miles around.

Phoning from the 'Beacon Hill'

It follows that if you prefer peace and quiet on a hill, then the tourist route up Ben Lomond may not be for you. In the past I have opted for alternative ways up. Further west of the main path is the Ptarmigan ridge – second only to the tourist path in terms of popularity with over one hundred walkers on a good summer's day. For a quieter approach (at least until you are nearly at the trig point), a climb from Comer in beautiful Gleann Dubh up the albeit more demanding northeast ridge will appeal.

Nevertheless, for this visit I wanted to have another look at the tourist route. Popularity brings with it problems: crowds of people and resultant erosion and the tourist 'path' of old from Rowardennan was at one time boggy, messy and uninviting in places. I am delighted to say that it has been improved immensely.

It is a slow drive on the B837 from Drymen to the road end parking area at Rowardennan at map ref 360984. Although quite a climb from near sea level to the 974m/3192ft summit, the tourist path has a steady gradient over the three and a half miles, firstly through forest then on to the open hillside. The forest start (once not immediately obvious) is now well signposted.

Jimbo had taken his two Springer spaniels and they bounded gleefully through the trees and then amid large areas of clear fell that enhance the distant views. Once onto the open hillside, as requested by the livestock sign, the dogs were put on lead. One dog for Jimbo and one for me, we were almost pulled up the grand path – the dogs keener than we were in the sultry weather to chase on to the summit.

The pointed snow-capped summit of Ben Lomond

Even on a late August mid-week the hill was quite busy with over a hundred walkers, but they were well spaced out. Many were family groups and it was pleasing to see the well-judged pace to cope with young children. The West Highland Way passes by the start of the walk, yet it appeared that such walkers had too much on their mind to contemplate such a hill detour.

The slope steepens at the summit cone and the path goes between some rocky outcrops. Sometimes on a busy weekend at that point it is almost a case of needing to have traffic lights installed, but not that day.

With the sultry heat Jimbo and I were glad to have a rest on top and were blessed with atmospheric views down to the attractive islands on Loch Lomond. During a period of wet weather, we were lucky in our choice of both day and hill. The forecast of dry weather with cloud level of around 800m proved to be spot on.

What about sending a message from the Beacon Hill? The last time I was on Ben Lomond there was a young lady using a mobile phone; this time it was a man. Ugh, my pet hate!

On the way down having the dogs on lead was definitely not a help – their idea of speed was different from ours and they were happier when we returned to the forest. That is where we came across a German couple just setting out for the hill. They had taken the train from Glasgow to Balloch then cycled the long and undulating route to Rowardennan. We were impressed with their green credentials.

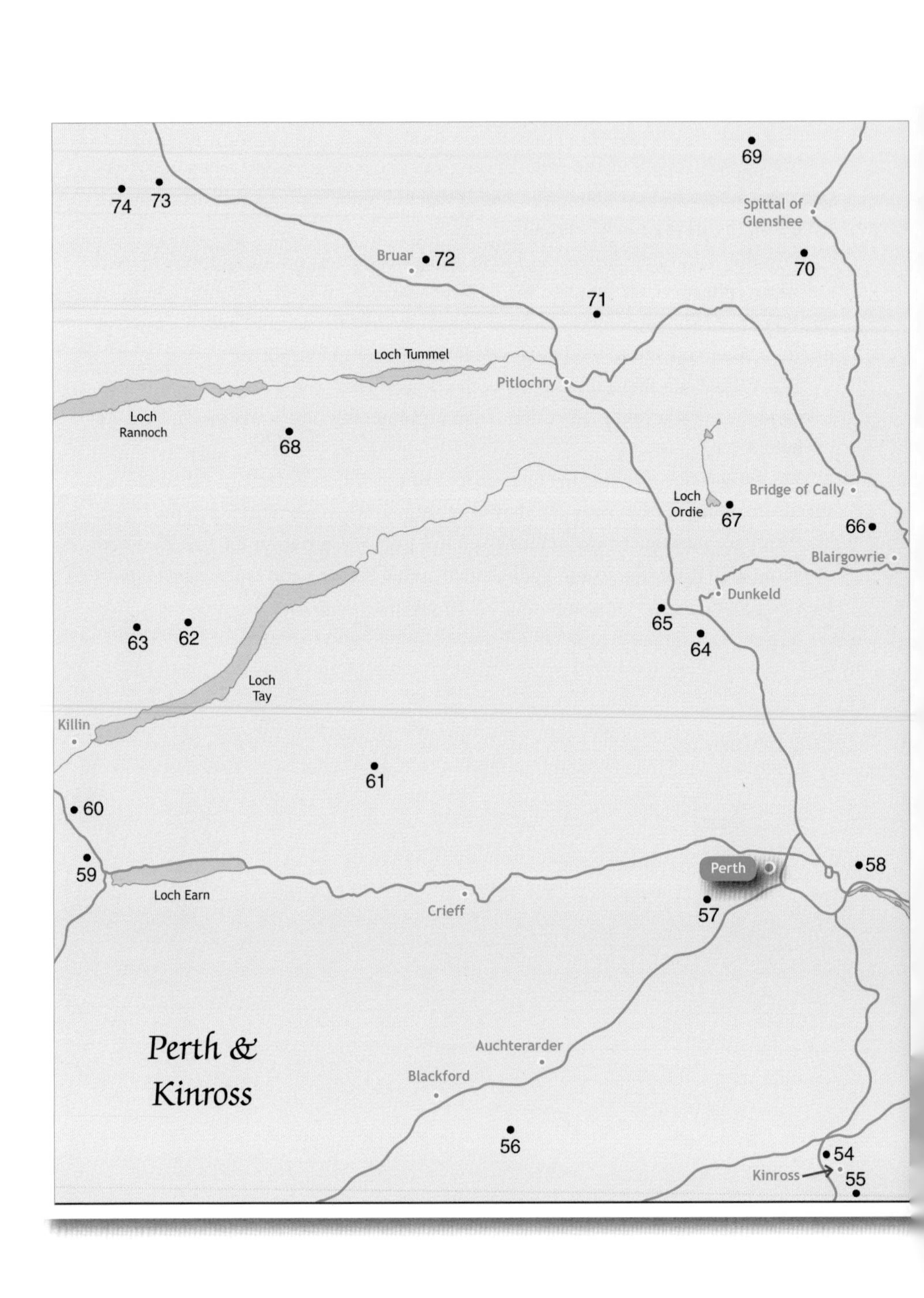

69
74
73
Spittal of Glenshee
Bruar
72
70
71
Loch Tummel
Pitlochry
Loch Rannoch
68
Loch Ordie
Bridge of Cally
67
66
Blairgowrie
Dunkeld
65
63
62
64
Loch Tay
Killin
61
60
59
Perth
58
Loch Earn
Crieff
57
Perth &
Kinross
Auchterarder
Blackford
56
54
Kinross
55

Perth & Kinross

54 The Loch Leven Heritage Trail, part 1

FACTFILE

Map Ordnance Survey map 58, Perth to Alloa
Distance 6 miles
Height negligible
Terrain superb path, then grassy track
Start point Kirkgate Park, Kinross
Time 2 to 3 hours
Nearest town Kinross
Recommended refreshment spot good choice in Kinross but I recommend a halfway stop at Loch Leven's Larder

Although the day started brightly enough, there was a cold north wind blowing and the forecast was for rain falling as snow on the high Cairngorms. However by mid-morning there was still no sign of rain so Margaret and I decided to stay with our earlier plan of a short visit to the Loch Leven National Nature Reserve – Margaret to go bird watching at the RSPB Vane Farm and I to have a look at the new Loch Leven Heritage Trail, or rather what there is of it so far.

Could it really be exactly a year ago (bar one day) that I described a walk with the Mountain Hare to Benarty Hill that overlooks Vane Farm and Loch Leven? At that time plans were afoot to build a pathway round the perimeter of the loch – 'a path that no doubt will feature in a future column' – was my comment then. A few months ago Jimbo told me that the path on the northern side of the loch had been completed: a three-mile stretch from Kinross to the Pow Burn beneath Wester Balgedie, or roughly a quarter of the loch's circumference.

So on this cold and likely to be wet December day, a low-level partly sheltered walk seemed like a sensible proposition, especially at this seasonable festive time of year –exercise still required ... but not too much of it.

Set in low ground between the Ochil, Lomond and Cleish Hills, Loch Leven is renowned as a nature reserve, brimming with wildlife and famous for its brown trout. Claimed to be the largest water of its kind in lowland Britain, it is home to more breeding ducks than anywhere else in inland Europe. You may wish to take binoculars with you, but if so the likely time of two to three hours for the actual walk will be insufficient.

So off we set. I deposited Margaret at Vane Farm and then headed for Kinross. Kinross was an important town in medieval times and Loch Leven Castle on Castle Island is associated with the imprisonment of Mary Queen of Scots in 1567–1568. With immediate views of the castle, the walk starts from Kirkgate Park beside the walls of Kinross House (built in the late 1600s). The gardens (open April to September) are well worth a visit. The house itself is not open to the public. There is a regular ferry service to the Castle, but only in summer.

And what did I discover? The walk is a delight and I am convinced that once completed, the circuit of Loch Leven will be a favourite Central Scotland low-level walk. Loch Leven is on the Ordnance Survey Landranger map 58 (Perth to Alloa) and on the more detailed larger scale Explorer map 369 (Perth & Kinross), but in fact neither is really needed. Just stay with the path and return the same way.

There are good views of Castle Island to begin with, but on heading north into light woodland the castle is soon lost to sight. Wooden bridges cross a number of small burns, with the path varying direction to avoid fields and the more immediate wet areas by the waterside. After passing Burleigh Sands, the path swings eastwards through more woodland and into open country, and then suddenly ends at the wooden bridge over the Pow Burn at map ref 155033 (the burn is not named on the Landranger, but appears on the Explorer as the outflow from Greens Burn).

Thereafter an easy route (signposted for refreshments) goes northeast to Channel Farm and Loch Leven's Larder, just west of Wester Balgedie on the A911. This part gives the only climb of the day, all of 20m beside a woodland strip. The café (and farm shop) is open seven days a week, though closed on 1st and 2nd January.

I covered the whole route from Kinross to Channel Farm and back again. That distance of six miles can however be shortened (it is the festive season after all!) by pre-placing a car at the farm for a one way trip, or in using a parking spot at map ref 134040 at Burleigh Sands on the minor road that links the A911 and Kinross. The latter car park is only some 100 yards from the Heritage Trail.

After the walk I collected Margaret and we set off home, refreshed by our separate activities and looking forward to the New Year, anticipation enhanced by the feel-good factor of seasonal serendipity, for on the homeward drive the forecast rain duly arrived ... too late to spoil a good day.

55 The Loch Leven Heritage Trail, part 2

FACTFILE

Map Ordnance Survey map 58, Perth to Alloa
Distance 8 miles
Height negligible
Terrain superb path, then grassy track
Start point Vane Farm car park, map ref 160990, off the B9097
Time 3 to 4 hours
Nearest town Kinross
Recommended refreshment spot a halfway stop at Loch Leven's Larder

Could it really be just over a year ago that I described a delightful walk on the new Loch Leven Heritage Trail, or rather what there was of it at the time? How time flies! That walk on 29 December 2007 was on the northern side of the loch – a three-mile stretch from Kinross to the Pow Burn beneath Wester Balgedie, or roughly a quarter of the loch's circumference – a low-level partly sheltered stroll, ideal on that raw December day.

The pleasures of the walk convinced me that the planned 12-mile circuit path round the rest of Loch Leven – once complete – would quickly become a favourite Central Scotland low-level walk. Having heard on the grapevine that the second four-mile phase of the path – from the RSPB Vane Farm to the Pow Burn – was either finished or just about to be opened, Jimbo and Drew came with me at the end of October to have an exploratory look. That section – due to be finished in the summer and then deferred to October – was officially opened in November with good coverage on national television. We were thus a couple of days early, but even then the path was being well used.

Set in low ground between the Ochil, Lomond and Cleish Hills, Loch Leven is renowned as a nature reserve, brimming with wildlife and famous for its brown trout. Claimed to be the largest water of its kind in lowland Britain, it is home to more breeding ducks than anywhere else in inland Europe. You may wish to take binoculars

The Lost Valley, Glen Coe

with you, but if so the likely time of three to four hours for the actual walk will be insufficient. It should be noted however, that the loch is at times surprisingly hidden from the new path and the more open views lie on the landward side to the east.

Loch Leven is on Ordnance Survey map 58 (Perth to Alloa), but the map is really not needed. Just stay with the path and return the same way.

The walk starts from the Vane Farm car park on the south side of the loch at map ref 160990, two miles east of the M90. Go past the RSPB buildings to reach the pedestrian tunnel under the B9097. Once through that, turn sharp right on the path going eastwards between road and loch (with open views of the water) for less than one mile to another car park – the Findatie picnic site at map ref 171991.

A few yards north of that second car park, by a large sluice is the outflow from the loch – once the snaking River Leven but now the three-mile long Leven Cut. The Cut was built to lower the level of the loch, thus freeing more fertile land for agriculture and to provide water power for mills such as at Milldeans.

Follow the track on the south side of the Cut, then cross the Leven Bridge to reach the path that goes northwards on the east side of the loch. Even though the path twists and turns as it meanders through open mixed woodland, there is no danger of getting lost. There are ample stone marker posts. The just-over two-mile stretch to Pow Burn is most pleasing – perhaps seeing gliders and ravens soaring above the escarpment of the Lomond Hills. The last section of the new path when we were there was somewhat wet, though remedial work was underway.

Leave the path at the wooden bridge over the Pow Burn – the outflow from Greens Burn at map ref 155033 – and go northeast to Channel Farm and Loch Leven's Larder (just west of Wester Balgedie on the A911). The part gives the only climb of the day, all of 20m beside a woodland strip. The café (and farm shop) is open seven days a week. I recommend their home-made millionaire's shortbread.

For the indolent, the distance of eight miles can be shortened by pre-placing a car at the farm for a one-way trip, or by starting at the car park at map ref 171991 rather than at Vane Farm.

With the eight-mile section from Kinross to Vane Farm now pathed, plans still remain to complete the final phase of some four miles round the southwest end of the loch, albeit that may take a couple of years. I look forward to that.

56 Over the Ochils to Blackford

FACTFILE

Map Ordnance survey map 58, Perth to Alloa
Distance 6 miles
Height 100m
Terrain tarmac road, path and then track
Start point A823, Glen Eagles road, map ref 949052, signposted Frandy and Backhills
Time 3 to 4 hours
Nearest villages/towns Yetts o'Muckhart and Blackford
Recommended refreshment spots Blackford, but specially recommended is Mona's Coffee Shop, Pool of Muckhart

The Ochil Hills (usually just called the Ochils) run in a NE/SW line for 25 miles in a series of rounded grassy and mossy hills. To the northwest (bounded by the A9) they gently slope down to the Braes of Ogilvie – more moorland than prime farmland. To the south it is quite another story. A natural break in the earth's crust – the Ochils Fault – caused the land south of the fault to be 'thrown' down into what is now the fertile flood plain of the Forth, and the resultant escarpment is the most dramatic aspect of the Ochils. The word *ochil* comes from the very old Celtic word *uchil* meaning 'high ground', so it was presumably so-named by the early inhabitants to the south. The escarpment is breached by a series of attractive glens which lend themselves to short walks, as ways to the hilltops, or as through routes. The River Devon flows through the Ochils east of the main escarpment. It has a sudden change of direction at Crook of Devon, such that it flows into the Forth only some five miles south from its source. Glen Devon, with Glen Eagles to the north, is the line taken by the A823 – the only major road that cuts through the Ochils.

There are however many trade routes of old, and one is the eight-mile right of way from Tillicoultry to Blackford – previously used by the weavers in Tillicoultry to trade with the leather workers in Blackford. It was this walk that caught my attention.

A mid-week day in March was free for the Mountain Hare and the Mountain Lamb to go to the high tops. The day though was not well chosen. The forecast for the northwest was very poor, with strong winds and torrential rain, but with slightly better weather for the southeast. Always have a fallback plan, and ours was then to go to the Ochils, possibly to do the Tillicoultry/Blackford traverse.

With conditions forecast to improve slightly, we took our time, yet at Yetts o'Muckhart it was still raining heavily and very windy. Always have a second fallback plan. We made a detour to the nearby tearoom. The weather did eventually improve but any thought of a long tramp had to be aborted with the by-now late start. The revised plan was a shorter outing, starting from Glen Eagles walking west past the two Glendevon reservoirs and descending by Glen of Kinpauch towards Blackford.

As we had only one car, that meant a long walk across the Braes of Ogilvie, heading ENE to Glen Eagles and then through the glen using the old drove road rather than the A823. That turned out to be a long day, so the following walk describes the route only as far as Blackford.

Park off the A823 at map ref 949052 where the old glen road/track comes in. It is tarmac road all the way to Upper Glendevon reservoir. The first section is on the north side of the River Devon as far as the lower reservoir, built in 1924 as a public water supply. The road then goes above the south shore – giving the only climb of the day – before dropping down to the upper reservoir built in 1955. It seemed obvious in what is quite a narrow valley, that there would have been no small lochs swallowed up by this double damming of the river, and this proved to be the case when I checked up on old maps.

Continue with a full circuit of the reservoir – a track leading to Backhills, then a path (boggy in places) round the western arm of the reservoir and crossing the infant Devon. The path leads into the quaintly named Glen Bee – more of a defile than a glen, and surely one of the smallest glens in the country.

The path joins a track west of Craigentaggert Hill. Shortly afterwards there is a junction in the track and a choice to be made: turn left for the descent to a plantation lower down Glen Kinpauch; or take the track (later a grassy path) that climbs the shoulder of Kinpauch Hill, from where there are open views to the north. The end result is the same however, for both routes lead to the next destination: Kinpauch – or rather what is left of it – at map ref 895075. Head north on the track to reach the minor road adjacent to the A9. The dual carriageway to the west has to be crossed with considerable care to reach Blackford.

57 THE GASK RIDGE

FACTFILE

Map Ordnance Survey map 58, Perth to Alloa
Distance what you make it
Height negligible
Terrain minor road and Roman Road
Start point sharp turn on Crossgates to Kinkell Bridge road, map ref 985191
Time what you make it
Nearest city Perth
Recommended refreshment spot Gleneagles Hotel, by Auchterarder

Bearing in mind the heavy snowfalls and traffic disruption at the beginning of the week, I am suggesting a change for this February weekend: a Perthshire walk – sheltered, quiet and easily accessible and an opportunity to inspect some remnants of the Roman military operations in Central Scotland. The sites of the Gask Ridge watch-towers follow the line of a Roman road that can still be identified to this day.

The Gask Ridge lies southwest of Perth, south of the A85 Crieff road and just north of the A9 trunk road to Glasgow. If approaching from Perth, take the A9 west for just over two miles, then turn off right at Crossgates (map ref 049211) for the minor road that runs from Crossgates to Kinkell Bridge. For four miles this minor road follows the line of the old Roman road until a sharp turn at map ref 985191, where the minor road leaves Gask Ridge and descends steadily via Trinity Gask to Kinkell Bridge. However, it is possible at this sharp turn to see – and indeed to walk along – the straight line of the Roman road as it heads west, staying to the top of the ridge.

The minor road is a haven of peace after leaving the A9 and is mostly well-sheltered. Traffic is minimal and indeed it was a favourite place in my marathon days, offering long steady runs. Map 58 clearly identifies a number of the Roman signal stations / watch-towers sites and parking at map ref 985191 gives a choice of stations east and west, as well as a short wooded walk to the north. The length and duration of the walk is what you make it, though most will concentrate on the western end away from the minor road. You can also park at map ref 960188, north of Trinity Gask.

Exploring Scotland's Heritage – Fife, Perthshire and Angus (published by HMSO) has a very interesting chapter on Roman Tayside and is recommended reading prior to the walk. For post-walk refreshments, Crieff and other small towns give a good choice, but if you are well-dressed and feeling affluent, try afternoon tea at Gleneagles Hotel.

58 Kinnoull and Deuchny Hills

FACTFILE

Map Ordnance Survey map 58, Perth to Alloa
Distance 7 miles
Height 300m
Terrain mixture of track, path and road
Start point car park, north-east corner of South Inch, Perth, near railway bridge
Time 3 to 5 hours
Nearest town Perth
Recommended refreshment spot Scone Arms, Scone

Starting from Perth, this walk goes over Kinnoull and Deuchny Hills then a royal descent on the Coronation Road to Scone, a burn-side path to Quarrymill visitor centre by the A93 and an urban stroll back to the South Inch. Depending on the method of transport to Perth, it could be a carbon-friendly outing.

Kinnoull Hill Woodland Park (east of Perth), opened in 1991, covers land owned by Perth and Kinross District and the Forestry Commission, jointly managed to provide public recreation for cyclists, horse riders and pedestrians. Although Kinnoull Hill at 222m/729ft is the highest, the park has four other hills of which Deuchny Hill has the largest wooded area. Available from tourist offices, an informative leaflet covering the start of the walk, shows the mixture of paths and tracks on both hills. Although there are numerous waymarkers, the leaflet's large scale map will enhance the enjoyment of the outing. Thereafter, Ordnance Survey map 58 (Perth to Alloa) suffices for the second half.

A well-situated car park (no parking charge on Sundays) is at the northeast corner of the South Inch (map ref 120230), close to the west bank of the Tay and just south of the elevated curved railway bridge that straddles the river and the northern tip of Friarton Island. A narrow but most convenient walkway on the bridge's northern side gives a pedestrian crossing. Look out for golfers and their bags along the way for the walkway also gives access to the surprisingly large pendant-shaped island – large enough to boast a golf course. At the end of the bridge, a walkway leads to the A85 (cross with caution) and goes past the National Trust for Scotland Branklyn Gardens to reach the base of Kinnoull Hill.

There is a choice of paths to the 222m summit, the one on the right being arguably the more interesting. The park leaflet says: 'no visitor to Perth can say that they have seen its real beauty until they have climbed Kinnoull Hill and feasted their eyes upon the panorama before them' – flowery comments maybe, but true. The summit is graced with both trig point and viewfinder. From Ben More in the west to Lochnagar in the northeast, the views are impressive so do pick a good day.

Heading towards Deuchny Hill, take a curving route through mixed woodland (mostly birch and oak) thus staying with the path by the edge of the escarpment that overlooks the meandering Tay and with views to Fife and the Carse of Gowrie. Take care at Kinnoull Tower – an 18th Century castles-on-the-Rhine imitation perched by the edge of the cliffs. Still close to the escarpment, the path with yellow waymarkers then curves northeastwards to the Jubilee car park at the dip between the hills.

From the car park follow the green waymarkers over the lovely wooded slopes, taking a direct line to reach the signposted Coronation Road. This is the ancient route used by the Kings of Scots as they moved between the palaces of Falkland and Scone – the latter one of the ancient capitals of Scotland and the place where the Scottish Monarch was traditionally crowned.

The Coronation 'Road' goes northwest to the edge of the wood and – now shown as a path on the Ordnance Survey map – descends to a minor road. A few yards to the west, a track leads to the southern end of Scone at Mayfield Terrace.

Cross the A94 past the Scone Arms and by Burnside, to enter the eastern end of the Quarrymill Woodland Park (otherwise known as Quarrymill Den). The way is also signposted as a public footpath to Isla Road. Take time to visit the memorial to David Douglas – the famous botanist after whom the Douglas Fir is named – in the grounds of Scone Old Church. Paths on either side of the burn lead to the Quarrymill visitor centre (the centre and café are only open during the summer months).

It is then an urban, though pleasant, stroll back to the South Inch.

59 A railway walk down Glen Ogle

FACTFILE

Map Ordnance Survey map 51, Loch Tay & Glen Dochart
Distance 6 miles
Height negligible
Terrain well-surfaced old railway line and cycleway
Start point parking area, east side of A85, Glenoglehead
Time 2 to 3 hours
Nearest village Lochearnhead
Recommended refreshment spot Clachan Cottage Hotel, Lochearnhead

Despite many-a-time driving past the spectacular eight-mile long escarpment of the Fintry, Gargunnock and Touch Hills, it took me until last year to climb to the two highest points – Stronend and Carleatheran, both written about recently. I have had similar regrets when travelling through Glen Ogle. It is impossible not to be impressed by the arched viaduct of the old railway line, yet I had neither 'walked the line' nor more closely inspected the massive rock fall – one of many that caused constant problems. However, on a lovely December day, Jimbo and Joe came with me to rectify this omission. Joe (of the heart attack and helicopter rescue on Carn Liath) persuaded his wife that a six-mile cold-weather walk would not be strenuous for we had decided (purely for his benefit you understand) to start from Glenoglehead Station. Until the construction of the branch to Killin, the station – subsequently reduced to a passing place – was designated 'Killin'.

This Caledonian Line (Callander to Oban) was only completed in 1880 and was axed as part of the Beeching cuts of the 1960s. For such a short lifespan, the expense in terracing the steep-sided glen was excessive, yet we should be grateful to have inherited the dismantled line in the guise of a wonderful walking route and now part of a national network of cycle ways.

Though scarcely needed, Ordnance Survey map 51 covers the area. My 1999 edition does not show the new cycle-way (a more current edition is required), but the route – where it leaves the old line – is well-signposted.

From the Glenoglehead car park – the large one on the east side of the A85 – head south on the cycleway, then carefully cross the road to join the old railway line. At first stroll by the almost-hidden Lochan Lairig Cheile, then wonder at the cuttings and viaducts required to obtain the requisite gradient; gentle for walkers but at the top end for trains. John McGregor kindly sent me an extract of the 1881 Working Timetable.

Instructions on the incline to Lochearnhead were quite precise:

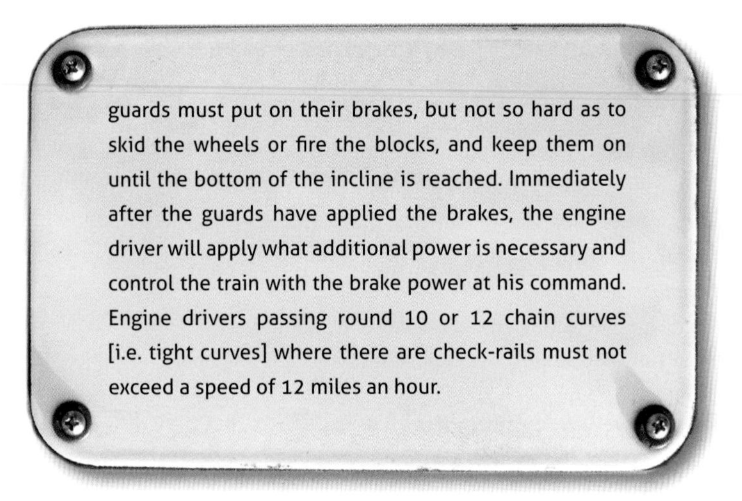
guards must put on their brakes, but not so hard as to skid the wheels or fire the blocks, and keep them on until the bottom of the incline is reached. Immediately after the guards have applied the brakes, the engine driver will apply what additional power is necessary and control the train with the brake power at his command. Engine drivers passing round 10 or 12 chain curves [i.e. tight curves] where there are check-rails must not exceed a speed of 12 miles an hour.

With several inches of snow hiding the tarmac surface, our pedestrian speed was less than four miles per hour, but we enjoyed superb winter weather: blue skies, no breeze and the most gigantic icicles I have seen for many a year in passing by one of the cuttings. With steep rock-strewn slopes to the west and open views to the east, it was a magical stroll downhill.

A decision point is reached where the cycleway leaves the Glen Ogle line to descend in steep zigzags to join the old Lochearnhead line. Knowing that our routes would later converge, Jimbo and Joe kindly opted to stay with the marked route, leaving me to explore the Glen Ogle line. The lower signposted route is straightforward. After descent, walk to a new metal arched bridge spanning the Kendrum Burn then continue towards the A84. However, the cycleway stays on the west side of the road to join the Glen Ogle line at map ref 576214.

I followed the Glen Ogle line with little hope of success, for the way was overgrown and further on there was an ominous gap on the railway line, at least as mapped. However, the overgrown area soon cleared giving an easy walk and there proved to be no gap in the line. The only ill-drained area (through a cutting) was easily traversed.

Sipping hot soup and enjoying the tranquillity, I waited briefly for the others. The Glen Ogle line crossed the road at this point, but again the cycleway stays on the west side to reach the A84 / Balquhidder junction, where we had preplaced one car.

Afterwards we retired to the Clachan Cottage Hotel and its welcoming wood-burning stove.

60 From the Head of Glen Ogle to Killin

FACTFILE

Map Ordnance Survey map 51, Loch Tay & Glen Dochart
Distance 6 miles
Height negligible
Terrain excellent cycleway path, then well-surfaced old railway line
Start point parking area, east side of A85, Glenoglehead, map ref 559285
Time 2 to 3 hours
Nearest village Killin
Recommended refreshment spot Killin Hotel, Killin

In December 2008 Jimbo, Joe and I had a magical downhill stroll on the old Glen Ogle railway line. The weather was superb: blue skies, no breeze and the most gigantic icicles I have seen for many a year.

In December 2009 I returned to the head of Glen Ogle in the company of Jimbo, John and Bruce – this time for a downhill stroll on a cycleway path, then an old railway line to Killin. By contrast it was a raw, wet day: two hours snatched before heavier rain arrived. There had been extensive flooding and the Falls of Dochart at Killin were at their most dramatic. There was more flooding to witness later on…

We met outside the Killin Hotel with time though for coffee and scones before starting the walk from the large Glenoglehead car park on the east side of the A85 at map ref 559285.

In heading north, the old railway line stays on the west side of the A85. A cycle way (National Cycle Network 7) is on the eastside, but both meet up later on.

The Caledonian Line (Callander to Oban) was only completed in 1880. 1882 saw the first meeting of the Killin Railway Company, whose aim was to build a branch line to Killin. Work commenced the following year and the line was opened to passengers in 1886.

The line went beyond Killin to a pier on Loch Tay and a linking steamer service. However, steamers were withdrawn in the 1920s and the extension to the loch closed in 1939. The branch line had a mini boost in the 1950s, being used during construction of the hydro-electric power station at Finlarig. However, with the withdrawal of freight in 1964 the end was inevitable. The following year the line was finally closed as part of the Beeching cuts.

Though scarcely needed, Ordnance Survey map 51 covers the area. My 1999 edition does not show the new cycle-way (a more current edition is required), but the route is well-signposted.

Head north on the cycleway and pass on the right a memorial erected to the memory of the two Flight Lieutenants who died when their Tornado crashed in September 1994. Later on is a high gate (though with a pedestrian gate at the side) with a notice: 'Welcome to Acharn Forest'; plus a most useful large-scale map. It is a steady descent – some sections of almost railway gradient standard – following the cycleway signs to join the long straight track bed of the old branch line. Continue to Killin with a short deviation to the A827. Do not cross the Dochart by the road bridge. Rejoin the railway on the east bank and cross the river by the high splendid railway bridge.

Jimbo and John stopped at the car park on the site of the old Killin station and waited at the car. Bruce and I were keen to explore the decidedly wet and muddy extension of the line towards Finlarig. We crossed the bridge over the swollen River Lochay to witness an unmapped expansion of Loch Tay. The loch now extended west such that the railway line was the only ground above water and the only way over if swimming was excluded.

We did not go all the way to Finlarig. Once adjacent to a minor road, we cut back on the road for a shorter return to Killin. Shorter no doubt, but not drier. One section of the road by the cemetery was completely flooded. Rather than retrace steps, we concluded that the easiest course of action was to go barefoot with rolled up trouser legs, wading over. The water temperature could euphemistically be called refreshing, but the glow to the feet once dry and warm on the far side was worth the effort.

The road bridge over the Lochay took us to the A827 and round to the car park. Then it was back to the hotel for more scones and coffee. It was a poor weather day after all!

61 Ben Chonzie and food for thought

FACTFILE

Map Ordnance Survey map 52, Pitlochry to Crieff
Distance 8 miles
Height climbed 600m
Terrain track and grassy hillside
Start point Loch Turret reservoir dam, near Crieff
Time 5 to 6 hours
Nearest towns Comrie and Crieff
Recommended refreshment spot a good choice in both towns

Munros come in all shapes and forms – some only requiring short, straightforward days with limited ascent. Included in that category is Ben Chonzie, also known and pronounced as 'Ben-y Hone'.

Ben Chonzie stands in a fairly featureless area that starts to the east of Glen Ogle, and stretches eastwards between Loch Tay to the north and Loch Earn to the south. In modern transport terms it is only bisected much further east by the minor road that runs from Amulree to Kenmore at the east end of Loch Tay. Three Corbetts in this area all share similar features of rounded grassy tops and three major glens – Lednock, Turret and Almond – intrude to break some of the monotony. There are only a few craggy parts so some find the terrain dull and characterless.

The name is possibly an anglicised corruption of *Beinn na Coinnich*, meaning 'mossy mountain' – an apt description of the terrain. Another suggestion is that it is a corruption of *Beinn a'Chaoineidh*: 'hill of weeping'. If Glen Turret – from *Glen Torradh* – could mean 'glen of burial', then who knows – it might all refer back to Roman times? Evidence of their presence abounds locally, including the site of a fort southeast of Crieff, and the Roman road running eastwards over the Gask Ridge.

Overlooking Loch Tay to Ben Chonzie

Ben Chonzie is truly on the edge of the Highlands for the boundary fault-line, running diagonally southwest from Stonehaven through Loch Lomond to Helensburgh and beyond, passes just to the south of Comrie along the line of Glen Artney. There are still regular tremors in Comrie for it is highland, whereas Crieff is lowland. Comrie boasted the first seismograph in the country.

Some years ago I wrote about the popular route starting from Coishavachan in Glen Lednock, with an easy gradient on a bulldozed track for much of the way. Once on the broad summit, a line of fence posts comes in diagonally and leads to the cairn.

Whilst Ordnance Survey maps 51 and 52 both show Ben Chonzie, map 52 (Pitlochry to Crieff) is required for the following Glen Turret approach from Crieff.

It is permissible to drive all the way on tarmac road to a car park by the Loch Turret dam. A track goes along the eastern shore of the reservoir with the slopes of Auchnafree Hill just to the north. The track continues (at least in tyre track form) almost to Lochan Uaine. Crossing the Turret Burn at the top end of the reservoir is seldom a problem, and a westerly approach to the flattish area to the south of Ben Chonzie should present no difficulties, but I would recommend carrying on to Lochan Uaine (not that it ever looks all that green to me), nestling below the eastern crags of Ben Chonzie. The crags are well interspersed and even in mist present little problem, so a more direct western route can be used following the line of a stream that flows into the lochan. Even better is to go a bit further north from the lochan, weaving in and out through broken terrain, then up a grassy ramp for the top.

From the summit there are open northwest views to the line of the Ben Lawers range above Loch Tay, and north to Schiehallion. Look out for the mountain hares that frequent the top, though much fewer than used to be in pre-Munro-boom days.

Instead of retracing steps, return along the high grassy area, dropping to the 786m/2579ft top of Carn Chois with its trig point, following the line of fence posts mentioned under the popular route, before descending to the dam. If returning late from the summit, the lights of Crieff and Comrie may be attractive and the walk back to the car can be in the gathering gloom.

I have many memories of Ben Chonzie, including an association with hill food. When Margaret first decided to share the delights of hillwalking, it had been a while since she had climbed anything higher than a horse, so an easy hill was required. Enter Ben Chonzie and a small family outing was arranged. I soon realised however, that the term 'hill food' was being misunderstood as Margaret started to organise for everyone instead of each walker being responsible for themselves. The subsequent events turned out to be most embarrassing, as a picnic cloth was spread out on the hillside. As the others sat in the heather gleefully unpacking crab, drumsticks, salad and mini wine bottles, I stood apart guarding my hill-credibility, hoping that none of my friends would chance by.

62 Ben Lawers

FACTFILE

Map Ordnance Survey map 51, Loch Tay & Glen Dochart
Distance 6 miles
Height 900m
Terrain path all the way
Start point Car park on the Lochan na Lairige road, map ref 608379
Time 4 to 5 hours
Nearest village Killin
Recommended refreshment spot a good choice in Killin

At 1214m/3983ft, Ben Lawers is not only the highest mountain in Perthshire, but also the highest in Britain south of Ben Nevis. With its prominent position, it played a significant part in the early survey work of the Ordnance Survey. A rather tired looking trig point – its base eroded – is scant memorial for such pioneering work. The metric height converts to 3983ft – tantalisingly short of the 4,000ft mark. In 1878 a group of 30 or so men decided to do something about the shortfall and built a large cairn. Nature having a habit of taking its course, only a small cairn now remains.

By far the most popular way to climb Ben Lawers – traversing Beinn Ghlas en route – is from the car park at map ref 608379, on the Lochan na Lairige road that goes from the A827 on the north side of Loch Tay, over to Glen Lyon.

From the car park simply follow the well-made signposted path, over duckboards initially, as it heads NNE in a sylvan conservation area, on the west bank of the Burn of Edramucky. The path crosses the burn at the end of the nature trail at NN616393, at a junction of paths, by now on the open hillside. Ignoring the path to the left, continue straight ahead on the excellent path that climbs northeast on to the SSW ridge of Beinn Ghlas.

It may come as a surprise to realise that Beinn Ghlas – at 1103m/3619ft – is number 47 in the list of Munros, because with a starting height of 440m and the excellent path, the climb to the summit is not significant. The popularity of Ben Lawers is such that many a summer tourist is blissfully unaware of having just climbed past a Munro en route, so much so that there must be plenty of people who would reply 'Ben Lawers' if asked what their first ever Munro was – when in fact that it was their second.

If inadvertently passing the Beinn Ghlas cairn, one indication is the gentle descent northeast to the col below Ben Lawers. Arguably as a consequence of having corridorised the route to such an extent over the previous couple of decades, the National Trust for Scotland has improved the Ben Lawers path to almost pavement standard. However, thousands of boots on the narrow, high-level approach from Beinn Ghlas has caused erosion. Re-vegetation has been attempted alongside the summit path, but erosion will require regular attention by the NTS.

The mighty bulk of Ben Lawers

The drop from Beinn Ghlas is just over 100m and the final 200m cone of Ben Lawers is easily climbed ENE via the zigzag path.

From the top on a very clear day it is possible to see the Atlantic to the west and the North Sea to the east – or so my friends tell me. Maybe I have been unlucky, but I have yet to see both bodies of water on the same day. If the drive up to the visitor centre is shrouded in mist and the rain is gushing down, then you've picked a good day for there will not be many people about. Similarly enveloped in waterproofs, I met only two other hardy souls on such a day a few years ago. They had turned back after just climbing Beinn Ghlas. As a not-too-experienced pair, they had made the right decision, for the visibility had been about 20 yards. On such a bad day, do not expect any views (although it might even suddenly clear on top), but once back at the car expect that illogical sensation of satisfaction.

63 Meall nan Tarmachan

FACTFILE

Map Ordnance Survey map 51, Loch Tay & Glen Dochart
Distance 4 miles
Height 600m
Terrain good track and path to summit
Start point off-road parking on the Lochan Lairige road, map ref 604383
Time 3 to 4 hours, summit only
Nearest town Killin
Recommended refreshment spot Killin Hotel

Back from an enjoyable but exercise-free holiday, the lure of the hills was too strong to ignore, despite an iffy weather forecast. With that lay-off and forecast in mind, a shorter day was called for. Meall nan Tarmachan fitted the bill. Rhona was away at Braemar and Jimbo had decided that Hearts needed his support more than I did (true), so I was on my own.

Meall nan Tarmachan (commonly referred to as simply Tarmachan) means 'hill of the ptarmigan', but I have not seen Scotland's mountain bird on any of my many outings there. Perhaps I have been unlucky or unobservant; perhaps the hill's undoubted popularity is to blame (I wrote about Ben Vrackie in August, mentioning that the summit was said to be often frequented by aggressive goats, not that I had seen any there. Readers' letters have confirmed the existence there of goats, as well as an aggressive sheep).

Tarmachan lies north of Loch Tay overlooking Killin, west of the main Lawers range of which it arguably forms part, despite the minor road to Loch Lyon acting as a divide. The hill is best seen to advantage from the top of Glen Ogle, this southeast aspect revealing a sharp and craggy two-mile main east/west ridge that suggests (correctly) a worthy traverse.

The popular route takes advantage of the minor road that climbs north from Loch Tay and the A827. Drive to where a rough track goes off left at map ref 604383. This gives a starting height of 460m. There is adequate off-road parking. Suddenly, despite its 1044m/3425ft height, Tarmachan no longer seems quite so big and do not be put off by the steep, craggy eastern slopes looming over Lochan na Lairige. There is a path all the way to the summit. The eastern slopes of Tarmachan being National Trust territory, have no stalking restrictions.

Although the post-war damming of the loch added little length, the dam itself is quite unattractive. On the southeast slopes of the hill are tracks used to extract rock for the construction of the dam – the water destined for the power station at Finlarig at the west end of Loch Tay.

Meall nan Tarmachan

The popular route using the slight SSE ridge, is short, easy and direct. Start on the track but after little more than quarter of a mile head west on the obvious path (recently constructed), climbing gently and easily to reach the base of the ridge. Already at a height of 700m, the path turns north. The National Trust for Scotland, for regeneration purposes, has fenced off the eastern slopes and there is a stile to cross. The path continues over a small knoll – the modest 923m South-east subsidiary Top. Many hillwalkers – intent solely on reaching the summit – are unaware of its status.

From there, descend a short distance to another stile over an electrified fence. Thereafter the going is steeper northwest, but the path cutting to the right, shows the way. Once on the ridge, turn left for the summit.

A disappointingly small summit cairn sits by the edge of crags and amid an eroded area. Retracing steps for the return, at first head northeast for a short distance. This direction may not be entirely obvious on a misty day.

Having reached the summit in some two hours, it would be quite inexcusable – especially on a good day – for an experienced party not to continue with a traverse of the knobbly, undulating ridge (the fact file assumes only a visit to the summit). Although there is a well-worn path, Tarmachan should not be under-estimated. The ridge includes three subsidiary Tops – surprising given Tarmachan's relatively small strip of land above 3000ft. First up is Meall Garbh, an attractive peak more deserving of pre-eminence than the 18m higher lumpish summit. The ridge then turns west descending a short eroded little gully. There is however, a perfectly easy avoiding path on the north side. The narrowest part of the ridge then leads to Beinn nan Eachan. The ridge then falls sharply to a bealach and continues to lowly Creag na Caillich. Return to the bealach and descend south then east to reach the old tracks.

I did the whole traverse in little more than four hours on a day of rolling mist that only cleared on descent. But that is how it often goes. There were neither ptarmigan nor goats to be seen, though a scattering of sheep.

64 King's Seat on Birnam Hill

FACTFILE

Map Ordnance Survey maps 52, Pitlochry to Crieff or 53, Blairgowrie and Forest of Alyth
Distance 6 miles
Height 400m
Terrain road, track and path
Start point North car park, Dunkeld
Time 3 to 4 hours
Nearest town Dunkeld
Recommended refreshment spot Howies Bistro, Atholl Street, Dunkeld

A walk from Dunkeld to Birnam Hill gives a partly sheltered wooded outing with a signposted pathway – ideal for a shorter winter's day. That is exactly what I did when the weather forecast of extensive low-lying cloud and drizzle ruled out a higher hill. My choice of Birnam Hill gave a good leg stretch.

The hill is shown on both Ordnance Survey maps 52 and 53, however the larger scale map on the excellent leaflet *Dunkeld & Birnam Walks* (available for £1 from the information centre in Dunkeld) is more useful, following what is known as the Birnam Hill Walk, with red signposts showing a small pointing walker. Higher up, some of the signs have weathered so that they are more pink than red.

From the north car park in Dunkeld head south along Atholl Street (the old A9) to Dunkeld Bridge over the River Tay. Designed by Thomas Telford and built 1804–1809 to replace two ferries slightly upstream, the bridge was paid for by tolls, charged until 1879. Previously drovers had had to get their reluctant cattle to swim the river.

Turn left into Little Dunkeld and Birnam and continue to just before the Beatrix Potter Garden, where a red signpost directs the walker into Birnam Glen. Follow the narrow road on the east bank of the Inchewan Burn. The road goes under the A9 and then the railway. A pathway leaves the road at the latter bridge but the road can still be followed as it curves higher up the glen to rejoin the path and another signpost. Continue southeast on the road (later a track) that gently rises through charming woodland – a walk not spoiled by the sight and sound of the nearby A9. Before reaching Craigbeithe, look out for another sign on the left-hand side where the narrow path leaves the track. On my visit on what was admittedly a damp day, the path was somewhat muddy.

I passed two backpackers from Holland. They could not contain their enjoyment in being in such a lovely wooded area – so unlike their homeland – and regretted that their week in Scotland was almost over. The damp conditions only added to their enjoyment.

The undulating path ever so gradually swings away from the A9. The path crosses a track and then parallels the track to within sight of the railway again (this slate quarry track goes under the railway to the Quarry car park by the B867. The Birnam Quarry should not be explored as the old slate workings could become unstable and dangerous). At this stage it is important to notice where the signposted path heads to the right, southerly, for the start of the steeper pull-up that eventually leads (by now on a grassy track) to open hillside. Just off the track at Stair Bridge over the Birnam Burn there is a good viewpoint looking south towards Perth. The burn flows towards Robin's Dam, alas no relation. The track goes west by the burn, then northwards, later reaching a stepped climb that leads to the small but rough summit area where a large cairn marks the 404m high point, King's Seat.

By this time I was into low lying cloud, clearing from time to time to give grey but atmospheric views. With the trees dripping in the gentle drizzle, a vivid imagination could lead one to think of the much maligned Macbeth. Crowned at Scone on the Stone of Destiny in 1037, his throne was said to be secure until Birnam Wood came to Dunsinane Hill. An Australian couple, here on a year's sabbatical, could only gasp at the difference between their parched landscape and this inspiring mixture of colour and dampness.

The northern descent path is shorter, thus steeper, and in the initial stage is little more than a quagmire. However, the path does improve and lower down take time to stand at the next viewpoint with a truly staggering vista down to Dunkeld. Return to Birnam then retrace steps back to Dunkeld.

65 Inver Walk, Dunkeld

FACTFILE

Map Ordnance Survey maps 52, Pitlochry to Crieff or 53, Blairgowrie and Forest of Alyth
Distance 6 miles
Height 100m
Terrain tracks and paths
Start point Hermitage car park, off the A9, west of Dunkeld
Time 3 hours
Nearest town Dunkeld
Recommended refreshment spot Howies Bistro, Atholl Street, Dunkeld

On a gloriously colourful late autumn day, Jimbo, John and I visited the environs of Dunkeld for a sheltered woodland walk – a well-chosen day with rain and cloud forecast for the high tops, but with gently improving conditions at lower levels.

Bounded by the River Braan and the Hermitage to the south, Craigvinean Forest covers an extensive area – possibly a confusing place of tracks and paths, big and small. Only a few of these of course can be shown on the otherwise excellent leaflet, *Dunkeld & Birnam Walks* (available for £1 from the information centre in Dunkeld) and likewise on Ordnance Survey maps 52 or 53. Nevertheless, the leaflet does help in following what is known as the Inver Walk: a low level circular stroll through forest then by the south bank of the River Tay. On our visit we met a Countryside Ranger. She explained that a survey of the various trails was underway with the objective of improving the signpost system.

The walk starts from the Hermitage car park (requested parking charge), reached from the A9 less than one mile west from the northern of the two road junctions to Birnam and Dunkeld. The turn-off is well signposted. Go through a short but oddly unobtrusive railway tunnel and follow the good broad path by the north bank of the River Braan as if heading for the folly known as Ossian's Hall. Just before the folly the good path gradually curves to the right, leading away from the river. However, if you have not been there before, do make the short detour to visit the folly whose balcony gives an impressive view of the Braan surging through a rocky defile in a series of small waterfalls.

From the folly, return to the path that goes through a delightful wooded area to reach a forestry track. Cross that track and follow another forestry track heading northwards. Some five minutes later look out for a new path marked by red-circled signposts, that cuts back to the left. Although a detour on the Inver Walk, it is a must-do extension included in the fact file time and mileage. The path has gently graded zigzags, such that the climb of 75m is scarcely noticed. Keep to the right at another path junction and shortly after reach a new landmark – the Pine Cone viewpoint perched on a rocky spur overlooking Strath Tay and the meandering river. Not only a most marvellous viewpoint, it offers shelter on a wet day. The designer and builder are to be congratulated.

Return to the track, head north again for a few yards, then on the right a short path leads to another viewpoint of older vintage, partly hidden at first. Named after a long deserted township which lay to the north, Torryvald is a bizarre construction that replaces a ruined Victorian viewpoint. Of lesser height and vantage than the Pine Cone, there are nevertheless good views to Dunkeld House on the far bank of the Tay.

Continue north on the track until it meets another track coming in from the left. Curve to the right and within a short distance reach old wooden Inver Walk signs at map ref 999433. Leave the track and follow the narrow path that cuts to the left. This charmingly leads though Inver Wood to Newton Craig car park (map ref 003437) on the B898.

From now on there is no confusion. The signposted path leads under the A9 and heads south by the pretty banks of the Tay to a footbridge over the River Braan. Along the way look out for Neil Gow's Oak where the famous Scottish fiddler was in the habit of sitting with his violin, composing many of his finest airs – many of which are familiar to present day Scottish Country Dancers. From the footbridge head west on either the north or south banks of the Braan to reach Inver and continue on the north bank to return to the Hermitage car park.

66 From Blairgowrie to Bridge of Cally – the start of The Cateran Trail

FACTFILE

Map Ordnance Survey map 53, Blairgowrie and Forest of Alyth.
Distance 6 miles
Height 200m
Terrain mixture of minor road, track and path; some sections muddy
Start point bridge over the River Ericht, Blairgowrie
Time 3 hours
Nearest village Bridge of Cally
Recommended refreshment spot Bridge of Cally Hotel or Riverside Granary coffee house, Blairgowrie

The West Highland Way has been an undoubted success. Thousands of walkers set out each year – most of them make it all the way and some are so enthused by the experience that they return for more. That does not necessarily mean a return to the same Way, for its success has spawned other long distance walks, such as, the Great Glen Way continuing from Fort William to Inverness; the Speyside Way from Aviemore to Buckie; the Rob Roy Way from Drymen to Pitlochry; and now the East Highland Way.

There is a newer long-distance walk, described as a Trail rather than a Way. This is The Cateran Trail: a round walk of 64 miles that starts and finishes in Blairgowrie. It follows the footsteps of cattle-rustlers – known as 'caterans'; in reality a ruthless bunch of local outlaws. The Trail is well way-marked and has undemanding gradients with mixed and interesting scenery along the way. The whole distance can be covered within four to five days.

The Trail is maintained and managed by the Perth & Kinross Countryside Trust. Whilst it is unlikely to reach the popularity of the West Highland Way, local people tell me that it is well used at weekends in the summer months.

Why not try the first short section of six miles from Blairgowrie to Bridge of Cally? A few weeks ago the Mountain Lamb, the Mountain Hare and the Mountain Maid came with me for a most enjoyable January morning walk. Although Ordnance Survey map 53 (Blairgowrie and Forest of Alyth) covers the area, I would recommend the Rucksack Readers guide for more detailed information.

Pre-walk arrangements may include leaving one car at Bridge of Cally and driving back to Blairgowrie, but why not consider using the local albeit infrequent bus service, starting say from Blairgowrie? Or else why not walk all the way back again, after a suitable refreshment spot? The one-way walk should take about three hours and possibly faster on the way back.

Park slightly upstream from the start of the walk, at the Mill Inch car park on the west side of the River Ericht. At the bridge look out for the sign 'River Ericht Walk' and for the metal sculpture in Mill Street. Signposts abound and are easy to follow, but on the open moorland in winter a compass and map are necessary. The walk may lack height, but once away from Blairgowrie you will be crossing open country – Cochrage Muir at over 250m, so the usual sensible hillwalking rules apply: namely be well clad and equipped – remember this is January.

The first mile is a delightful path by the river and the old mill and water lades. Look out for Cargill's Leap at a gorge in the river. The walk then swings back on itself and climbs steeply for the first of many open views to the south.

The next part – from East Gormack to West Gormack – is disappointing in that the path leads round to avoid the farm buildings and fields (understandably so) but the way is narrow, fenced in with many gates and styles and can be muddy and slippy. This section will take longer than at first imagined. Had it been possible, I would have preferred a slightly lower way by the Lornty Burn. The minor tarmac road from West Gormack to Middleton is a welcome sight, and easier walking.

The route now is generally north from Middleton on a broad track, however shortly after the farm make sure you spot one of the many marker posts at a junction of the track (not shown on my map), taking a turn to the left. Cross a minor stream and then it is northwards over Cochrage Muir. This section gives marvellous open views and on a good day is a grand spot to be walking over. I would express caution however on a day of drifting snow.

Look out for a track to the west that gives good grassy walking to Blackcraig Forest – an old running haunt of mine. A detour to the forest, dropping down to Croft of Blackcraig and so to Bridge of Cally, adds on another two miles, but is well worth doing.

Crossing Cochrage Muir has a drawback, apart from being an open area on a bad day, the track hereabouts is very wet and good boots are a must. Near the end of the moor traverse, the line of the Old Military Road comes in from the southeast. After that it is a surprisingly quick, dry, grassy descent to the end of Blackcraig Forest. At a junction in the track, turn left for the rest of the Trail, but right for Bridge of Cally.

67 Loch Ordie and Deuchary Hill

FACTFILE

Map Ordnance Survey map 52, Pitlochry to Crieff
Distance 10 miles
Height 250m
Terrain track and path all the way
Start point north side of A923 at bend in road, map ref 045447
Time 4 to 5 hours
Nearest towns Dunkeld and Birnam
Recommended refreshment spot Howies Bistro, Atholl Street, Dunkeld

This week's walk goes to Loch Ordie, north of Dunkeld, and includes a circuit round Deuchary Hill. Jimbo and I had planned to go further west and higher that day, but with poorer weather forecast for that direction a more easterly outing seemed sensible. In fact we went too far east, but with a well-nigh perfect day for a walk – cold, but with blue skies and no wind – who could complain about such an attractive outing, even if at lower level?

Immediately north of Dunkeld is a rough craggy area, well-wooded in places, holding a number of small hill-lochs. The ground rises to the 509m Deuchary Hill, beneath whose northern slopes at a height of 980ft (nearly 300m) nestles the largest of those lochs, Loch Ordie. Important enough for its depth to be surveyed, it is to some degree an artificial loch, its size expanded by a sluice. This was undoubtedly done for fishing reasons and I am told that its waters hold an abundance of fine large trout. On its grassy SSW banks, close to the sluice, is a line of attractive fishing cottages.

Loch Ordie drains southwest to Raor Lodge, then more steeply west to Dowally on the A9. This is the shortest approach to the loch – just over two miles by track – but arguably the more attractive approach is from the south from the A923 (the Dunkeld to Blairgowrie road). This southern area has a good network of tracks and paths. A popular approach to the loch goes from a parking area just before Cally Loch, using a not well-signposted side-road that leaves the A923 at map ref 025433, just past a sawmill.

However, Jimbo and I opted to start further east on the A923, at the north end of Loch of Craiglush, using a track to Mill Dam to join the popular route. In fact for the complete walk there are tracks all the way, with one short stretch of tarmac. Arguably the most scenic part of the walk is on the south side of Deuchary Hill, using a mapped path – the remnant of an overgrown track.

Use the A923 parking area by a bend on the north side of the road at map ref 045447. From there a short path leads to a beautiful grassy and pine-needle-strewn track. This rises gently northwest – an easy start to the day, with open views developing on the approach to The Glack and Mill Dam. From there the circuit of Deuchary Hill passing Loch Ordie, is in open country with superb views to the west over Strath Tay and not spoiled even by the sound of the A9 traffic. A broad gravel track goes northwest to Raor Lodge to join the Dowally track, and then continues northeast, again gently rising, to reveal the sudden emergence of Loch Ordie.

Turn eastwards and cross the sluice for a charming stroll on the south side of the loch by the cottages, with a stone wall at the water's edge. At map ref 042500, turn southwards past the entrance to Riemore Lodge – by now on a short stretch of tarmac – and continue towards Grewshill croft.

Immediately east of Grewshill by the track-side is the site of the Sancta Crux Well: a Pictish/Christian healing well to which folk – even into the 19th Century – used to resort for cures on the first Sabbath in May. Known locally as *grews* or *gruis*, the name is a corruption of the Pictish word for 'cross'. I did not know at the time of the curative nature of the water – in any case we were not there on the requisite date.

Just beyond Grewshill, another track (grassy this time) goes southwest past the south base of Deuchary Hill. The track soon becomes overgrown, but still has a definite path that climbs gently to the watershed, easing the way through rough terrain – craggy heathery slopes dotted with boulders. If wishing to climb Deuchary Hill, an approach from this side is not recommended; use the path on the northwest side via Lochan na Beinne, but if going there on 8 March look out for the runners taking part in the annual Deuchary Hill 'Canter'.

More open views develop to the southwest on descent to map ref 031472, where a mapped path comes in. This proves to be another grassy track that quickly leads down to Mill Dam. Return to the road using the ascent route.

68 SCHIEHALLION ... AND A PATH TOO EASY

FACTFILE

Map Ordnance Survey maps 42, 51 or 52
Distance 6 miles
Height 750m
Terrain superb path climbing to 900m, then stony ridge to summit
Start point car park at Braes of Foss (map ref 753556) off the minor road running from the B846 to Kinloch Rannoch
Time 4 to 5 hours
Nearest town Aberfeldy
Recommended refreshment spot a good choice in Aberfeldy

Four weeks ago I complained about the path up Criffel. Today I am complaining about the path up Schiehallion – but for different reasons.

It would be an understatement to say that Schiehallion is a popular hill. It is extremely popular. Even the Ordnance Survey appears to like Schiehallion, for it is the only Munro with its summit on three Landranger maps. Its popularity is partly due to its central position, but even more so due to its striking appearance. It stands slightly apart from its neighbours, and its distinctive graceful cone can be picked out from as far north as Ben Nevis.

Cloud inversion, Schiehallion

And is Schiehallion the most famous mountain in the history of science? Its regular slopes were used in 1774 by the then Astronomer Royal, Nevil Maskelyne, to measure the Earth's mass from the deflection of a plumb line held at various points around the mountain. Schiehallion was chosen because it is reasonably symmetrical, making the centre-of-gravity calculations easier and it has steep northern and southern faces, allowing platforms to be tucked in close to the centre of gravity of the mountain, thus maximising the induced deviation. Amidst the enormous and confusing number of elevation readings taken, it was noticed that a line drawn to connect points of equal height made the information less confusing. It is possible that this led to the invention of contour lines as we know them today.

Many hillwalkers choose Schiehallion as their final hill to complete a round of Munros. There have been over 50 Schiehallion completions, including my fifth round in December 1992.

Schiehallion has a long east-west whaleback shape, and the east ridge is the very popular way up, starting from the car park at Braes of Foss on the minor road running from the B846 to Kinloch Rannoch.

The downside is that popularity comes at a price. Over many years thousands of boots had turned the footpath into a muddy mess – definitely not a pleasure to climb. However, following acquisition of East Schiehallion by the John Muir Trust in 1999, action was taken to tackle the problem. A new route further south of the old quagmire, has been built on firmer, drier ground at a cost of £817,000. Notice boards at the start of the path shows the extent of the Trust's land, with a red line denoting the new path, claimed to be like the sturdy stalking paths of the 19th Century. It is narrow with an easy gradient of 12 degrees (compared to 20 degrees for the old path).

I do not like the corridorisation of a hill, with a well-made-up path seemingly as the official way (in previous visits I had avoided the popular route), but there is no doubt that the Trust has done a grand job.

At 1083m/3553ft, Schiehallion is not a little hill, but the car park lies at a height of 330m and almost effortlessly the two-mile path takes the casual hillwalker and visitor south, then southwest across the lower moorland, before gently climbing to a height of 900m. The scar of the old path is healing fast though the line can still be seen from the car park.

For some the climb to 900m may take as little as one hour, leaving just one mile west to the summit and less than 200m to climb. And therein lies the basic problem. The path is just too good, perhaps lulling the casual hillwalker into a false sense of security.

The truth is that the last stretch – by now above 3000ft – will take longer than imagined. The terrain quickly changes to stonier, rougher quartzite ground and the summit ridge is deceptively narrow with sheer drops at the bouldery summit, and all the while with the prospect of adverse weather.

Peter and I were there at the end of December and the final section was none too pleasant. Returning to the 900m mark and the top of the path we saw a group of ill-equipped walkers, most without rucksacks (and hence no spare clothing, no food) and inappropriate footwear. Some of them looked quite miserable, unable to comprehend the sudden ending of the good path and the change in the weather, and for them the summit still an hour away. I am glad to say that another couple did turn back, wisely admitting that they were under–equipped.

While there will always be stupidly under-equipped folk climbing hills, the John Muir Trust should install a warning notice at the car park about the inherent dangers of this too easy path.

69 Glas Tulaichean

FACTFILE

Map Ordnance Survey map 43, Braemar and Blair Atholl
Distance 8 miles
Height 700m
Terrain track to summit plateau
Start point Dalmunzie House Hotel, Spittal of Glenshee
Time 4 to 5 hours
Nearest towns Braemar and Blairgowrie
Recommended refreshment spot Dalmunzie House Hotel

Have you ever been to some event and realised at once what a big mistake it was going to be? My abiding memory of Glas Tulaichean is of participating in a hill race from Glenlochsie Farm all the way to the top. It seemed a good idea prior to the race, but when I turned up almost all the other runners were youngsters, trim and fit like racing whippets … and so it turned out. Geraldine and Irene waited in glorious conditions by the farm. Luckily, I managed to find three other runners who were not quite so young, and in the one-way race to the top (using the track – another reason why I do not like this as a way up) I just avoided ignominy by finishing fourth last in a field of 50. It was 58 minutes of agony for a 58 year old on his first ever hill race. I vowed never again to do another hill race – and now with an artificial hip, I never will!

I wrote about Glas Tulaichean in January 2002 and here I am now describing a late November return. As the hill's popular route lends itself to a winter's day and/or a short outing in bad weather, those dates are no coincidence ... and once the walk was over I discovered another coincidence.

Last week's walk was over nearby Glas Maol and Creag Leacach, on a day when heavy rain for the west made the east a more attractive proposition. So why should Jimbo, Joe, Lindsay and I return to the same area so soon? Yes, it is that weather again: gale force winds in the west, but only strong winds forecast for the east. So for a shorter day than we would have liked, it was off to Glas Tulaichean.

The most-used access is from Glen Lochsie, using the private road from the A93 at Spittal of Glenshee to Dalmunzie House Hotel. Although the hill has a height of 1051m (3448ft) the starting level from Spittal of Glenshee is some 350m, and in the summer most hillwalkers would consider adding on Carn an Righ and Beinn Iutharn Mhor.

Springer spaniels impatient to get going

Four broad grassy ridges radiate to roughly the four points of the compass from the summit. Glas Tulaichean probably means 'grey/green hills', from *glas-thulchan* – a most apt description of those grassy ridges. The generally southern ridge very quickly splits into two, high above the Allt Clais Mhor. The direct southern branch carries the bulldozed track of the most popular way up.

There is a small free parking area at map ref 105701 – a short distance up the Glen Lochsie road, but many hillwalkers do not like the initial walk in of just over a mile to the hotel and are happy to pay the road maintenance/parking charge. Park beside the petrol pump at the side of the hotel, once permission has been obtained from reception.

From the hotel, go west to Glenlochsie Farm and join the disman-

Glas Tulaichean as seen from Cairn an Righ

tled railway track that follows the Glen Lochsie Burn on the north side for the two miles to the ruins of Glenlochsie Lodge. The narrow-gauge railway was originally built to link the hotel and the lodge for deer-stalking purposes and old photos of the railway can be seen in the bar of the hotel. It gives a charming walk to the lodge, now looking sad and fast deteriorating. (Access to Glenlochsie Lodge is also achieved by using the track on the south side of the glen, starting from Spittal of Glenshee).

The somewhat ugly track climbs steeply at first over Breac-reidh – a track that normally makes light work of the ascent from the lodge to the top: 550m over two and a half miles. The summit lies a short distance to the east of the track, just before it veers off to the left. On our climb however, the strong wind was either gusting side-on – making us look like drunken crabs (not that I have seen any) – or head-on, making progress a genuine heads-down battle.

Glas Tulaichean has a trig point set amidst a small flat area, perched rather too close for comfort on a bad day to the crags above Glas Choire Mhor. Once at the summit we had to be cautious in approaching the edge of the crags, with a brief rest only achieved by lying flat on the ground.

Jimbo accompanied Joe back down the track, but Lindsay and I preferred a circular route, descending by the mossy ridge on the east side of the Allt Clais Mhor. From Glenlochsie Lodge, the wind blew us back to the hotel.

Our short outing ended with coffee and scones by a log fire at the hotel. That was when I discovered that Joe's cousin, Anne, used to be Margaret's flat mate in their Edinburgh student days. Hillwalking life is full of such coincidences.

70 Meall Uaine, Spittal of Glenshee – ideal for a short February walk

FACTFILE

Map Ordnance Survey map 43, Braemar and Blair Atholl
Distance 5 miles
Height 500m
Terrain good path, then easy grassy slopes
Start point Spittal of Glenshee parking bay, map ref 109698
Time 2 to 3 hours
Nearest village Spittal of Glenshee
Recommended refreshment spot Spittal of Glenshee Hotel, or Dalmunzie House Hotel

In January 2005 I described a six-mile walk from Blairgowrie to Bridge of Cally: part of the Cateran Trail – a round walk of 64 miles that starts and finishes in Blairgowrie. Meall Uaine lies just south of Spittal of Glenshee on the A93 and the Trail traverses it to the west, following a right of way and old cattle drove road, from Spittal to Enochdhu on the A924. That gives easy access to An Lairig, the pass or bealach, from whose height at 648m it is an easy stroll to the 794m summit of Meall Uaine.

Meall Uaine means 'green hill' – an apt description of its gentle grassy slopes, and although a modest hill, its somewhat detached position means that the summit offers excellent views in all directions. Quite apart from those views, Meall Uaine is of interest to hillwalkers because of its former status and its unique connection with the Munro Glas Tulaichean, over ten miles distant to the northwest.

Corbetts – originally compiled by J. Rooke Corbett between the wars – are Scottish hills between 2500 and 2999ft high (762 to 914m) with a drop of at least 500 feet all round (152.4m) and no account being taken of distance or difficulty. Meall Uaine was a Corbett until its deletion some 25 years ago. The drop to An Lairig is only 146m, or just 21ft short. The hill's demotion of course makes no difference to the quality of the walk to the summit.

For those who love reading maps, there is still the matter of Glas Tulaichean that makes Meall Uaine unique. A ten-mile stretch of high ground – containing two other summits, Ben Earb and Meall a'Choire Bhuidhe, as well as Meall Uaine – goes all the way to Glas Tulaichean. All three have sufficient height to be Corbetts, but lack the 500ft all-round drop. There is nowhere else in the UK quite like this, as the drop along the long ridge is never deeper than 146m and the walker connecting Meall Uaine with Glas Tulaichean need never stray below 648m – the low point at An Lairig. If starting from Glas Tulaichean, the overall ascent to Meall Uaine is around 780m, but irrelevant as Corbett's list does not allow for 'cumulative drop'.

But back to the walk. The starting point, at a generous 350m, is opposite the Spittal of Glenshee Hotel (claimed to be the oldest operating inn site in Britain). To avoid

The old bridge, Spittal of Glenshee

taking spaces used by a shop, park at the left hand end of a bay. At the road bridge over the burn that flows from Coire Lairige, follow signs for the right of way to Enochdhu and the Cateran Trail.

The good path climbs alongside the pretty babbling brook and crosses it a few times. Suitable footwear is recommended. In approaching upper Coire Lairige, the pleasant grassy path goes through sheep grazing land, leaves the burn, and gently rises WSW then more steeply southwest to reach the narrow col of An Lairig. At this point you may well consider a short detour to Ben Earb.

Just before a gate leading to the Enochdhu Estate, turn southeast on the obvious path that leads to the broad western shoulder of the hill. Follow the boundary fence that curves to the east along the crest, crossing a gap in a drystane wall further on to reach a rounded lower top. A short way southeast is the summit, marked by a cairn.

If returning the same way, you may be amused at the sign at the Lairig that suggests an over-optimistic time of 20 minutes to return to Spittal – in clear view but well over a mile distant. Without running, time yourself.

A more direct return to give a circular route goes north from the summit on a grassy but narrower ridge. As it levels out to gentler slopes, head northwest to regain the path.

I first climbed Meall Uaine in January 1984 during a stormy, cold and very snowy weekend. Just driving to Spittal of Glenshee was a bit of an ordeal. We headed directly south from Spittal, trudging through soft snow often knee-high. We soon lost any views, then it was into very strong winds on top, but luckily we came across a double fence line going in the right direction. Visibility by now was down to 20ft or so. The fence went near the summit so we ventured forth and found the cairn. We returned as quickly as possible before the snow filled in our footsteps.

Meall Uaine may be a modest hill, but a February outing should not be underestimated – just in case.

71 Ben Vrackie and *Whisky Galore*

FACTFILE

Map Ordnance Survey maps 43, Braemar & Blair Atholl, and 52, Pitlochry & Crieff
Distance 5 miles
Height 640m
Terrain excellent path all the way to summit
Start point car park in lane behind Moulin Inn, map ref 944598
Time 3 to 5 hours
Nearest town Pitlochry
Recommended refreshment spot Moulin Inn, Moulin

I last climbed the very popular Ben Vrackie some ten years ago and earlier this month made a return visit. We were staying overnight in Pitlochry and as part of a birthday treat I was taking Margaret to the theatre to see a musical production of *Whisky Galore*. Never one to miss the chance of an interesting hill walk, the obvious attraction was the local hill. Although it lies behind Pitlochry, the profile of the hill is best appreciated when passing Blair Atholl driving south on the A9. From there it dominates the skyline.

Ben Vrackie is ideal at any time for a shorter walk and was just perfect for me in the afternoon prior to dinner and theatre. As with an earlier visit to the Borders, Margaret needed no persuasion to spend a few hours on the lower slopes – woodland and moorland – bird watching.

The starting point is a secluded though well-signposted car park (map ref 944598) in a small lane, behind the Moulin Inn. It should be noted that the car park is often full at weekends and during busy holiday times: yes, the hill is rightly that popular. This lies at 200m and the 640m climb is over a distance of two and a half miles, with only the steeper climb to the summit cone requiring some effort. With a well-made path throughout, the overall walk should last only some three hours, but on a grand day you will want to linger at the summit.

On such a good day there should be no problems as the path is very obvious all the way, nevertheless the prudent hillwalker will take Ordnance Survey map 43 (Braemar & Blair Atholl). Map 52 (Pitlochry & Crieff) is only required if you are not quite sure of the start point at Moulin and even then a road map will suffice. Moulin lies on the outskirts of Pitlochry on the A924.

It is an interesting and varied walk, firstly through mixed woodland by the Moulin Burn, and then at a height of 340m a gate gives access to the open heathery moorland of the lower slopes. Heading NNE, the path passes the junction of another path (Bealach Walk) then cuts through between Meall na h-Aodainn Moire and Creag Bhreac. The 557m Creag Bhreac means 'speckled crag'. Ben Vrackie itself is described as the speckled hill, referring to a time when white quartz rocks were scattered across its slopes. My understanding is that Vrackie could be but an anglicisation of *bhreac*. Creag Vrackie however, does not sound so imposing.

With a slight descent, the path swings north to the embankment of Loch a'Choire. The path now uses that embankment rather than the oft-boggy path of old lower down.

Ahead lies the final 1,000ft climb, however it is not too demanding and eased by a well-stepped path. Do not be put off by the craggy face straight ahead for the path keeps going northeast to the eastern shoulder before turning west for the summit.

There are 219 Corbetts (Scottish hills between 2500 and 2999ft and with a drop of at least 500ft all round). Standing at a height of 2757ft and with a drop of 1319ft, Ben Vrackie qualifies with consummate ease. In common with most Corbetts, the summit is an excellent viewpoint – indeed some would claim it to be one of the finest in the country. It follows that it would be a shame to go there on a poor day. With rain over a few days having washed away atmospheric dust, I had a day of crystal clarity.

The summit is graced with both viewfinder and trig point. Even for the knowledgeable hillwalker, the former is most useful and the latter, maintained by Perth & Kinross Council, lies just below the highest point. The narrow fertile Strath Tay lies to the south. The Beinn a'Ghlo range to the north forms a backdrop and to the west is the easily identified Schiehallion.

The summit is said to be often frequented by aggressive wild goats. I have never seen any there. Perhaps they are now less keen to frequent the high slopes, dissuaded by the thousands of the human goat variety.

Later however, I did hear from one reader, Alistair MacLeod, who had met some aggressive sheep a few summers ago at the summit: 'One slinked up behind us and started rummaging through a rucksack for food! Don't know whether there were also aggressive goats at one time. If so, maybe they taught the sheep a few bad habits!'

And what about *Whisky Galore*? It was marvellous – a joyous and hilarious musical romp, with many of the cast doubling as skilled musicians, and a superb way to conclude a grand day. Do go and see it, but climb the hill first.

72 The Falls of Bruar

FACTFILE

Map Ordnance survey map 43, Braemar and Blair Atholl
Distance 1 mile
Height 100m
Terrain woodland path
Start point junction of B8079 (the old A9) and the new A9 by the House of Bruar
Time 1 to 2 hours
Nearest village Blair Atholl
Recommended refreshment spot House of Bruar, north of Blair Atholl

A circuit round the Falls of Bruar is a very short walk – little more than a mile – albeit with a climb of 100m. Even at a leisurely stroll and having a good look around, it will take not much more than an hour. It is a sheltered walk, ideal possibly for a not-so-good day, but even on a good day a little leg stretch would be beneficial, if by chance you are en-route on the A9.

The Falls of Bruar are situated where the B8079 (the old A9) running northwest from Blair Atholl joins the new A9 at a busy junction – a junction that reminds one how lucky Blair Atholl and Bruar are to be by-passed.

The walk starts at the grandly styled House of Bruar, a relatively-new quality shopping complex with a good restaurant. On no account let ladies in the party decline the walk with the excuse of bad weather, so that they can just 'have a look around' or go for a coffee – unless that is the men are given the task of caring for their younger children for a short while. Most men will gladly trade their exclusion from shopping for such a walk and the children will enjoy their outing to the Falls.

Ordnance Survey map 43 (Braemar and Blair Atholl) is not needed; just perhaps a glance at a road map to get you there. Alternatively with green credentials, arrive by train at Blair Atholl and walk west on the B8079 for three miles. Once on the walk it would be impossible to get lost.

Park in the massive complex car park (forever seemingly busy) and the route up one side of the Bruar Water, and down the other side, is well signposted and marked by a fine path through a wooded area.

A short tunnel takes one under the Inverness railway line and up to the lower bridge (and the lower falls) where the circuit begins. The upper bridge and falls mark the turning point. Because of the afforestation there are really no distant views but one is here to admire the waterfalls – the upper ones being the most impressive – and to remark on the impact that water has had over the years on the rocky ravine.

At the end of the short walk you may have done enough to salve your conscience and justify stopping at the House of Bruar for refreshments or indeed shopping. If however, you are still in need of exercise then the walk can be extended by exploring the tracks in the Baluain and Glen Banvie Woods which lie to the east of the Bruar Water, but this time do take with you map 43.

73 The Sow of Atholl

FACT FILE

Map Ordnance Survey map 42, Glen Garry
Distance 3½ miles
Height climbed 400m
Terrain track, then easy hillside
Start point near Dalnaspidal Lodge at map ref 645733
Time 2 to 3 hours
Nearest villages Blair Atholl and Dalwhinnie
Recommended refreshment spot House of Bruar, north of Blair Atholl

Twenty-three years ago less one day, we were returning to Inverness after a company dance the night before in Arbroath. It was already past lunchtime as we drove up the A9 and whilst a gentle interlude seemed like a good idea, we had little time to play with. Not only were there just a few hours of daylight left, but that evening we were going to a Highland Hillwalking Club party. The obvious answer to our search for exercise lay in the shape of the Sow of Atholl. My terse diary notes of the climb were: 'quite icy near the top; very good glissades on descent though really too hard; bruised hip next day; remember to take crampons next time ... enjoyed the party.'

Yes, the Sow of Atholl is that sort of bump – convenient for a short outing, but still to be treated with care as a winter hill. So if you are passing by and want a short break, why not give it a try?

But what about the panic over the late Christmas shopping? It came as a big surprise to me years ago when I realised that some people went shopping at weekends, rather than hillwalking, and worse than that, some of them appeared to enjoy it. However, the last week before Christmas is a desperate time for shopping and even hillwalkers have to make sacrifices. I have a good idea, but it will cost you.

South of the Sow of Atholl on the A9 is the House of Bruar, just north of Blair Atholl. Why not drive there, leave your partner to browse about, climb the Sow and return a few hours later in the certain knowledge that you will be poorer in terms of money and brownie points, yet richer in terms of a productive day of compromise? Or will you? It has been pointed out to me (somewhat forcefully) by two female acquaintances that this 'shopping strategy' makes two rather dodgy assumptions: that the person doing the walk is the male and that the person doing the shopping is the female. Nowadays such assumptions are politically incorrect and indeed inaccurate in that the male/female hillwalking split is roughly 50/50. Unless the weather is so foul that both individuals opt for shopping, assuming that both persons wish to climb, tossing a coin may lead to some bad feeling on the point of the loser who is given the shopping task. The prudent option may be for both individuals to climb, return for refreshment and then get on with the shopping. Compromise is often the best action.

At the Pass of Drumochter, the two obvious features on the west side are the Boar of Badenoch (An Torc) and the Sow of Atholl – both showing a steep, conical shape from the high point of the road. Both hills do have gentler slopes to the west, but these are to some extent hidden from the road. The hills are separated by Coire Dhomhain and the stream of that name flows east towards the railway line and road, just to the south of the watershed, and turns sharply south to join (via the Allt Dubhaig) the River Garry. On the west side of the Boar, the Allt an Tuirc flows north towards Dalwhinnie.

Whilst very impressive from the road, the Sow has a mile-long southeast ridge that gives a more gentle approach to the summit at 803m. Sounds high? Maybe, but remember that the starting height of Drumochter is at 420m. The small flat area between the steep eastern slopes and the railway line – through which meanders the Alt Dubhaig – is marshy, especially at the southern end where the stream flows into a small loch. However, a track from the A9 at the north end of the dual carriageway goes southwest to Dalnaspidal Lodge and on to Loch Garry, and gives an easy and dry approach to the base of the southeast ridge.

The Sow marked the northern limit of the lands of Atholl. It was originally called Meall an Dobhrachan – 'watercress hill' – perhaps referring to the marshy area by the new railway line, and it is likely that its current and meaningless name was given as a counter to the Boar. The sharp north ridge of An Torc has the shape of the back of a hog or boar, an animal hunted to extinction many centuries ago.

The walk starts at Dalnaspidal – once the highest railway station in Britain, and as the name indicates, a one-time hospice or inn. Park considerately by the start of the track (between the railway and the road) at map ref 645733 and walk SSW past the lodge to the bridge over the Allt Dubhaig at map ref 643728. The track follows the line of an old through-route to Loch Rannoch and featured in Roy's map of 1755.

The southeast ridge starts gently with the heather giving way to shorter grass as the slope steepens in approaching the summit. A slight detour to the west by the Allt Coire Luidhearnaidh may minimise the sound of the traffic on the busy A9 (though oddly I do not find the noise of the trains to be intrusive) and temporarily hides from view the line of electricity pylons. Despite those drawbacks, the view from the summit is impressive.

The descent is quick and easy, as is the drive back to find out the cost of the Christmas spend.

74 Sgairneach Mhor

FACTFILE

Map Ordnance Survey map 42, Glen Garry & Loch Rannoch
Distance 6 miles
Height 550m
Terrain gravel track, then heathery slopes leading to stony summit
Start point Pass of Drumochter, at highest point on the A9
Time 4 to 5 hours
Nearest villages Dalwhinnie and Blair Atholl
Recommended refreshment spot House of Bruar, by Blair Atholl

The most prominent hills on the west side of the A9 at Drumochter are not the four Munros, but the smaller conical duo, the Boar of Badenoch and the Sow of Atholl (the latter blocking the direct view of Sgairneach Mhor). However, from Dalnaspidal – a one-time hospice or inn and once the highest railway station in Britain (excluding the likes of Snowdon) – the higher slopes of Sgairneach Mhor can just be seen. These slopes might look uninspiring, but are redeemed by the crags of the north-facing Coire Creagach – momentarily glimpsed when travelling south and giving an

The trig point on Sgairneach Mhor

altogether more dramatic picture, especially as the corrie holds snow well into early summer.

Sgairneach Mhor means 'big stony hillside', referring to Coire Creagach – the rough slopes of which contrast with the surrounding mossy hillside. Below Coire Creagach, the Allt Coire Dhomhain flows east towards railway and road, then south (via the meandering Allt Dubhaig) to join the River Garry. Although I do not find the noise of trains to be intrusive, there is no escaping the sight of the railway and a line of electricity pylons, and the sound of traffic on the busy A9 – albeit modern day life left behind on ascent.

Given the close-by popular starting point at the Pass of Drumochter, climbing Sgairneach Mhor does not demand a full day – ideal for late December. Jimbo and I were there some weeks ago on a good day of little snow and memorable in that it was Jimbo's birthday. Still younger than me, what a way for a hillwalker to celebrate another year.

From the highest part of Drumochter, descend to the old A9 and head south for 250 yards to a tunnel under the railway line to join a track. The track curves north then west, to enter Coire Dhomhain on the north side of the Allt Coire Dhomhain.

Continue on the undulating but much improved track to around map ref 615750. Cross the river and head for the northeast arm of Coire Creagach, at first following a worn path over rough heathery ground on the west bank of the stream whose source is west of a 758m spot-height. The going improves on ascent to stony terrain, where traces of a track lead round the edge of the corrie. The river – often in spate – may be difficult or even impossible to cross. Higher upstream, one crossing point is easy to spot because an ATV track leads down to it. Another is 50 yards or so to the east where the river partially splits. However if needs be, continue on the track, crossing later opposite the base of the NNW arm of Coire Creagach, or even the grassy slopes west of that, or by continuing to the head of Coire Dhomhain.

The surprisingly small summit plateau – the highest point at 991m/3251ft being marked by a trig point surrounded by a broken circle of stones – lies quite close to the rim of Coire Creagach and should be treated with respect on a poor day. In addition, deceptively easy slopes fall westwards to the head of Coire Dhomhain – slopes that can be remarkably confusing in mist, for the lie of the land can draw the unwary too far southwards. Then there are the crags of Coire Creagach… Carefully descending one misty winter afternoon some 20 years ago, it was hard to pick out much detail ahead apart from a few rocks sticking above the snow. Suddenly, two cross-country skiers glided past, much to our envy at their seemingly effortless descent. With a quick wave they were gone, disappearing again into the mist. Later, we were surprised to see one skier standing close to the lip of the corrie. The telltale tramlines going straight to the lip were all too obvious. His companion had gone over the edge. Thankfully, the unseen skier shouted from below that he was unharmed and could climb back up. Reassured, we continued our descent in the mist. Sometime later the two skiers overtook us, this time more circumspectly and some distance to the east. By the time we got back to the old A9 and the ruins of a house, the skiers were gone. That derelict house (occupied in my early hillwalking days) is also gone; the site cleared as if it had never existed.

Gone too is Jimbo's birthday, celebrated afterwards with a cup of coffee and a sticky bun. The best things in life seldom cost a lot of money.

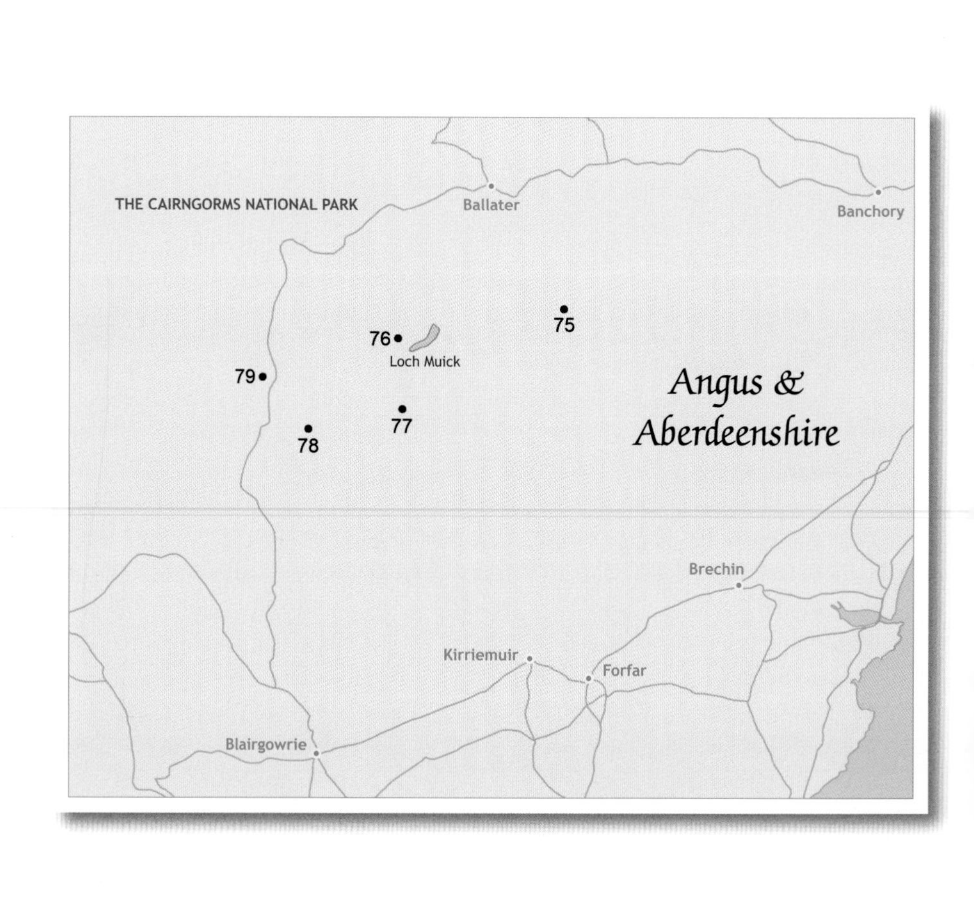
THE CAIRNGORMS NATIONAL PARK
Ballater
Banchory
75
76
Loch Muick
79
77
78
Angus &
Aberdeenshire
Brechin
Kirriemuir
Forfar
Blairgowrie

Angus & Aberdeenshire

75 Mount Keen

FACTFILE

Map Ordnance Survey map 44, Ballater & Glen Clova
Distance 10 miles
Height 700m
Terrain track, then Munro path
Start point parking place, map ref 447804, by end of Glen Esk road
Time 5 to 6 hours
Nearest village Edzell
Recommended refreshment spot a good choice in Edzell

I can still quote the first two lines of the Prologue to Chaucer's *Canterbury Tales*. Some of the magic is lost in a modern English translation but it is easier to understand than Middle English: 'When April with his showers sweet with fruit / The drought of March has pierced unto the root', and a few lines later: 'Then do folks long to go on pilgrimage'; or in the case of hill-walkers, long to go to the high tops with better weather. The 'drought' of March 2008 was the wettest for over a decade. As for April showers – with continuing wet weather and cold north winds April saw a lot of fresh soft snow on those high tops.

East of a line drawn between Glen Muick and Glen Clova is a vast area of rolling hills that occupies most of map 44. Only the highest hill – the isolated Mount Keen at 939m/3081ft – makes it to Munro status. Its position as the most easterly of all Munros makes it an obvious target. The next two highest main summits – the Corbetts of Mount Battock and Ben Tirran – each lie some nine miles distant. Mount Keen's conical peak and isolation make it a Corbett-like viewpoint, readily identifiable from afar. The name is a corruption of *Monadh Caoin*, meaning the pleasant, gentle or even smooth hill – perhaps referring to the lack of crags. This seems odd since there are crags on the Corrach to the north, and the summit area is of typical Cairngorms grit topped by a stack of granite boulders. Mount Keen can be approached from the north via Glen Tanar. Drive from Aboyne to Bridge o'Ess, or catch the main Deeside bus to Dinnet and walk the extra couple of miles, then to the car park before Glen Tanar House. It is six miles up this attractive glen and the track is of cycling quality. A more complex route (challenging navigational skills) is from Glen Muick to the west, yet it gives full flavour of this rolling, isolated countryside.

A few weeks ago Jimbo, Lindsay and I went to Mount Keen, anticipating a less than challenging outing by the popular Glen Mark route from the south. With a track climbing to a height of 670m, then a Munro path going north to the summit, this is a good approach for a relative newcomer. In 1861 Queen Victoria had it even easier: she cadged a lift on a horse for much of the way on a north/south traverse from Glen Tanar to Glen Mark. The assembled party used the drove road and ancient right of way – the Mounth Road – which crosses the west shoulder of Mount Keen, but there is no record that she actually made the detour to the top. At White Well (map ref 420829) she rated the water as being very pure, as indeed it is. Cue for a name-change to Queen's Well.

From Edzell follow the Glen Esk road to a parking place at map ref 447804, before crossing the Water of Mark. Walk west a short distance to the start of the signposted track on the east bank of the Water of Mark to enter Glen Mark – too open to be pretty but there are crags on the south-west side. It is a two and a quarter mile walk past the Queen's Well to reach Glenmark. The track is rough at first but improves to cycling quality once the track from Invermark Lodge comes in. The track then heads NNW, crossing the Easter Burn and the Ladder Burn. The climb now commences. The track continues by the side of the Ladder Burn and then zigzags steeply for a mile before easing off to a cairn at map ref 405853. From there a broad granite path strikes north giving a gentle ascent to the summit trig point. On a clear day it would be almost impossible to get lost.

We certainly had a clear day, but also lots of that fresh soft snow. As we went uphill the track disappeared altogether, leaving us to plowter through foot deep glistening white and unbroken snowfields. Luckily it was a grand day but arduous and so we took over three hours to reach the top. Between the three of us Mount Keen had been climbed some 30 times, but this ascent was the toughest. Once on top though, we did appreciate the attractions of Mount Keen – its solitary nature, remoteness and panoramic views.

Mount Keen from the west

76 Carn a'Choire Bhoidheach and a ninth round Munro Party

FACTFILE

Map Ordnance Survey map 44, Ballater & Glen Clova
Distance 17 miles, of which seven can be cycled
Height 700m
Terrain good track and path; then grassy terrain to summit
Start point Loch Muick car park, map ref 310851
Time 6 to 7 hours
Nearest town Ballater
Recommended refreshment spot Station Restaurant, Station Square, Ballater

East of the A93 (the road that cuts through the Glen Shee ski area) lies the Mounth: the name given to the high level plateau that extends as far as Lochnagar. More specifically, the area south of Lochnagar is known as White Mounth – a name also used for the second highest hill at 1110m. However, in the 1997 Munro Tables all reference to White Mounth was dropped and the hill is now identified solely as Carn a'Choire Bhoidheach. Choire Boidheach – to the east of the summit – is unremarkable and its out-flowing stream only becomes spectacular when viewed as a waterfall over the granite slabs of Eagles Rock. It should be noted that the name White Mounth appears on the map above the Dubh Loch, but that is not the summit. I still refer to this hill as White Mounth – in my opinion a preferable name to the dubious Carn a'Choire Bhoidheach. The name is supposed to mean 'the cairn of the pretty or beautiful corrie' – I think not. Still, a rose by any other name…

Queen Victoria passed close to the top of White Mounth on a Lochnagar traverse over a century ago, but there is no record of her having made the slight detour (a few hundred metres distance and 20 metres of ascent) to reach the summit cairn. There is no particular reason why she should have done this and, but for the hill's Munro status, I doubt whether so many hill-walkers would do this either.

It is a gently rounded hill and although located between the impressive crags of Eagles Rock and the Stuic, the actual summit area has no particular merit in itself, other than be-

Carn a 'Chore Bhoidheach

White Mounth and Eagles Rock

ing a good place for ptarmigan. Not surprisingly, until this year there was no record of any hill-walker having held a party on top to celebrate the completion of a Munro round. If anyone has, please let me know. That is a pity in a way but it did provide me with an idea for another round completion. That is why to finish my ninth round on 4 May 2007 a group of friends came with me to celebrate on top of White Mounth. Those friends could muster between them an impressive number of Munro rounds, but perhaps more remarkably one of them (George) has climbed all the Corbetts but not the Munros. With but a handful of Munros to go, perhaps he might have a party soon. [Then in 2008 I discovered that I had in fact been beaten to it, for Ian Macnab, Glasgow Glenmore Club, had finished his round on White Mounth back in June 2001! Well done, Ian!]

The most impressive way to White Mounth is from the Glen Muick car park. As mentioned, White Mounth – or at least its lower slopes – is only spectacular when viewed from the Dubh Loch and the walk (never mind getting to the top) is a joy in itself. In addition, the car park is at a height of 400m, leaving a climb of only 700m to the summit. Another bonus is the excellent track on the north side of Loch Muick, such that the three and a half miles via Allt-na-giubhsaich to Glas-allt-Shiel can be cycled in less than half an hour, and that has been assumed in the time quoted of six to seven hours. The only warning about the track is that loose gravel on bends may cause a skid. Glas-allt-Shiel was a favourite spot of Queen Victoria, the dwelling having been built for her after the death of Prince Albert.

The climb up the fine path on the north side of the Allt an Dubh-loch is delightful. Granite slabs abound with water flowing over them, either as part of the stream, or more impressively, tumbling down from Eagles Rock and Creag an Dubh-loch. The top end of the Dubh Loch has a real sense of rugged remoteness. Queen Victoria's words: 'The loch is only a mile in length and very wild. The hills which are rocky and precipitous rise perpendicularly from it' are still true today, for the scenery around the Dubh Loch is magnificent and it contains some of the finest cliffs on the mainland. It was a pity that when we were there the crags were mist-covered, as was the summit, and without complaining about the dry underfoot conditions on our walk, the waterslides were less impressive. The path almost fades away, continuing beside the stream for another mile. Thereafter curve round to the north, and then head in a more easterly direction for the easy climb to the top. This is a safe approach on a bad day – likewise for the return home.

77 Glen Clova

FACTFILE

Map Ordnance Survey map 44, Ballater & Glen Clova
Distance 7 miles
Height 500m
Terrain track and path
Start point Glen Doll car park at end of tarmac road, over a bridge at map ref 284762
Time 4 to 5 hours
Nearest town Kirriemuir
Recommended refreshment spot Glen Clova Hotel

Glen Clova is the most dramatic of the many Angus glens, especially the last three miles with the steep slopes on either side contrasting with the flat and narrow floor of the glen and the meandering River South Esk. However, when walkers mention Glen Clova more often than not they are actually referring to Glen Doll – the higher extension of Glen Clova.

There is a variety of walks starting from Acharn at the end of Glen Doll and going westwards into Glendoll Forest. There is an official parking area just after the end of the tarmac road and over a bridge at map ref 284762. You will require Ordnance Survey map 44 (Ballater & Glen Clova) for an easy two mile walk through the forest on the north side of the White Water as far as the edge of the forest. By now at 420m, you get the first glimpse of the high upper glen with a path over the next one and a half miles leading through rough terrain to a shelter as the turning point.

The way westwards is on a broad track, past Acharn Farm and Glendoll Lodge, for the first mile. Then there is a good path, easily recognisable, going off on the right. You will soon know if for some reason you have gone past it, for the track carries on to a bridge over the White Water and you have gone too far.

The second mile is a delight, albeit rising slightly along a pine-needle-strewn path, shady at times and sheltered on a poor day. The path is the start of what is known as Jock's Road that climbs high over the Mounth before dropping down to the A93, south of Braemar. Part of the fascination of this throughway is that no one can say with certainty who Jock was.

The edge of the forest is a good turning point in adverse weather, for although there is a good path ahead, it does lead through rough terrain. The path climbs steadily, gets rougher and skirts by crags at the top of the glen. Not the place to be on a dreadful day. The shelter at map ref 232778 lies beyond those crags, on the west side of the path and at a height of 750m. The current shelter – known as Davy's Bourach – was built by Davy Glen in 1966. *Burach* is the Gaelic word for a guddle, mess or shambles. With a turf roof atop corrugated iron, the surprisingly capacious shelter may not be the

The pine-needle-strewn path, the start of Jock's Road

prettiest but undoubtedly could be a life-saver. The Forfar & District Hillwalking Club is responsible for its upkeep. There were major repairs in the 1980s and again in 2001 when it was totally reroofed using materials transported by helicopter. If walking from the Clova side, the repainted red metal door means that the refuge is now less likely to be missed in bad weather.

A small plaque on the other side of the path marks the site of the demolished old shelter. I do not normally approve of such plaques, but this is the exception and should be mandatory reading: 'Universal Hiking Club Glasgow. Erected to the memory of five members who died New Year 1959. RIP.' They lost their lives in atrocious weather conditions on a traverse of the Mounth, heading for Glen Doll. Experienced but perhaps less than well-equipped, it is likely that they set out too late for that time of year and never made the descent to safety into Glen Doll. It took some weeks for all the bodies to be found, partially or completely buried in the snow. One body was found just a few hundred yards from the shelter. This tragic story appears in the highly recommended book *The Black Cloud* by I.D.S. Thomson.

On 30 October 2002 – a day of fresh, deep snow – I was sitting near this plaque when a cyclist appeared carrying his bike. An enterprising foreigner, he had read about Jock's Road and assumed that it would give an easy cycle to Braemar. Pointing out the terrain still to be traversed and reminding him of what he had already experienced, it was not difficult to persuade him to abort his journey and shoulder his bike back downhill.

What happened to Jock's Road?

78 On the Monega Road

FACTFILE

Map Ordnance Survey map 43, Braemar & Blair Atholl
Distance 10 miles
Height 900m
Terrain the Monega Road of track and path
Start point Auchavan, Glen Isla, map ref 191696
Time 6 to 7 hours
Nearest hamlet Spittal of Glenshee
Recommended refreshment spot Spittal of Glenshee Hotel

Situated too close to the A93 and the Glen Shee ski area, it may be difficult to work up much enthusiasm for the closely-linked Glas Maol and Cairn of Claise. Yet many hill-walkers are unaware of the contrast offered by the wild and beautiful Caenlochan Glen to the southeast. This week's walk follows the southwest rim of Caenlochan Glen and crosses the high ground between Cairn of Claise and Glas Maol, from where both summits are easily attained. It is a traverse from Glen Isla to Glen Clunie (north of the ski area) by way of the Monega Road and skirting the flanks of Monega Hill – a wonderful viewpoint overlooking Caenlochan Glen. A shorter day is of course possible – perhaps in poor weather – just staying with the Monega Road all the way.

Starting from Glen Isla, a south/north traverse offers a quieter and more spectacular approach than from the much busier and less attractive A93. Unless two parties agree to meet on the plateau – a risky ploy on a misty day – it follows that pre-placed transport is required. After parking with consideration at the Glen Isla road-end at Auchavan at map ref 191696, walk north on the broad gravel track by the west bank of the River Isla to the entrance to Tulchan Lodge. There is a notice at this point erected by the East Grampian Deer Management Group (it is a pity that this area does not feature in the Hillphones Service booklet). It says: 'The stalking season takes place between 1st July and 16th February, but the most important period is from 12th August to 20th October. During this shorter period please remain on the hill tracks indicated by the red line.' This need not concern you in autumn, for the Monega Road is indicated by such a red line – as well it should be as an old Right of Way. Continue on the track to the edge of the trees north of the lodge and the Monega Road signpost. This distance from Auchavan is easily cycled, but only of use if a cross party is to collect the bike.

Head NNW on grassy slopes, cross the Glas Burn and climb the ridge on the east side of the burn. The good track and path of gentle gradient eases the climb of some 500m to Monega Hill's small plateau. The right of way skirts west of the summit, but the short detour to this commanding viewpoint should be made. There are two cairns, the northerly one being more spectacularly placed. Then head northwest, well clear of the crags above Caenlochan Glen, until just north of Little Glas Maol at map ref

Looking down on Glen Coe

175762. A shed (still mapped) succumbed to the elements in the mid 1990s. Just a large pile of stones now marks the spot. Continue to a neck of land beside a large gully at map ref 173762, from where the right of way angles NNW on the eastern flanks of Glas Maol, but the hill is temptingly close at hand. Leave the road and climb northwest to the rounded dome of Glas Maol – at 1068m/3504ft the highest peak in Angus. Before descending by the Monega Road to the A93, Queen Victoria 'climbed' Glas Maol in 1861, making it the last of a probable eight royal Munros. Even leaving aside Charles Edward Stuart's west-highland antics, there are probably other 'royal' Munros as it is likely that the current heir to the throne has climbed some Braemar Munros that Victoria never visited.

From Glas Maol, descend north to almost 950m to reach a rusty gate on the ground at map ref 168776. This is the Monega descent point to Glen Clunie – however the 1064m/3491ft Cairn of Claise beckons. Now on an ugly vehicle track, walk east then northeast for just over a mile, then leave the track, crossing stonier terrain to the summit.

Returning to the descent point, it is an easy stroll northwest by path on a broadening ridge towards the east side of Sron na Gaoithe. The path fades away over a rocky area, but it is then a short descent, crossing the Allt a' Gharbh-choire, to reach the old military bridge over the Cairnwell Burn. The parking space on the A93 is at map ref 147800.

79 Carn Aosda – the easiest Munro and a Christmas cracker

FACTFILE

Map Ordnance Survey map 43, Braemar and Blair Atholl
Distance 2 miles
Height 400m
Terrain heathery slopes then easy walking on quartzite terrain
Start point parking area at map ref 145807 on the A93
Time 2 to 2½ hours
Nearest village Braemar
Recommended refreshment spot The Glenshee ski centre cafeteria

Although mainly associated with the Glen Shee ski-centre, Carn Aosda lies to the south of a narrow triangular wedge of land, bounded to the northeast by the A93 and to the northwest by the Baddoch Burn. On the south side is Loch Vrotachan, west of the col that separates Carn Aosda from the Cairnwell, its neighbouring Munro to the south.

Is Carn Aosda the easiest of all Munros? The standard wisdom is that the Cairnwell holds the title, but I have always thought Carn Aosda is even easier. I suspect that

Carn Aosda

the presence of the chairlift on the Cairnwell tends to skew perceptions. At 917m/3008ft, Carn Aosda just qualifies above the required 3000ft and it is an ascent of only 275m from the ski centre at the point where the track leaves the A93 just north of the café. In comparison, the ascent of the Cairnwell from the highpoint of the road is 278m. Although the distance to walk to the summit of Carn Aosda is a little bit longer, the terrain is easier. Many hill-walkers are happy to claim an embarrassingly easy 'tick' – for up and down will take less than an hour – yet with the proximity of the Cairnwell (and Carn a'Gheoidh), Carn Aosda is seldom climbed on its own. Only if climbing from the north is it likely to be treated as a solo Munro.

Yet ease of ascent does not, in this case, coincide with attractiveness and although its southeast slopes are marred by the skiing development, in truth even without those man-made changes Carn Aosda would still be one of the more unattractive and insignificant Munros. It is also the nearest any Munro is likely to come to being mistaken for a supermarket chain.The small summit area, comprising two minor bumps on a quartzite-covered vegetation-free top, has at least been spared the masts on the Cairnwell, yet the ski grounds lie just yards away. The east bump is the Munro, with a pile of quartzite stones as the cairn. *Aosda* is the Gaelic for ancient or old, and is pronounced 'oosh'.

Obviously the shortest approach is from the ski area. Climb northwest from the car park for a direct route, following the ski tracks. Alternatively, go WNW to the col above Loch Vrotachan, from where it is a short distance northeast then east, to the top. The only snag is in having to traverse the ski area.

One redeeming feature of Carn Aosda is the long north ridge sloping down to Baddoch, with the prominent and attractively sculptured Dubh-choire to the east – best seen from the road when driving south. A traverse of the ridge starts from the A93. Cross the Clunie Water at map ref 137832, leave the track and climb south on the easy slopes over Strone Baddoch and Carn Chrionaidh.

But what if time dictates a shorter route, but not so short that the direct route is the only option? Well, for Peter and I time did dictate a shorter route, one that could be fitted into the morning of Christmas Day. Our very good compromise was to start further north of the ski area, at a parking area at map ref 145807. With only one mile and just over 400m to climb, it is still a very short day and the way up is more interesting than the popular route, with the ski machinery and slopes only coming into view at the very last moment. You will need Ordnance Survey map 43 (Braemar and Blair Atholl), with the hill on an awkward mid-section fold of the map. Climb west to the narrow east rim of Dubh-choire, picking out traces of animal tracks through the thick heather. Once on to the rim, the terrain quickly changes to a covering of small quartzite stones and gives a gently rising southwest ascent. (From map ref 145807 a more direct but less attractive southwest approach can also be made.)

Climbing Carn Aosda on Christmas Day was my penultimate calendar step towards the ambition of having been on top of a Munro on every day of the year. Only one to go! It was a Christmas cracker of a day, with crisp weather, blue skies and little breeze and no one else on the hill. With only a few patches of snow, there were no skiers. We had special dispensation to leave home at 8am, albeit that meant conceding to Margaret a lot of hard-earned brownie points. The drive was almost traffic free, though with a temperature of -4°c I had to be careful. We used the above approach via the rim of the Dubh-choire, and once past the heather it was a magical stroll to the top. Sitting by the cairn at 11am, we could briefly sunbathe and meditate before having to make tracks for home, as the brownie points were only valid until 2pm. On the return to the car I saw a large herd of deer just round the corner from the ski slopes, but no Santa. Deer on the slopes of Carn Aosda – whatever next? Perhaps the deer have realised (rather like urban foxes) that proximity to people may protect them from shooters and stalkers. And yes, we got home with five minutes to spare.

Merry Christmas on Carn Aosda

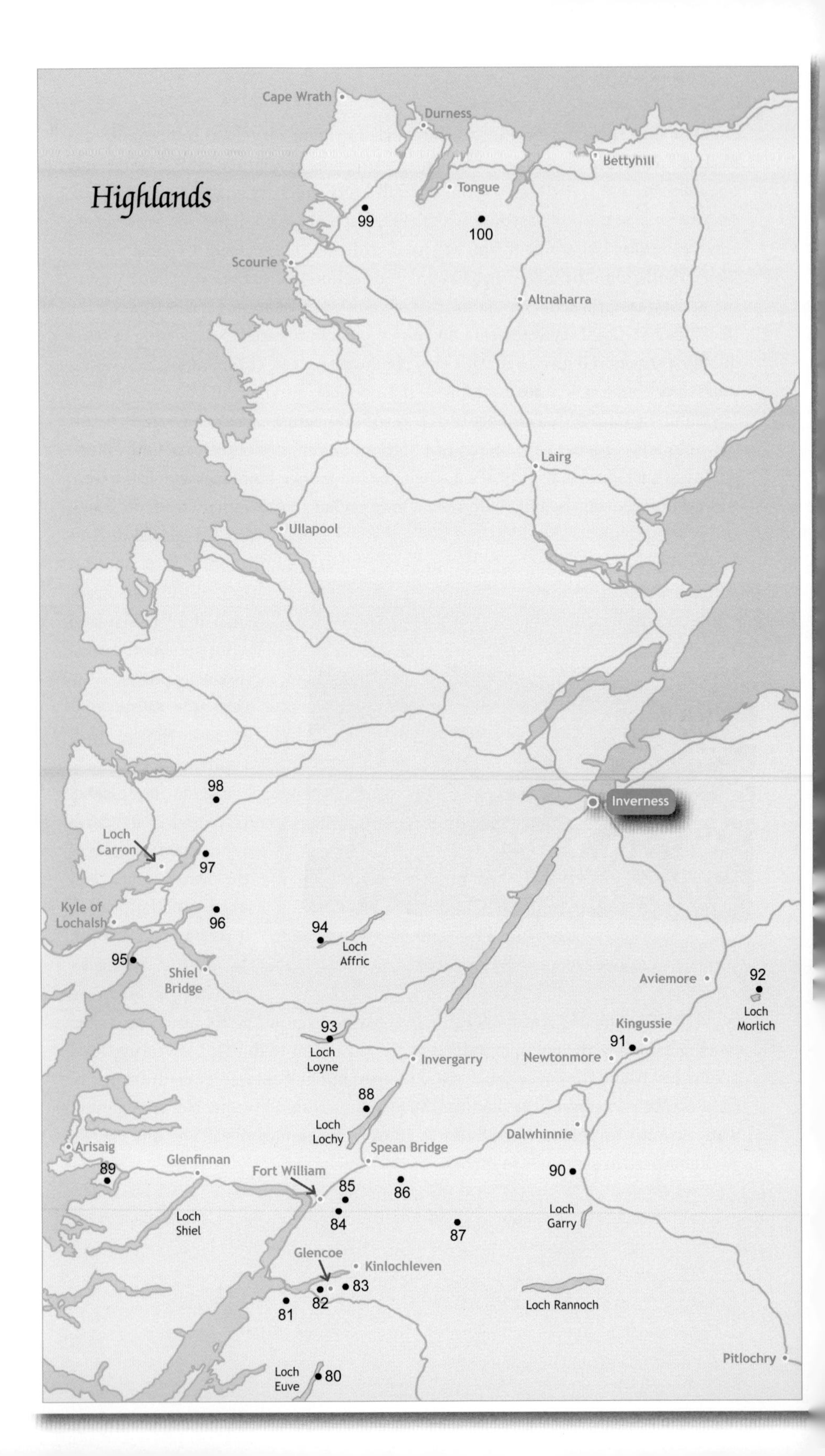
Highlands
Cape Wrath
Durness
Bettyhill
Tongue
99
100
Scourie
Altnaharra
Lairg
Ullapool
Inverness
98
Loch
Carron
97
Kyle of
Lochalsh
96
94
Loch
Affric
95
Shiel
Bridge
Aviemore
92
Loch
Morlich
93
Loch
Loyne
Kingussie
91
Invergarry
Newtonmore
88
Loch
Lochy
Dalwhinnie
Spean Bridge
Arisaig
89
Glenfinnan
Fort William
85
86
90
84
87
Loch
Shiel
Loch
Garry
Glencoe
Kinlochleven
82
83
81
Loch Rannoch
Loch
Euve
80
Pitlochry

Highland

80 Loch Etive

FACTFILE

Map Ordnance Survey map 50, Glen Orchy & Loch Etive
Distance 9 miles
Height negligible
Terrain track and path, the latter often wet in places
Start point near Glen Etive road end, map ref 137468
Time 4 hours
Nearest village Glencoe or Bridge of Orchy
Recommended refreshment spot Kings House Hotel, Rannoch Moor

Some three years ago I described a climb to Ben Starav. At 1078m/3537ft it is the highest of the five Munros to the east of lower Glen Etive and, with a sea-level start, reaching its summit requires a brutal ascent. Of the many ridges radiating from the summit, the long easy-angled north ridge is by far the best known and is the popular way up. However, there is more to this granite mountain than just the summit and ridges.

A few weeks ago Rhona and I undertook a new route over Glas Bheinn Mhor, followed by a careful contouring traverse of the rock-spattered and craggy upper Coire Hallater to reach the southern subsidiary Tops of Starav. We then descended to Loch

Etive. It occurred to me on the delightful stroll back to the Glen Etive road that this loch-side walk could be just the job for one of those days when the high tops – because of weather or indolence – might not be quite so appealing. In fact the walk could be just the job almost regardless of the weather, albeit better done if the ground has not seen rain for some time. The path is varied; very good in places, at times quite wet, but always fascinating as it follows the meandering River Etive, with the waters of the tidal Loch Etive close by at times.

The target for this week's walk is to the base of the southwest ridge of Starav, where the Allt Coire na Larach joins Loch Etive, just south of the headland Rubha Doire Larach. It is not necessary to cross the easily recognised bouldery delta, but there is plenty of evidence that the other streams to be crossed en route are in spate at times. Going during a dry spell is advised.

Park two miles before the bottom end of the single-track Glen Etive road at map ref 137468, opposite the track to Coileitir. The start of the track is not immediately obvious. There are a few small parking spots to choose from on the west side of the road. The track drops east and crosses the River Etive above some very deep, dark pools to reach Coileitir. Unoccupied for a while, the cottage is now being renovated.

Use the sign-posted short detour to avoid the immediate environs.

Follow the path by the edge of the river then cross the Allt Mheuran at the bridge (map ref 135460). A short-cut SSW from Coileitir is only recommended in a very dry spell. The path curves northwards back to the Etive and follows the meandering river for a while, before heading southwest. To save time, it is possible to take a straight line from the bridge, but the ground is usually boggy and in any case the delights of the riverside stroll will be missed.

The 'path' to Kinlochetive bothy (and its continuation to the north end of Loch Etive) is doubtful in places. Sensible footwear is recommended. Kinlochetive bothy – by the flood plain of the Etive – is no longer maintained on an open-door basis. The property of Blackmount Estate, it is leased to Venture Scotland to provide a base for personal and social development programmes for young adults.

There is much to look at along the way. To the west across the loch are the Trilleachan Slabs – of great interest to rock climbers – and to the east are three steep rough corries: Coire da Choimhid; Coire Sgriodain and Coire Lotha; of which Coire da Choimhid is the most slabby and impressive. The term *sgriodain* (meaning 'ravine') could apply to many a feature on this western face of Starav.

The walk eventually curves round a bay, Bagh Clach nan Ron, then the headland Rubha Doire Larach, and finally reaches the bouldery delta of the Allt Coire na Larach. *Larach* means 'the site of a building or habitation', but there is no evidence of anything there nowadays. *Doire* means 'a thicket', but neither are there any trees ... just an isolated spot with visitors few and far between.

Remembering that it is a long way back, the delta may be as far as you want to go. However if you have enjoyed the walk perhaps another time you might be tempted by the traverse from Glen Etive all the way to the A85 at Bridge of Awe. Now that would be a long walk!

81 The Back of Beinn a'Bheithir

FACTFILE

Map Ordnance Survey map 41, Ben Nevis, Fort William & Glen Coe
Distance 7 miles
Height 300m
Terrain tracks and path
Start point off the A828 at Achadh nan Darach, map ref 004552, at the entrance to Glen Duror
Time 4 to 5 hours
Nearest villages Ballachulish and Glencoe
Recommended refreshment spot a good choice in Glencoe

Beinn a'Bheithir – well seen from Onich and North Ballachulish – overlooks the western approaches to Loch Leven and features on many a pictorial calendar. The area is one of natural beauty and a tourist attraction: Loch Leven in front, Glen Coe to the side and the magnificent bulk of Beinn a'Bheithir as a backdrop, its snow capped peaks overlooking the village of Ballachulish by the still waters of the loch.

Beinn a'Bheithir has two Munros: Sgorr Dhearg and Sgorr Dhonuill; both written about a few weeks ago. Peter Drummond, in his excellent *Scottish Hill and Mountain Names*, describes the hill as being the home of Cailleach Bheithir, the Celtic goddess of wind and storm but with a contradictory character – at times a beautiful maiden, at times a destructive demon, even a serpent. That could describe many a hill. The prudent hillwalker knows when to leave the high tops for another day, but in the case of Beinn a'Bheithir – or rather round its back – there is no excuse for not getting some exercise. A superb sheltered walk traversing two glens – Glen Duror and Gleann an Fhiodh – goes round its southern flanks: a walk on good paths and tracks and climbing only 300m.

Ordnance Survey map 41 (Ben Nevis, Fort William & Glen Coe) covers the whole route to be walked, starting from Achadh nan Darach at map ref 004552 at the entrance to Glen Duror. The minor road from the A828 (the Ballachulish to Connel west coast road) to the start point is annoyingly just off the map. Although Ordnance Survey map 49 shows the start of the minor road, it is not really required. A road map will suffice, the junction being just over a mile south of Kentallen, approaching Duror Inn.

The heavily forested Glen Duror has a myriad of mazy tracks leading to the eastern end, the trees ending just east of the watershed between the River Duror and the River Laroch. The most direct track follows the north bank of the Duror to a junction at map ref 031536, from where the northeast branch should be taken. It is nearly four miles to clear the forest at map ref 057546.

Back in 1983 I managed to get permission to drive up Glen Duror to the end of the forestry track, a short walk then leading to the east end of the forest. We had gained

Over Loch Leven to the mighty bulk of Beinn a 'Bheithir

300m in height and saved a walk. Hillwalkers can be very lazy! No permission would be given nowadays. In any case you are here for the exercise and the surprisingly open forest in the narrow glen – with Beinn a'Bheithir to the north and the Corbett Fraochaidh to the south – is so charming that the miles may seem all too short, with the gentle gradient easing the way.

After closely studying the map, a variation is to pass by Taigh Seumas a'Ghlinne – an MBA-maintained bothy at map ref 022539, situated as if the central part of a maze. A firebreak north of the bothy leads to another track that goes east to join the above route.

Now into open country and descending gently, the quartzite south slopes of Sgorr Dhearg and Sgorr Bhan – scree-covered higher up – can be admired. A path that can be a bit vague at times over grassy stretches eventually improves to a grassy, then stony track, passing a cairn marking a right of way south to Glen Creran. The track turns to the north, high on the west side of the River Laroch, to enter lower Gleann an Fhiodh, with the village school in Ballachulish soon coming into view. This last section can be easily managed in the gathering gloom but it may be sensible to be carrying head torches.

Despite its location, Ballachulish – formerly renowned for its slate – is a contender for the title of least attractive Highland village, perhaps due to its north-facing aspect in an area that gets more than its fair share of rain. Yet it may be that the welcoming lights of the village below will revise your opinion.

Walk through the village to where you have left the pre-arranged transport. Oh dear, had you not considered that? It is a long way back to Duror. There used to be a railway: the Callander & Oban branch to Ballachulish opened in 1903, but that now belongs to industrial archaeology.

82 Glencoe Lochan

FACTFILE

Map Ordnance Survey map 41, Ben Nevis, Fort William & Glen Coe
Distance 3½ to 4 miles
Height 100m
Terrain excellent paths all round
Start point Glencoe Lochan car park, map ref 104594, north of Bridge of Coe
Time 2 hours
Nearest village Glencoe
Recommended refreshment spot Café and crafts shop, Glencoe

As a result of clutch problems with the car, last week's reported trip to Carn an Tuirc turned out to be longer and more expensive than expected. The following week (with the car still in the garage), Jimbo and I were due to go for a couple of nights to the charming white-walled Blackrock Cottage – the LSCC club hut in Glen Coe; a calendar favourite with Stob Dearg of Buachaille Etive Mor as the backdrop. Drew was to join us for the second day. Jimbo most kindly came to collect me for the evening's journey and off we set in defiance of the weather forecast.

The overnight weather continued to day one: gale force winds with a high wind chill factor. Thoughts of bagging a few high tops were easily dismissed and we settled for the comfort and nostalgia of the cottage's coal fire. However, feeling guilty at this sloth by mid morning, we drove down to Glencoe for coffee, a sticky bun and a read of the paper. The village being partially sheltered from the cold northerly blasts, a short walk became more attractive and that is how we had an unplanned and charming stroll

The Pap of Glencoe

round Glencoe Lochan, nestling beneath the Pap of Glencoe – new to Jimbo and last visited by me over 20 years ago.

Whether fair weather or foul, I strongly recommend a visit to the lochan and its beautiful wooded surroundings. The following three walks in the vicinity of the lochan are clearly shown on Ordnance Survey map 41 (Ben Nevis, Fort William & Glen Coe), yet the map is only required to identify distant views. The notice board map at the start point is sufficient and explanatory.

Go through the old village to Bridge of Coe and turn north on the tarmac road. At a branch in the road the left fork leads to Glencoe Hospital and ambulance service; the right fork leads to the walker`s car park at map ref 104594, and the notice board.

Glencoe estate was acquired by Lord Strathcona in the late 19th Century. Born Donald Alexander Smith, a saddler's son in Forres in 1820, he emigrated to Canada when he was 18. He rose to become Governor of the Hudson's Bay Company, then High Commissioner for Canada. Wishing to make his Canadian wife more at home in Scotland, he built Glencoe House in 1895 and created Lochan Gleann Chomhann, now known as Glencoe Lochan. The estate woods were bought by the Forestry Commission in 1950 and subsequent plantings and path improvements have helped to provide the present sheltered woodland scene. The main lochan trail has a fine surface for wheelchairs, of possible interest to Jimbo's disabled ramblers group.

The Lochan Trail, signposted by red feathers, gives a sheltered and tranquil walk of about one mile round the perimeter. On a still day the reflections of mountain and forest are entrancing. Also starting from the car park is the one and a half mile Woodland Walk (marked by yellow signs) on the southwest side of the lochan. This undulating path round Torr a'Chomhain goes through a variety of coniferous and deciduous woodland with fine examples of Douglas Fir and Sequoia and gives good views down Loch Leven. The one and a half mile Mountain Walk (marked by blue signs) gives a short demanding climb by Stuc a'Chomhain on the southeast side of the lochan and at one place with good views to the towering Pap of Glencoe.

Extending our sheltered walk to the maximum, we covered all three trails, some four miles in well less than two hours. Then it was back to the cottage and the coal fire. Drew was due to arrive about midnight so Jimbo and I chatted away, putting the world to rights, until his arrival.

Some weeks ago I described Drew as being impatient (as only a would-be Munroist can be) to add to his list. He still had Meall a'Bhuiridh to do – a hill recently climbed by Jimbo and I: just follow the line of the ski tows behind the cottage all the way to the summit. However, the weather on our second day was little better so Jimbo and I decided that enough was enough. Like a couple of wimps we headed home, stopping for coffee along the way. Meanwhile Drew patiently waited to see if the storm would abate. It did and off he set. The weather improved all the while, so much so that he carried on to Creise. Drew put us to shame.

83 From Glen Coe to Kinlochleven via the Devil's Staircase

FACTFILE

Map Ordnance Survey map 41, Ben Nevis, Fort William & Glen Coe
Distance 6 miles
Height 250m
Terrain path and track
Start point parking area, just west of Altnafeadh on the A82, map ref 220563
Time 3 to 4 hours
Nearest village Kinlochleven
Recommended refreshment spot Macdonald Hotel, Fort William Road, Kinlochleven

Most walkers tackle the 95 miles of the West Highland Way from south to north, hoping to benefit from the prevailing wind. That leaves the Glen Coe to Fort William section as the final leg – arguably the most demanding in terms of height to be climbed and descended. However, that final section can be split over two days with a break at Kinlochleven.

From Altnafeadh (on the A82 near the watershed between Rannoch Moor and Glen Coe) to Kinlochleven is a paltry six miles, albeit with a climb of 250m – an easy day and one that suits those wishing to tackle only part of the Way. Yet when Margaret and I did the Way a few years ago we were decidedly grateful for that 'easy' day.

We had stayed overnight at the Kingshouse Inn on Rannoch Moor, getting there just before the heavens opened. With overnight gale force winds and driving rain, we were grateful not to be camping. In the morning we swithered as to what to do: delay another day or just go for it? We chose the latter but it was quite a battle into the westerly gale just to stagger along to Altnafeadh and the start of the Devil's Staircase. Once over the top, the long descent to Kinlochleven was somewhat sheltered but it was still not a day to dawdle. We passed some workmen repairing the path and admired their fortitude. Truth to tell, even on a good day the section from Kingshouse (parallel to the busy A82) is not the prettiest part of the Way. The following walk thus starts from Altnafeadh.

The Devil's Staircase is the fanciful name for the zigzag path that climbs 250m to a height of 550m. It was part of the military road network built in Scotland in the second half of the 18th Century and its presence today bears tribute to the quality of the original workmanship. The views from the top well justify the efforts of the climb, and even on a poorish day the position is atmospheric, with views of the mountains surrounding Glen Coe. The path thereafter contours round the hillside – a forbidding place on a miserable day, seemingly miles away from Glen Coe or Kinlochleven. It is then a descent of 1,800ft to sea level at Kinlochleven.

The descent is on part of the construction work of the Blackwater dam, built in the early 1900s to supply water to the aluminium smelter. Many navvies employed in the construction died, some caught out in bad weather returning from the Kingshouse after a night of drinking. You have been warned!

Kinlochleven is a place of strong personal connections and fond memories. The aluminium smelter transformed the handful of houses into a small and unattractive Highland village, where law and order were more akin to the Wild West. My great-grandfather – a manager during the smelter's construction – was authorised to carry a gun. Maybe it was this distant association that persuaded Geraldine and I to choose Kinlochleven`s registry office for our wedding.

So I am biased towards Kinlochleven, even though it suffers from high annual rainfall, sunlit hours are restricted by the surrounding steep slopes and – of more recent times – the closure of the smelter has caused financial hardship. Nevertheless, the town is being well promoted as an outdoor activities centre with the West Highland Way playing an important part.

The chairlift overlooking Rannoch Moor

For those without pre-arranged transport in Kinlochleven and needing to return to Glen Coe, there is a choice: retrace steps or utilise the local Kinlochleven/Fort William bus service to get to Ballachulish then the national bus service back to Glen Coe.

84 Ben Nevis

FACTFILE

Map Ordnance Survey map 41, Ben Nevis
Distance 9 miles
Height 1300m
Terrain steep hillside track to summit
Start point Nevis visitor centre or further up the glen at the youth hostel
Time 6 to 7 hours
Nearest town Fort William
Recommended refreshment spots a good choice in Glen Nevis and Fort William

Ben Nevis at 1344m/4409ft, is Britain's highest mountain – hence its popularity with tourists and non-hillwalkers. The appeal of reaching the summit outweighs the physical endeavour of climbing from almost sea level, and with a zigzagging track there is no reason why any reasonably fit person should not attempt the Ben.

But for the humble hillwalker, when is the best time to go? At the height of summer the multitude of walkers may inhibit enjoyment; at the height of winter it is a potentially dangerous place to be. I would suggest that a late autumn day is possibly the best time to go, but with two very strict provisos. Firstly, select a day of excellent weather. Quite apart from the dangers on the summit plateau, why save the mountain for a bad day? A few weeks ago Rhona and I picked a magical day: a cloud-free, breeze-free summit, with my only regret in having forgotten to take sunglasses. Secondly, start early in the morning, prepared for the rapid change in temperature and wind on ascent, and allowing some four to five hours for the climb.

Accidents on the Ben are estimated to account for ten per cent of all mountain rescue incidents in Scotland. The Lochaber Mountain Rescue Team has produced a very useful card. Get hold of one or a more detailed pamphlet *Navigation on Ben Nevis,* issued by the Mountaineering Council of Scotland.

The origin of the name is lost in the mists of time. I like *beinn-nimh-bhathais*: 'the mountain with its head in the cloud' as is so often the case. In 1883 an observatory was opened on the summit, with a zigzag pony track built for volunteers manning the station. The observatory operated 24 hours a day until 1904. A hotel was also built at the summit, open June to September, but with sky-high prices. It stayed open until 1918.

The start-points in Glen Nevis are well signposted: from the visitor centre – with a bridge over the River Nevis to Achintee – or further up the glen at the youth hostel. The path is initially steep, but eases near Lochan Meall an t-Suidhe, crosses the Red Burn, then gets to work again as the zigzags seem to go on for ever. The path is being upgraded, though I wonder for how long some sections will be able to withstand the rigours of adverse conditions at altitude and hundreds of thousands of boots.

Looking across Loch Eil to Ben Nevis

You will see some funny sights on the way: questionable footwear and insufficient clothing. We came across a daft pair from St Andrews, pushing their mountain bikes to the summit. To keep their anonymity let us call them Donald and Bob. Donald (the really daft one) claimed to be able to get to the top in four hours and then descend in under 20 minutes.

For some the summit plateau may be an awesome but unattractive place. An ugly corrugated iron safety shelter perches on the remains of the observatory tower. There is also a trig point platform and a 'peace cairn'. On a good day the plateau is a wonderful place to be, a sensational viewpoint. On a bad day – even in the height of summer – it can be cold and miserable, with the observatory ruins looming out of the cloud like a deserted village.

Take extra care on the way down. The northeast cliffs are very, very close to the trig point and the plateau slopes slightly west towards the dangerous flanks of Five Finger Gully. Study the map carefully, for the cairned path (if partly hidden by early-lying snow) goes further to the north of west than your senses might indicate.

Having swept past us at some speed on their descent, we were astonished over an hour later to come across our two mountain bikers. Bob had had a puncture. Donald, lower down, had the sole pump. I told you they were daft! From summit to road we were faster than them.

85 West Leanachan Forest

FACTFILE

Map Ordnance Survey map 41, Ben Nevis, Fort William and Glen Coe
Distance 6 miles
Height 50m
Terrain forest tracks
Start point Nevis Range ski car park
Time 2 to 3 hours if not exploring
Nearest town/village Fort William and Spean Bridge
Recommended refreshment spot Nevis Range gondola cafeteria

Many years ago I was fortunate to live and work in Inverness – the capital of the Highlands and a superb base from where to tackle many of the high tops. I reckoned that over half of the Munros could be climbed on a day trip from Inverness, including most of the far flung northwestern hills, seen by those living in the central belt as being very remote indeed.

Yet even then I had to grudgingly admit that perhaps, just perhaps, Fort William was an even better base with more hills in most directions. In addition, after many a holiday week spent in that vicinity, I came to appreciate the other attractions of Fort William. Yes, it can be a wet place at times and the ruddy complexions of the locals seemed more akin to rust than sun tan, but there is a fine swimming pool and plenty of shops selling outdoor equipment. Almost all my hill gear has been bought in Fort William on bad weather days.

Aonach Mor car park on a quiet day

And of more recent times there has been the advent of the ski slopes of Nevis Range, built in 1989. Not that I have ever skied there, but the development has been very good indeed for the local economy. Britain's only mountain gondola system glides up to a height of 2150ft on the slopes of Aonach Mor, carrying visitors, tourists and (dare I say it) even hillwalkers.

But it is at lower level that Fort William really scores when the weather is poor, for apart from the delights of the Caledonian Canal there are many low level walks available with the most extensive being within the Leanachan Forest which lies on the northern slopes of Aonach Mor and the Grey Corries. There are 25 miles of forest tracks – just the job for a windy, wet day amidst shelter of the trees. So if you are in the Fort William area and the weather is keeping you away from the hills or the ski slopes, then this forest is a sensible place to go.

Take with you Ordnance Survey map 41 (Ben Nevis, Fort William and Glen Coe) – one of the very best maps and a joy to read in its own right. The Nevis Range is seven miles north of Fort William, just off the A82 and is well signposted.

Use the ski centre car park. The track for this walk goes east, starting just under the gondola, and very quickly one gets a feeling of distance from the crowded car park and the sound of machinery. Keep left at the first junction, then right at the second (at map ref 184777) – all of this in just under a mile. You are now on the main east/west track in the forest, heading for the distant clearing that contains Leanachan. That is a walk of two miles so that the total distance back to the car is six miles. There are very good views of the Grey Corries as you progress and if there is anyone else about it may just be the odd cyclist. Leanachan is served by a minor road and it is easy to carry on walking to the A82, coming out just short of Spean Bridge – an interesting variation if you have transport pre-arranged.

The gondola line above the forest

Another variation (and one well worth doing) is to explore part of the dismantled railway system, used to transport material in the construction of the aluminium smelter. In leaving the car park, start as before but at the first junction turn right, climbing southwards. At the next junction turn left where the track heads east, contouring much closer to the lower slopes of Aonach Mor. The track follows the line of the old railway and carries on until map ref 204769. There the track loops down north and the old railway continues eastwards. Exploration is now up to you. Return the same way.

And at the end of the walk? There is a cafeteria at the gondola base station but why not just go for that gondola ride? Fifteen minutes to the top, a quick blast round the cold outside and then dive into the Snowgoose restaurant for food and warmth. After all, you do not have to be masochistic every hill outing.

86 East Leanachan Forest, Spean Bridge

FACTFILE

Map Ordnance Survey map 41, Ben Nevis, Fort William and Glen Coe
Distance 5 miles
Height 200m
Terrain forest track, then dismantled tramway, wet in places
Start point forestry track, map ref 253794, south of Corriechoille
Time 3 hours
Nearest village Spean Bridge
Recommended refreshment spot Spean Bridge Hotel

Blanketing the northern slopes of Aonach Mor all the way to Spean Bridge, the eastern side of the Leanachan Forest gives not only a stunning autumnal and sheltered walk beneath the high tops, but offers a return by a railway line of historic interest.

From Spean Bridge it is a two-mile drive or cycle along the minor road on the south side of the River Spean to its end at Corriechoille. It is possible to continue driving from here, turning right along the dirt track, passing Corriechoille and continuing south for another three-quarters of a mile (opening and closing a gate along the way) to a junction in the track at map ref 253794. Now for the walk through the forest.

Follow the minor track on the right. It quickly enters the forest to give a sheltered, gently undulating route southwestwards. There is soon a large clearing of felled trees with good views to the Grey Corries range to the south. Red squirrels, although an endangered species, can still be found here. They rely on the shelter and rich food supply of this coniferous forest and the tall trees provide a perfect setting for them to build their nests, known as dreys.

Turn left and then right at the next two junctions amidst the trees, the latter at map ref 238770. Continue southwestwards to the end of the track and a dam from where the waters of the Allt Coire an Eoin are abstracted. It is well worth stepping out a little bit into the corrie to admire the rough terrain. The glen with its meandering waterway is a wild, desolate place on the other side of Aonach Mor from the skiing area, yet seems more remote than that.

Return to the trees and the track junction at map ref 238770, but for a change on the way back to the car, return along the line of the old tramway that runs parallel to the first stage of the walk. Once over the Allt Choimhlidh, head south for a short distance, looking out for the remains of the tramway, especially what is left of one short bridge that spans the water and which looks like the remnants of a Hollywood film set. The tramway (on a narrow-gauge track) was built by the British Aluminium Company to assist in construction of the tunnel taking water from Loch Treig to the aluminium smelter at Fort William. The light railway ceased to be used in the 1970s yet I have long wondered about the tourist possibilities of re-opening it. The gondola on Aonach Mor has proved to be a big success and the railway runs beneath that. Re-instating 12 miles of the track from the gondola to Loch Treig would get my vote!

The line goes northeast through a large clearing. Nowadays, with insufficient drainage, the track can be wet underfoot so good footwear is advised. Despite several ups and downs necessitated by the removal of small bridges over side streams, it may well be of more interest to the younger generation. Continue northeast to join the top end of the Corriechoille track, where until recently were still to be found a few rusty relics of the rail stock.

87 Beinn na Lap

FACTFILE

Map Ordnance Survey map 41, Ben Nevis, Fort William and Glen Coe
Distance 5 miles
Height 550m
Terrain track then path leading to easy whaleback ridge
Start point Corrour railway station
Time 3 to 4 hours
Nearest town none
Recommended refreshment spot Corrour Station Restaurant

During the summer I wrote: ‘It may have taken a while in coming, but two weeks ago the persistent Mountain Lamb (ML) climbed Mullach Coire Mhic Fhearchair and Sgurr Ban, to reduce his outstanding Munro tally to just two. A guided return to Skye in June should see Am Basteir climbed, thus leaving Beinn na Lap for the final party celebration’. Am Basteir was eventually climbed and so on 17th October a 14-strong group set off from Corrour railway station to climb the ML’s ultimate Munro.

Beinn na Lap lies near the heart of Scotland and but for the West Highland Railway line giving easy access it would be one of the more remote Munros to be treasured. The usual way up is thus from Corrour station, well armed with a railway timetable. With a 400m starting height and a walk of less than three miles, reaching its modest 935m summit takes only two to three hours.

Beinn na Lap

Beinn na Lap is thus a sensible and popular hill on which to complete a Munro round. It was the scene of the fifth known Munro completion in 1933, when John Dow reached the top accompanied by his friend Percy Donald (compiler of the eponymous list of southern Scotland hills). The ML was planning to join an illustrious group!

It is easy to dismiss Beinn na Lap as one of the easiest Munros. It has an uninspiring slope and even its name – possibly 'mottled hill' – hardly seems exciting. Uninspiring it may be – yet more akin to a Corbett – it gives wonderful views of beautiful Loch Ossian and the outlying circle of distant Munros.

The ML was blessed with glorious autumnal weather. The early morning mist and frost soon lifted and we enjoyed a warm blue-sky day of gentle breeze. We arrived on the 11.08 train from Rannoch station: an all too short journey of only ten minutes, but at a bargain £5.20 day return.

The route is straightforward. From the station head for Loch Ossian, following the track to just before Ossian youth hostel. With time to spare do have a look at the hostel. Opened in 1931, its position and place in the history of the SYHA makes it the jewel in the crown. This former boat-house was originally used as a stopping point from the station, using the pier to board a steam yacht to proceed to the lodge at the far end of the loch. Changed days indeed!

From the track fork go round the top end of the loch and then strike up NNE on what is now (sadly) a worn path that leads over an easy slope towards the whale-back ridge. There is a lochan just short of the summit cairn.

So after 28 years or more since Meall Buidhe – his first Munro – the ML had done it. With good weather and a late afternoon train there was plenty of time in which to celebrate. Then – intoxicated with champagne – we slowly made our way back to Corrour.

For some, the frisson of risk in getting back too late for the return train adds a little spice to what is but a short day. We had no such problem. Indeed our problem was the other way round: what to do with the spare time until the 18.25 train? Luckily there is the Corrour Station Restaurant on the site of the old stationmaster's house. We were thus able to wait in comfort with suitable refreshments until our train back to Rannoch. (Since 2010 the building has been leased by SYHA, operating in conjunction with Loch Ossian as a hostel, with a café/restaurant open to guests and visitors).

That evening we were royally entertained at Bunrannoch House, Kinloch Rannoch – a fitting and enjoyable end to that long Munro trail. Well done Mountain Lamb, whose anonymity should now be lifted: well done Gordon Davies.

88 Gairlochy to South Laggan on the Great Glen Way

FACTFILE

Map Ordnance Survey map 34, Fort Augustus
Distance 13 miles
Height negligible
Terrain minor road and forest track
Start point Gairlochy
Time 5 to 6 hours
Nearest villages Spean Bridge and Invergarry
Recommended refreshment spots a good choice in both villages

Completed in 1980, the West Highland Way was the first long-distance route in Scotland. Not only extremely popular, it has provided a welcome commercial boost to the local economy. The Southern Upland Way and the Speyside Way have since been opened and in 2002 it was the turn of the Great Glen Way.

The 73 mile walk from Fort William to Inverness has already attracted a great deal of interest, for some would argue that it is the most scenic of all the Ways and arguably the most natural in following Britain's greatest geological fault. It passes by Ben Nevis and Loch Ness and ends up in Inverness – the Capital of the Highlands – with most folk covering the distance over five to six days. Although there are some harder bits, most of the walking is fairly level along the towpath of the Caledonian Canal and on forest tracks.

Towpath and Caledonian Canal

Representative of the delights of the Way, the ten-mile section from Gairlochy to South Laggan covers the length of Loch Lochy – with lock gates at both ends – and passes through the Clunes and South Laggan Forests. Throw in a small detour with a couple of attractions (increasing the mileage to 13) and it has everything. Well not quite, for there are no refreshment spots along the way and half way up Loch Lochy with the A82 on the other side, you know you are at the point of no return. But that adds to the spirit of adventure.

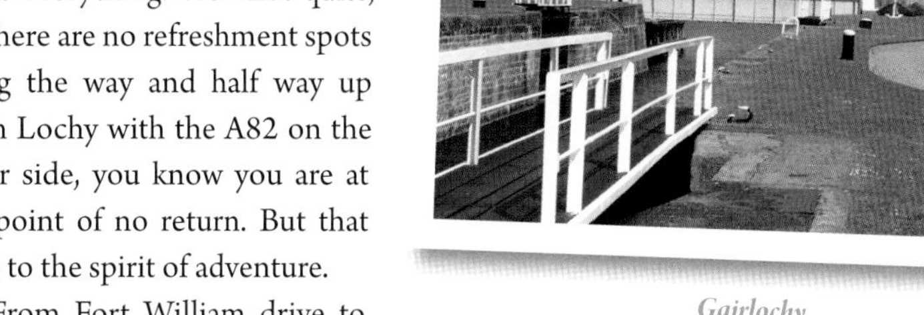

Gairlochy

From Fort William drive to Banavie (do take the time to look at Neptune's Staircase, recently refurbished) then take the B8004 that follows the line of the canal to Gairlochy. Once you have stopped looking at the boats passing through the lock gates, it is time for the walk.

Walk along the B8004 that takes a curving route to Loch Arkaig, but after two miles make a diversion by going along the estate road to Achnacarry and the Clan Cameron museum (open in the afternoons from April to October). Continue on the estate road to the south end of Loch Arkaig, over the wooden bridge and turn east on the B8005. The Eas Chia-aig waterfalls are on the left at map ref 177888. This was the site used for one episode in the film *Rob Roy*, where the hero escapes by jumping from the bridge. Miraculously he further escapes by throwing himself down the waterfall, which just happens to be above the bridge.

The next mile is through a moss-covered dark forest – the Mile Dorcha (or the Dark Mile). On reaching Clunes you have regained the Way.

Now for the serious bit: all the way through the forest and you are committed – seven miles to go. The Way at this stage is also covered by the Great Glen Cycleway, so look out for those pesky cyclists, and nearing the end you may come across hillwalkers returning from Meall na Teanga and Sron a'Choire Ghairbh – the two Munros that overlook Loch Lochy. At Laggan Locks at the north end of Loch Lochy, cross the resumed canal and so on to the A82.

Now you did remember to organise transport, car, bus or bicycle, back to Gairlochy, didn't you?

Placid Loch Arkaig

89 A Walk to Peanmeanach

FACTFILE

Map Ordnance Survey map 40, Glen Shiel.
Distance 7 miles
Height 150m
Terrain path with varied terrain, rough and bouldery in places
Start point lay-by near Polnish, map ref 742835
Time 4 hours
Nearest town Mallaig
Recommended refreshment spot a good choice in Mallaig – try some of the local fish restaurants

Last week I wrote about the Fife Coastal Path – an ideal winter's low-level walk when the weather is nasty in the west. But what if those conditions are reversed? There are plenty of coast walks in the west, but this one is special. It leads to the coast through a rough uninhabited area, walking away from 'civilisation' and truly is a walk on the wild side. No tea rooms here!

The Sound of Arisaig lies to the west of Lochailort and the much-improved A830 (the trunk road from Fort William that passes through Arisaig to Mallaig). Jutting out into the Sound is the small, rugged Ardnish Peninsula that separates Loch nan Uamh from Loch Ailort. Twisting through the peninsula is a three-mile path, rough in places, that leads to the southern beach at the abandoned settlement of Peanmeanach. All that is left amidst the ruins is one restored building, maintained by the Mountain Bothies Association (MBA).

As bothies go, this is one of the best, for in addition to the varied walk in, it has a delightful setting and an other-worldly nostalgic presence. The last inhabitants left over 60 years ago, but there still are locals living elsewhere on the west coast who were born at Peanmeanach. The other buildings – in a line like a miniature St Kilda – are reduced to waist high walls almost hidden by nettles, whereas the MBA bothy has two rooms and a loft space. Last year a MBA work party, using a boat to transport materials across Loch Ailort, carried out extensive renovations.

A walk to Peanmeanach

Peanmeanach is a corruption of *Peathan Meadhonach*. Many west coast names have a Norse background. The Norse system of land division defined an ounceland as being an area capable of producing enough for an ounce of silver in rent. An ounceland was divided into 20 pennylands or farms. *Meadhonach* is Gaelic for 'intermediate' or 'middling'.

Peanmeanach (on the Ardnish Estate) is at map ref 712805. The bothy has a well-drawing fire and driftwood may be found on the shore and there is also fallen timber nearby. But don't cut live trees! But what about the walk in, rather than a stay at this bothy?

Park at a large lay-by near Polnish (some two miles north-west of Lochailort) on an improved stretch of the road at map ref 742835. The walk in is on a right of way, and the Scottish Rights of Way Society's green signpost shows the initial direction, passing down through a small gravel quarry to reach the path. The distance shown on the sign says four and a half miles but that would appear to be an exaggeration. When doing the walk in it seems more like three and a half miles, so allow for say seven miles as a return walk. However, the once well-maintained way is rough and bouldery in places with 150m of ascent, so allow at least four hours' walking time. For anyone backpacking in to stay at the bothy, and hence carrying a heavy load, more time may be needed. The original path was well made for pack ponies although it is likely that heavy materials would have been transported by boat.

The path crosses the railway line by a curved concrete bridge, then over a stream by some planks of wood, and that feeling of exploration begins. Shortly after comes the rough section that is the uphill pull, but once on to the higher ground the path improves and there are magnificent views out to sea. To the east the interior of the peninsula is dominated by Loch Doir a'Ghearrain. The path weaves between rocky knolls to the highest point at 150m below the knobbly Cruach an Fhearainn Dubh.

The path of almost pavement standard gently descends to the outflow from the loch. This could present a problem if crossing in spate, as the stepping-stones are not very large. The last stretch goes through a delightful wooded area – a mixture of moss-covered oak and birch, a veritable sylvan delight – and then it is out into the open. The bothy is sited on a raised beach beyond a wet grassy flat area.

Stand outside the bothy for magnificent picturesque views out to Rum, and south to the Ardnamurchan peninsula. Soak in the atmosphere, then grudgingly turn your back for the return journey.

The MBA's mission is to maintain simple shelters in remote country for the use and benefit of all who love wild lonely places. If you would like more information, possibly even to join, the organisation can be contacted on www.mountainbothies.org.uk. Numbers going to a bothy as one party should not exceed five.

90 A'Mharconaich

FACTFILE

Map Ordnance Survey map 42, Glen Garry & Loch Rannoch
Distance 5 miles
Height 550m
Terrain track leading to north-east ridge, stonier near summit
Start point off-road A9 parking area, map ref 628792, just east of Balsporran Cottages
Time 3 to 4 hours
Nearest village Dalwhinnie
Recommended refreshment spot The Inn at Dalwhinnie

A'Mharconaich is one of four Munros on the west side of the Pass of Drumochter. The lower part of A'Mharconaich's two-mile northeast ridge – the route for today's walk and the new cycle path by the A9 – provide an excellent platform for observing various types of moraine hummocks; evidence of glacial action that caused the breach.

A modest hill at 975m/3199ft, A'Mharconaich is rather too close to the A9 but with a high start of 425m/1394ft and a short walk, it suits well as a winter hill and is an excellent viewpoint. Its closeness to the busy A9 is partially redeemed by the intervening bulk of An Torc, better known as the Boar of Badenoch.

Stop, Look, Listen

A'Mharconaich – 'place of horses' – has a half-mile summit plateau with bumps at either end. The northeast bump is the Munro. Earlier confusion arose because maps of the 1920s spot-marked only the southwest bump, Bruach nan Iomairean, at 3174ft. When seen from the southeast the plateau emphasises a blunt eastern buttress

Low-lying cloud on the A9

overlooking An Torc, whereas from further north the northeast ridge – bounded by the Allt Coire Fhar and the Allt an Tuirc – is seen as a graceful way to the summit.

My most vivid memory of A'Mharconaich is not of climbing the hill but of being stranded at its base. In the mid-1980s, driving home to Inverness on an evening of very strong winds and heavy snow showers, I was following a slow moving line of vehicles. Just short of Balsporran the traffic stopped and very quickly all vehicles were stuck in snowdrifts. The rippling message from car to car was that a lorry had jack-knifed further north. With only a thin coat and no food or drink, wrapping car mats around me made little difference. With the risk of running out of petrol, the engine was only kept running intermittently. Soon even that had to stop. Knowing that other drivers were also stuck did little to ease the very cold, solitary and sleepless night. Help arrived next morning and the Siberian refugees were escorted to North Drumochter Lodge. Luckily the blizzard had abated as we picked our way through drifts, cold and hunger making me indifferent to the wintry beauty of A'Mharconaich. That afternoon a train made an unscheduled stop at Balsporran. I recall how high the train was without the aid of a platform. I bought some whisky from the bar, but do not remember being charged for the rail fare. I had little thought as to the car left in the snow. After all, it was not mine: I had been driving a colleague's. My own car would have been stocked with hillwalking gear and food and I could have walked to Dalwhinnie. Another driver and I returned a few days later in a van, loaded with chains, ropes and shovels. Nearing Dalwhinnie, we could see the effect of a rapid thaw – tarmac instead of snow-plastered roads – and at the garage were all the once-stranded cars, transported there the day before, free of charge.

The north-east ridge is approached from a parking area at map ref 628792, just east of Balsporran – former railway cottages sandwiched between the A9 and the railway line. With flavours of Brigadoon, Balsporran is likely a corruption of Beul an Sporain. Coire Beul an Sporain – 'corrie of the mouth of the purse' – overlooks the cottages.

Take full precautions at the railway level crossing gates. Stop. Look. Listen. Once over the line there will be a feeling of escape, leaving the busy road and the railway behind. On the northern side of the Allt Coire Fhar, a superb stalkers' track, then a path, leads west then southwest. Follow it a short distance then cross the stream to reach the northeast ridge (note that the track west of the A9 leading to a communications mast gives no advantage).

Once past the initial hummocky ground, the ridge offers a gradual and easy approach. Well, it usually does. A few weeks ago, four of us tackled the hill after a heavy fall of snow such that the lower stages made for a slow and tedious start. The easiest way was for Rhona – the lightest – to go first and for Jimbo – the heaviest – to be last. Higher up, thankfully the wind had whipped away much of the recent fall. A path, if clear of snow, helps on ascent as the ridge narrows. Nearing the summit the ridge turns to the south and steepens on stony terrain, close to crags of the eastern corrie. At the summit there is a choice of two cairns.

Return the same way, mindful of the eastern corrie.

91 The Wildcat Trail, Newtonmore

FACTFILE

Map Ordnance Survey map 35, Kingussie & Monadhliath Mountains
Distance 4 miles
Height 50m
Terrain good paths, tracks and walk through village
Start point Newtonmore village centre
Time 2 hours
Nearest village Newtonmore
Recommended refreshment spot The Tuckshop, Newtonmore

The Wildcat Trail is a pathway of nearly eight miles round the village of Newtonmore, linking areas of woodland managed by the Newtonmore Community Woodland Trust. I had already covered some parts of the Trail, but was keen to do more and this fitted in with describing a shorter low-level walk for the beginning of January – a four-mile stroll with minimal climbing.

Margaret and the Mountain Lamb came with me to Newtonmore. Margaret drove on to the RSPB Insh Marshes Nature Reserve, promising to return in three hours time to collect us two walkers in the middle of the village.

The Wildcat Trail gives a varied route by streams and rivers through woodland and open moorland. The southern side follows the banks of the River Spey and no doubt will feature in a later easy walk. We opted for the walk on the north side of the village, giving closer views of the Monadhliath – not that we could see those rolling hills, the aptly named grey mountain range. It was a cold, grey day with lowering cloud and damp air all the while, though just right for our low-level walk and with no regrets about not being on the higher tops.

The Wildcat Trail is signposted in a clockwise direction, but I was keen to go anti-clockwise. This meant meeting the black cat signs head on, then following their tails. I chose this direction because severe flooding a year ago damaged part of the trail by the Allt Laraidh and I wanted to see this section early in the walk, in case there was a problem. In fact the damaged section is easily bypassed.

The trail is well signposted with pictures of the black cat appearing on numerous posts and gates, but there are one or two areas where the way ahead is not altogether certain. Also, the trail can be joined at several points from the edge of the village. I would strongly suggest buying the Trail detailed brochure (available at the Wildcat office in the centre of Newtonmore or by phoning 01540-673131). Enclosed with the brochure is a map, which when used in conjunction with the Ordnance Survey map makes everything very clear and the informative sheets give a fuller understanding of the area traversed.

Start in the middle of the village and walk along the A86 (the old A9) to the east end, on a pleasing path through woodland after the end of the pavement. Continue to the Allt Laraidh – the mare's burn – at map ref 729999 that marks the end of the village and then head northwest on the path by the west bank of the stream. You will note the short eroded section, but easily passed with care, climbing slightly then regaining the path. There are beautiful cascades at the confluence of two streams, the Allt Laraidh Falls. Cross the west stream by a wooden bridge and follow the other stream into the area once part of the Strone Crofting Township. A plaque nearby – erected by Newtonmore Community Woodland Trust – gives an indication of what the Township looked like in 1891. Continue following the signs and cross the Allt na Feithe Buidhe by a wooden bridge to reach the edge of the open woodland area at map ref 719004. This crosses the track used by Jimbo and myself in November on our approach to Carn Sgulain and A'Chailleach – I must like the area!

Enter the woodland by a gate – just one of many in traversing southwest. Please shut and fasten all gates, except those you find open and which have no sign. Corridors with gates have been left between sections of new plantings to allow the crofters to move livestock between the upper and lower grazings.

The path, then track, reaches open country around map ref 710996. Follow the track SSW to reach the Glen Banchor road, well known to Munro baggers as the popular approach to the Monadhliath. It would be simple to follow Glen Road down to the village, but do continue with the trail. Follow the tarmac road a short way northwest (with a charming woodland diversion not readily apparent), then turn left at a signpost to descend to the River Calder. Follow the riverside path above the

Calder gorge to the Calder Bridge at the west end of the village. It is then a short walk back into the village.

Our leisurely walk – an ideal start for the New Year – took only two hours, so there was plenty of time for scones and coffee in the village whilst waiting for Margaret's return.

92 From Loch Morlich to An Lochan Uaine

FACTFILE

Map Ordnance Survey map 36, Cairngorm Mountains
Distance 3 miles
Height negligible
Terrain good, slightly undulating track
Start point small car park at map ref. 991097, east of Glenmore Lodge
Time 1 to 2 hours
Nearest town Aviemore
Recommended refreshment spot café by Loch Morlich

Nestling below the northern flanks of the Cairngorms, Loch Morlich is a watery playground amid Glenmore Forest Park. Also known as The Queen's Forest, the large wooded area extends west in patchwork fashion towards Rothiemurchus and Aviemore. In contrast, the eastern side of the forest extends only some two miles to another – albeit much smaller – stretch of water: An Lochan Uaine. The Park offers a variety of walks – one of which goes from loch to lochan (a distance of only two miles) – all of which can be cycled on a good track. However, such activity negates the pleasure of a gentle stroll through this beautiful wooded area. The distance and the scenic terrain make it a more appealing and shorter outing for younger members of the family.

The 'green' lochan

From the visitor centre at map ref 976099, follow the minor road that goes past Glenmore Lodge (the National Outdoor Training Centre) to a small car park at map ref 991097.

From the car park a broad gravel track goes northeast through a beautiful open woodland of Scots pine. Following the line of the Allt na Feith Duibhe, the track goes by

Where Fairies wash their clothes

the steep wooded slopes beneath Creag Loisgte, gradually giving a more hemmed in feeling.

The first mandatory stopping place is beside An Lochan Uaine, meaning 'the green lochan' and arguably Scotland's most lovely small stretch of water. It is hemmed in by scree slopes falling from Creag nan Gall and the water is more emerald than green – a delightful photo stop and in complete contrast to the wide open area of Loch Morlich. And why the colour? Fairies wash their clothes there. The fact that there is no obvious outflow and that a build-up of minerals and rotted vegetation may play a part is not so romantic.

It is well worthwhile to continue a short distance along the track, beyond the forest to a junction. The right fork leads all the way (eventually) to Bynack More – a typical Cairngorms hill whose summit area has its share of granite tors; wart-like outcrops scoured by the elements, of which the biggest are known as the Barns of Bynack. However, for this outing take the left fork that leads to Ryvoan Bothy at map ref 006115, below the eastern flanks of Meall a'Bhuachaille. It is a small bothy in the Abernethy estate and RSPB nature reserve.

But why continue to the bothy? Much admired and much copied, the following words for many years were pinned to the inside of the door of Ryvoan bothy. Written by a Mrs A.M. Lawerence – who lived for a while as a young girl in Nethybridge – they could well be the national poem for hillwalkers. The first four and last eight lines say it all:

I shall leave tonight from Euston
By the seven-thirty train
And from Perth in the early morning
I shall see the hills again.

And again in the dusk of evening
I shall find once more alone
The dark water of the Green loch,
And pass by Ryvoan.

For tonight I leave from Euston
And leave the world behind;
Who has the hills as lover
Will find them wondrous kind.

93 Walking on water over Loch Loyne

FACTFILE

Map Ordnance Survey map 34, Fort Augustus
Distance 5 miles
Height 100m
Terrain old road/track
Start point road junction just west of Tomdoun Hotel at map ref 154010
Time 2 to 3 hours
Nearest village Invergarry
Recommended refreshment spot Tomdoun Hotel

The A87 is the trunk road that runs from the Great Glen to Skye. Starting from Invergarry, it follows the north shore of Loch Garry and then climbs north high above the east end of Loch Loyne to reach the east end of Loch Cluanie. However, much of this initial part is a comparatively new road.

The old Invergarry to Skye road ran the length of Loch Garry as far as Tomdoun, at map ref 154010. From there it turned north, crossing the River Loyne, then climbing to over 1400ft by the east side of Creag a'Mhaim and dropping to the Cluanie Bridge Inn (as it was then known) beyond the west end of Loch Cluanie. Not any more. As well as Loch Cluanie, Loch Loyne was dammed as part of the post-war hydroelectric works completed in 1957, so that the waters spread further westward and drowned the road. Peter Bellarby – my climbing partner of old – can remember being driven on the old road, but then he is older than me. At one time it was almost a toss-up as to which route would be adopted – upgrade the old road or construct what is now the new road. I am glad it was not the old road, for the closer proximity of traffic would have been detrimental to a lovely area.

The road heads into the water

This week's walk makes use of part of the old single-track road, closed to public traffic since the 1950s but still serviceable: a two and a half mile forested stroll from Tomdoun to Loch Loyne. Enjoy the step back in time.

I have a pre-war Bartholomew's quarter-inch-to-one-mile map of Inverness and Skye. This very clearly shows the smaller size of Loch Loyne as it then was, with a wide gap and a stretch of the River Loyne where the old road crossed. The map notes that 'the publishers would appreciate the friendly co-operation of users of the map in suggesting corrections or additions'. I am I fear, a little too late.

Another Peter – Peter Cook – and I were at Tomdoun a few weeks ago. Approached from Loch Quoich on a circuitous route that also involved cycling, we had a four-Munro wet day on the South Cluanie ridge. On the next morning (also wet) and before heading home, we opted for the short visit to Loch Loyne. I must confess that we cycled there rather than walking, but the previous day had been hard, lasting ten hours. Shame!

A telephone box marks the start of the walk, on what at this stage looks just like a forestry track (as indeed it is now), cutting back northeast from the public road. It is an easy stroll, only climbing some 100m to the high point at 250m. From there the old tarmac surface is more apparent on the by now open descent by Lochan Bad an Losguinn, with the first views of Loch Loyne. Looking more like a loch-side jetty, the road goes direct into the water.

At times of major water abstractions from Loch Loyne it is possible to see the line of the old road above or just under the water. The road is quite visible as it crosses the east side of an island to reach a usually submerged bridge over what was the River Loyne. After a day of heavy rain it was unlikely that Peter and I would be able to walk very far in the water, and so it proved. A barefoot paddle in shallow water, carefully following the line of the road, took us only a short distance from the shore and we turned back when we could no longer see the road under our feet. I will need to return when a dry spell coincides with maximum water abstraction from the loch. Do have a look, but only take a gentle paddle.

The water's too deep!

Years ago Geraldine and I walked over Loch Loyne to reach the South Cluanie hills to the northwest. After the water crossing, the hills seemed rather tame. Walking on water? Well not quite, but do not let the facts get in the way of a good story. When we were there the old bridge was still intact ... just. It was warped as if melted by the sun, but it was still possible to cross very gingerly and with dry feet. At the time of writing, the bridge is little more than the high curved arch of the keystones – in this respect almost identical to the bridge over the Dulnain at Carrbridge. It is interesting to have a look on a day of very low water levels, even if not intending to cross, as the old bridge is not going to last forever.

94 A Return to Glen Affric

FACTFILE

Map Ordnance Survey map 25, Glen Affric
Distance 10 miles
Height 200m
Terrain track/path all the way
Start point Glen Affric road-end car park at map ref 201234
Time 5 to 6 hours
Nearest village Cannich
Recommended refreshment spot the café in Cannich

Last week I wrote about a wet spell we had had in Glen Affric, with a short climb to the modest bump that is An Socach – a hill seldom climbed on its own but ideal for a day of bad weather and/or a short November day. We had both!

Bearing in mind the restricted daylight hours at this time of year, I had suggested that taking a bicycle to reach the base of the hill was almost essential. However, some walkers do not have, or do not like using, a bike and this week's walk – a circuit of Loch Affric – avoids the need. The walk – staying well clear of hills – is ideal for a poor day and can also be concluded in the dark if necessary. Yes, even for the hillwalker, being below the cloud-covered hills has a certain attraction. It is a fairly flat walk, albeit with some undulations, and the height climbed is of the order of say 200m.

Glen Affric – one of the most beautiful glens in Scotland – is a wonderful spot at this time of year, indeed at any time, with remnants of the old Caledonian Forest set beneath wonderful mountain scenery. Much of the walk is on Forestry Commission access land.

You will need Ordnance Survey map 25 (Glen Affric), though once on the circuit of the loch it will be used only to identify the surrounding peaks.

The road into Glen Affric goes by the north shore of Loch Beinn a'Mheadhoin. When the loch was dammed for hydro-electric generation purposes its length doubled, mostly affecting the east side, and the old road was inundated. The lack of mapped contours and the presence of shoreline tidemarks betray its changed status. By contrast, Loch Affric retains all its unspoilt natural beauty with its contours disclosing a depth of 60m.

Continue to the road-end car park at map ref 201234, a wooded area at the east end of Loch Affric with the loch initially hidden from view. Head west on the track, the first sight of water being the Affric surging under a concrete bridge. Do not cross that bridge – this is the return route – and continue along the north shore to Affric Lodge. This area is one of the most photographed parts of Scotland – staple material for picture calendars, and rightly so. Pause to admire the wonderful wooden bridge that straddles the narrow part of the loch.

The track skirts north of the lodge and stays well above the shoreline at a height that enhances views to the south. Nearing the west end of the loch, the track (more of a path in places) goes southwest by Loch Coulavie to join the track (at map ref 128208) that comes in from Strawberry Cottage. This is the halfway and turning point so remember to head east from here. (Straight on west leads to Alltbeithe youth hostel, closed in winter.)

Strawberry Cottage (at map ref 132207) is quickly reached and who knows, if it is occupied a kindly hillwalker may offer a mug of tea. The cottage belongs to the An Teallach Mountaineering Club and following refurbishment is one of the best-equipped huts in the country. Bookings are normally restricted to fellow hillwalking clubs. What I have never been able to find out is why it is called strawberry, but I am sure that there is a reader out there who knows the answer.

Cross the Affric by the long wooden bridge – an impressive 90ft span – to reach Athnamulloch: 'the fording place'. Athnamulloch bothy on the south side of the Affric – a former croft house – is now used for only seasonal accommodation. The forestry track on the south side of Loch Affric (undulating and rough in places) is not as pretty as the north track/path, but nevertheless gives fast walking back to the concrete bridge and the car park.

Last week I mentioned that we had had difficulties in driving out of the glen, a short stretch of the track just east of Athnamulloch being flooded. My car had been at the car park – safely I had assumed from any water problems. The car had let in water on the passenger side. It has now recovered (or rather I have) following an expensive week in the garage having the electrics dried. The ingress of water was due to a broken pollen filter. While a bike can get rusty, it would not have had those problems, and hillwalkers are even better equipped to cope with the rain. We quickly dry out with no ill effects, so even if your visit is on a bad day, just go for the walk.

95 A Ferry Journey, plus walk, to the Kylerhea otter haven

FACTFILE

Map Ordnance Survey map 33, Loch Alsh & Glen Shiel
Distance 6 miles
Height 50m
Terrain tarmac road, ferry and track
Start point road junction, east end of Glenelg village, map ref 820198
Time 2 to 3 hours, plus time at ferry and hide
Nearest village Glenelg
Recommended refreshment spot Glenelg Inn

For most hillwalkers the Glen Shiel area requires at least a weekend away. Instead of a number of such visits, a week makes more sense and that is what Margaret and I – together with the Mountain Maid and Hare – did some days ago. Pre-booking a self-catering place does commit one to the vagaries of the weather, yet the area offers options: superb weather, dash over to the Cuillin; good weather, the mainland peaks; or poor weather, a good choice of low level walks.

James Hogg on his Highland Tours in the early 1800s commented on the Glen Shiel district: 'The mountains are very high and steep, especially those of them most contiguous to the sea. The snow never continues long ... except on the heights, the frosts are seldom intense, but the winds and rains are frequent and terrible.' That weather pattern remains true today. For us the week got off to a miserable start and climbing Beinn Sgritheall in almost non-stop rain soon quashed our early holiday hillwalking enthusiasm.

The following morning, amid a pile of still-wet clothing and with yet more rain, all hillwalking plans were aborted. A short low-level walk was the order of the day. The Mountain Maid mentioned that the Kylerhea Otter Haven on the eastern tip of Skye would be of interest. From our mainland base the haven could also be reached by the Shiel Bridge/Mam Ratagain road to Glenelg and so to the ferry at Kyle Rhea. As Margaret had never been on that ferry, this was the approach taken.

The walk starts from the road junction at the east end of Glenelg village (map ref 820198), a two-mile stroll to the ferry point, crossing as foot passengers, then a mile walk to the otter haven.

The stroll (beneath umbrellas for us) to the ferry is delightful; a quiet single-track road hemmed in between craggy escarpments and the sandy Bernera Bay. The road goes past a path leading to Bernera Barracks. Using much of the stone pillaged from the Pictish Brochs in Gleann Beag (also worth a visit), the garrison was built post the 1715 Jacobite Rising to police crossings to and from Skye.

The ferry car park (also the start of a way marked trail) overlooks the small pier tucked away in a rocky cove. The lighthouse has an honesty box – help yourself to tea, coffee and gifts. There is also a bucket for donations, best given by coins and not notes; valuable contributions to support this the original ferry, and now community-owned. There is no need to book. The ferry operates until October sailing 10am to 6pm, seven days a week and crossing every 20 minutes. At the time of writing[2008], the fare is £2 return, but if you insist on taking a car (a waste for the short Skye road section) the fare is £15 return. A word of warning though – from the beginning of October the ferry runs on a day-to-day basis until not viable to continue, so it is best to enquire at www.skyeferry.co.uk or phone 01599-511-302.

You will enjoy the crossing through the swirling tide-race of Kyle Rhea and marvel at the skill of the two-man crew coping with both tide and manoeuvring the turntable holding cars and passengers alike. No wonder it was listed Best Ferry Journey in the *Scotsman* last year! If you do miss the boat, promise to go there next year, any time after Easter.

In the early days of the cattle drove from Skye to the Lowlands, the tide race – at times over ten knots – was a watery hazard and even during a period of slack water cattle were still lost on the swim across. Latterly cattle were transferred by boat.

Once on Skye, the dyke-enclosed road leads to a sign-posted tarmac side road at map ref 786208 that goes north to a car park and toilets. A good track then leads through woodland and descends slightly to the otter hide. The hide is open from 9am until one hour before dusk each day (for further information phone 01320-366-322).

Do not leave the paths or forest road and above all do not attempt to approach the shore. The otter is designated as a protected species and dogs should be left at home. Binoculars are essential, though there is of course no guarantee that otters will be spotted by the rocky shoreline. We were lucky, also seeing plenty of seals and herons. Who would be a fish!

96 The Falls of Glomach

FACTFILE

Map Ordnance Survey map 25, Glen Carron & Glen Affric
Distance 12 miles, of which 10 miles can be cycled
Height 350m
Terrain estate road, track and path
Start point car park by end of Loch Long road, map ref 941303
Time 5 to 6 hours walking; 3 hours if cycling
Nearest village Dornie
Recommended refreshment spot Dornie Hotel

Even to many a hillwalker, the insignificant Gleann Gaorsaic – only four miles long – may not be instantly identifiable. At its southern end is Loch a'Bhealaich ('loch of the mountain pass') – a charming stretch of water beside the line of an old west/east through-route from Kintail to Glen Affric. The outflow of the loch – the Abhainn Gaorsaic – meanders northwards down the watery glen. The river then changes its name to the Allt a'Ghlomaich and more importantly changes its very character as the water speeds up then hurtles over a steep cleft on the southern slopes of Glen Elchaig to join the River Elchaig. At this stage recognition may dawn for the cascade of water is known as the Falls of Glomach, at 370ft/113m one of the highest waterfalls in the United Kingdom and perhaps the most magnificent. (Eas a'Chuil Aluinn in Sutherland is alleged to be the tallest uninterrupted waterfall, albeit with a lesser volume of water.)

A popular route to the Falls starts from the National Trust for Scotland (NTS) property at Morvich. On a previous visit by that route I had the worst of all worlds:

a dull, damp day that followed a dry spell thus giving a slippery path yet less of a waterfall. 'Glomach', an anglicisation of *ghlomaich*, means 'gloomy'! This approach involves a three-mile walk, climbing some 500m to Bealach na Sroine, then a gentle one-mile descent during which you might start to doubt the whereabouts of the Falls, only to be reassured as the Allt a'Ghlomaich appears at the last moment. This signposted route to the Falls is peculiar in that it arrives at the top of the waterfall and so it is then necessary to descend on the west side, to fully appreciate the torrent of water.

Consequently I prefer an approach from Glen Elchaig to the north to see the Falls in full flow, although this still involves climbing by the water's edge. On a less-than-perfect weather day for the high tops, a visit to the Falls will give an enjoyable shorter outing – some three hours if using a bicycle, or five to six hours if walking all the way. Taking a bicycle will save a lot of walking, hence likely to appeal more to younger members of the family.

It should be noted that the Falls of Glomach lie in NTS property and hence there are no stalking restrictions.

The Falls appear on two Ordnance Survey maps: sheet 25 (Glen Carron & Glen Affric); and sheet 33 (Loch Alsh & Glen Shiel). However, as the initial approach from Killilan only appears on sheet 25, it would be prudent to take that map.

From the A87 just north of Dornie, follow the minor road on the north side of Loch Long to an estate car park at map ref 941303. It is then a charming five-mile cycle/walk up Glen Elchaig, passing the estate hamlet of Killilan. The first half is on an almost level tarmac road, with the remainder on a good estate track that eases the undulating 100m climb. Continue to map ref 009271, just west of the outflow of Loch na Leitreach (if you reach the loch you have gone too far), where a carved bench is both a marker for the Falls and a convenient resting spot.

Head south, descending slightly on the good path to reach the wooden footbridge over the River Elchaig. The path climbs slightly then crosses to the west bank of the Allt a'Ghlomaich. You can't miss the Falls. Take time to admire the gorge but be alert to its obvious dangers: steep slippery ground with a gentle scramble in places. Particular care should be taken on the return descent.

Rhona, Peter and I passed by on a recent visit – the bench a welcome stop en route to hillwalking further up Glen Elchaig. This was during a dry spell; ideal for hillwalkers no doubt, but not so good for the Falls. Even so, despite the reduced flow of water the steep cleft was still a dramatic feature. It is ironic that the very weather that might keep someone away from the hills actually increases the enjoyment and impact upon coming across the Falls. Unlike that earlier visit, the ideal time to see the Falls is on a dryish day, but the first day in weeks to have escaped torrential rain.

97 On the track from Attadale

FACTFILE

Map Ordnance Survey map 25, Glen Carron & Glen Affric
Distance 7 miles
Height 350m
Terrain estate road, then track
Start point car park at entrance to Attadale estate, map ref 924387
Time 4 to 5 hours
Nearest village Lochcarron
Recommended refreshment spot Carron Restaurant, Attadale

Attadale House – originally the seat of the clan Matheson – lies on the east side of Loch Carron in Wester Ross. Beyond the gardens (now open to the public) lies the 32,000-acre Attadale estate, described as a 'wilderness' of hills, lochs and waterfalls. Two such hills are Bidein a'Choire Sheasgaich and Lurg Mhor, far distant from the nearest road. The challenge of that remoteness is part of their attraction and how often do they appear in an imminent Munroist's short list of unclimbed peaks?

Some weeks ago I took one such imminent Munroist (the Mountain Lamb) on a trip from Attadale. The hills are normally tackled on the one – albeit long – day but, to make matters easier for the Lamb, one afternoon we cycled/pushed the bikes some seven miles to Bendronaig bothy. After an overnight stay at the bothy, we left at 7am to tackle the hills.

No matter the route taken, the hills involve a long day, even if climbed singly. Few would think of tackling them overnight, but the intrepid Hugh Munro did just that en route to Skye in June 1905. He left his home in Angus on the morning, reached Strathcarron station at 6pm and after a light meal started out at 7pm. He returned at 6am in time for a good rest before continuing to Skye.

In what says a lot about her hill planning, my sister Frances completed her round of Munros on Bidein a'Choire Sheasgaich in 1981. On a soaking wet day, out came the mandatory bottle of champagne. The cork soared into the mist and was lost to sight. Seconds later, as though cleaved by the cork, the clouds rolled away. I believe in the efficacy of champagne as a weather-improver, for it has worked elsewhere.

But enough of hills – what if you are in the Attadale area on holiday but having wretched luck with the weather? What to do about exercise if the high tops are not appealing? One lower-level solution is to take the start of the track that goes to Bendronaig Lodge and bothy (from mid-August to mid-October walkers are asked to stay on the track because of the deer cull), but only as far as the watershed before the long descent to Bendronaig. When the Mountain Lamb and I were there we were surprised by the number of walkers doing just that.

Bendronaig bothy

The walk gives a variety of terrain, with open views to west and north, two beautiful lochans and then views east to the distant hills.

Attadale Estate is hillwalker-friendly, evidenced by the provision of an off-road parking area by the A890 (with a welcoming sign) and by the rebuilding of the superb estate bothy – the eastern building by Bendronaig Lodge – for the use of hillwalkers. The estate should not be confused with another of similar name. Alladale, the subject of a TV programme, is in Sutherland and Easter Ross – a 23,000-acre estate owned by Paul Lister; he of the controversial plans to transform this vast uninhabited Highland estate into a nature reserve and re-introduce bears, wolves and other animals to Scotland.

Use the hillwalkers' car park by the A890 south of Attadale House (map ref 924387), at the entrance to the estate grounds. The first mile is on flat tarmac road that skirts Attadale gardens and goes past a second car park (designated for those visiting the gardens), then turns sharply to the right, southeast, parallel to the River Attadale. The tarmac road ends by some holiday cottages at Strathan, and then a track – still level – leads to the bridge over the river.

Now for the slightly harder work as the track – rougher in places – zigzags south. The gradient eases as the track turns to the southeast, and then passes two side-tracks to gently descend to beautiful Loch an Droighinn – a secluded spot and a mandatory resting place. The track then goes northeast, slowly climbing to a second loch – Loch na Caillich, nestling beneath a narrowing gully.

Beyond lies the soon-reached watershed at map ref 973374. By now at 350m after a sea-level start, enjoy the distant views of Bidein a'Choire Sheasgaich and Lurg Mhor, then head back to Attadale. On return, why not pay a visit to the gardens and nursery? Except on Sundays, the gardens and woodland walks are open from 10am to 5.30pm, until the end of October.

98 Easan Dorcha Teahouse and the Coulin Pass

FACTFILE

Map Ordnance Survey map 25, Glen Carron & Glen Affric
Distance 8 miles
Height 500m
Terrain excellent path and track
Start point Achnashellach on the A890, map ref 004484
Time 4 to 5 hours
Nearest villages Achnasheen and Lochcarron
Recommended refreshment spot Ledgowan Hotel, Achnasheen

Last month I wrote about a visit to the quartz-capped peak of Beinn Liath Mhor – a delightful hill west of the Coulin Pass that links Glen Torridon and Glen Carron. My account of that day ended with no mention as to how I returned to Achnashellach.

The assumption would have been that I simply retraced steps. I did not. Instead I made a lengthy but most enjoyable diversion to the small hut Easan Dorcha, better known as The Teahouse, and returned to the A890 over the Coulin Pass.

This week's walk follows that route, but of course not climbing Beinn Liath Mhor. Consequently, with no hill to climb and gradual gradients on path and track, this may appeal as an easier day – a walk of eight miles but a climb of only 500m. In addition the entire way is well maintained; paths and tracks in good order and all streams and rivers crossed by bridge – of some importance in these very wet times. Footpath maintenance is a thorny issue for hillwalkers. Who should maintain these old paths and construct new ones where too many boots have taken their toll? The estates, the government, the hillwalker? Some clubs have taken the initiative and Alex Joss of the Highland Hillwalking Club in Inverness writes about their decision to maintain the Coire Lair footpath from Achnashellach and over to the Teahouse:

> Footpath repair and maintenance may trouble some who retain a romanticised image of roaming free on unspoilt Scottish mountains. However, it is a realistic acceptance that our most heavily used approach-routes require

> strengthening of the path structure and restoration of the adjacent natural vegetation. The two objectives are interlinked: the first allows the second. A creditable amount of work has been completed in recent years, with sufficient funding to bring professional expertise into the initial construction of a sound footpath along the line of a well-used existing route. However, funding seldom provided for regular year-on-year maintenance. The club adopted this footpath in 2000, obtained written permission from the landowner, and successfully applied for Lottery funding. The latter provided for initial stocks of tools. The basic work can be done in two visits, one in spring, one in autumn, with as few as three volunteers. Avoid summer and midge nets become redundant. In taking on this type of project, perhaps the most important decision is the first. The footpath you adopt should be somewhere you feel you'll want to keep coming back to, because you'll have to!

Start from the red phone box at map ref 004484 on the A890 and take the track to the seldom-used Achnashellach station. Cross the railway line with due care. Follow the signposted route up to the bend of a forestry track and turn left. Carefully note this bend for return. Shortly after, turn left again to join a stalkers' path.

The path leads through the forest to emerge on the open hillside and then climbs steadily but easily into Coire Lair. The path reaches a couple of close-together path-junctions around map ref 991502, both marked by cairns. At the second junction, take the right fork going NNE to Drochaid Coire Lair. This saddle is at 380m and the hard work has been done. From this high point, there is a gentle descent of less than two miles to the Teahouse at map ref 012526.

It is in an enchanted spot at the junction of two streams: the main stream in a rocky ravine now mapped as Easan Dorcha ('dark waterfalls') and the Allt Coire Beinne Leithe arriving in a cascade of water over rocky slabs. The small wooden building is reached by estate track from Coulin Lodge, and was used as a comfortable place of leisure and shelter, presumably mostly by Victorian ladies not involved in manly pursuit of the stag. Supplies of refreshment were easily brought from the lodge, hence the name. Respect the unlocked bothy with no fireplace and note that no fires are permitted outside.

The return to Achnashellach is now all by track. Continue a further mile, cross the Easan Dorcha at a broad bridge and head south on the open and easy approach to the Coulin Pass. Take time at this 286m point admiring the views of Glen Carron and the hills beyond.

The broad forestry track descends 100m in gentle bends then turns westwards. Continue WSW on the long descent, ignoring a track to the right, and eventually reach the bend in the track carefully noted at the start of the walk. Return to the station.

99 Foinaven makes some Munros look second-class

FACTFILE

Map Ordnance Survey map 9, Cape Wrath
Distance 8 miles
Height 800m
Terrain rough moorland traverse to grassy, then quartz covered ridge
Start point small parking area on A838, two miles north-east of Rhiconich
Time 5 to 6 hours
Nearest village Rhiconich or Kinlochbervie
Recommended refreshment spot Rhiconich Hotel

It was the hillwalking story that never was – the widely-held assumption that the Corbett, Foinaven, following re-survey would be promoted to Munro status. You may recall the 'alarming' news story: dedicated Munro baggers may soon face the daunting prospect of having another two new peaks to conquer, Beinn Dearg and Foinaven.

Beinn Dearg had been planned as the first hill to be re-surveyed, but adverse weather caused abandonment when the surveyors and hillwalking porters were at 700m. In the event, it was resurveyed and is still under the 3,000ft mark. A joint announcement by the Munro Society and the surveying firm CMCR Limited at a meeting on 8 June 2007 confirmed that Foinaven's new height (ratified by the Ordnance Survey) had been revised, not up as expected but down – and well down at that. Foinaven now stands at 911m or 2989ft, quite a significant reduction from the previous 914m (3,000ft is 914.4m) and as such remains classified as a Corbett.

It was amusing to hear one newsman at that meeting reporting by mobile phone to his office: "It is not a new Munro, repeat, not a new Munro". 'Climbers can pack away their boots' was one newspaper report!

End of story? Well, no. Quite the opposite in fact for this unexpectedly large reduction in height has opened up a can of worms all wriggling to get out. It will no longer be a case of what Corbetts might be promoted, rather are there any borderline Munros that might be of insufficient height? Twelve of them have heights listed between 914m and 918m. Even with Ordnance Survey unlikely to mount an expensive re-survey project over such hills, this story will run and run (in fact, the Munro Sgurr nan Ceannaichean has now been demoted to Corbett status).

Its non-Munro status intact, Foinaven will still not attract hordes of walkers, though that number is likely to be slightly boosted as a result of the recent publicity. For the vast majority of hill walkers however, it is a long way to travel to Sutherland – a dramatic area of sculptured hills rising from moorland: Corbett country of which the best known – even to the racing fraternity – are Foinaven and Arkle. Rocky and scree-covered it may be, but Foinaven is just as fine a hill as it ever was and well worth the journey.

Foinaven is the name of the hill, a narrow north/south rough quartzite ridge stretching for two miles above 800m. The highest point, just north of the mid-point, is Ganu Mor, shown on my old edition of the OS map as 908m. West of the ridge, steep slopes fall to a glacier-scoured, lochan-studded and fascinating area. To the east, three impressive corries separate ridges that fall to Srath Dionard whose waters (eventually) flow to Kyle of Durness.

Foinaven is an anglicisation of *foinne-bheinn,* meaning 'wart mountain' – a reference to the many bumps on the ridge: the highest is Ganu Mor from *ceann mor* meaning 'big head'. All accurate descriptions but which fail to capture the magic that is Foinaven.

If coming from the south from Lairg on the A838, or from Ullapool on the A894, continue north past Laxford Bridge to Rhiconich. The A838 then gently climbs northeast and after two miles passes a waterfall on the west side at map ref 279546. There is a small parking area by the roadside.

The start of the walk is at 100m but little height is added on the traverse of often-wet moorland southeast then south, to cross the Allt na Claise Carnaich and reach the base of Creag na Claise Carnaich. That route skirts a number of small lochans – confusing terrain on a misty day. Only go on a dry and clear day when the route is fascinating.

By now at 150m the climb begins, heading ESE then southeast to the first of the 'warts', Ceann Garbh. The drier grassy ridge makes for easier walking until you reach steeper quartzite slopes. After a short descent south, curve east on rough arid quartz to Ganu Mor. There are two cairns a short distance apart. Visit both to be sure of the highest point. On a clear day, both Lewis and Orkney can be seen from the summit Do pick a good day to go.

My diary note recalls one of those days to remember: 'Climbed in mist, but near the top we came out of the cloud and the rest of the day was beautiful. Distant panoramic views from Harris to Orkney.' And my final entry: 'Foinaven makes some Munros look second-class.'

100 A wet day on Ben Hope

FACTFILE

Map Ordnance Survey map 9, Cape Wrath
Distance 4 miles
Height 900m
Terrain worn path, eroded and wet in places
Start point parking area, east side of minor road, map ref 462477
Time 3 to 4 hours
Nearest town Lairg
Recommended refreshment spot Crask Inn

Last month five of us had an enjoyable self-catering stay in Ullapool. Jimbo, Bruce and I were the keen hillwalkers. Mary (Jimbo's wife) has more sense and their granddaughter, Cara, has better playtime interests.

After the long drive from the south, it made sense to head for the northerly hills that could be climbed on a day trip. The obvious candidate was Ben Hope – the most northerly Munro. Our 80 mile cross-country route – via Ledmore Junction and Lairg, then passing the Crask Inn – was nevertheless a slow drive. Ben Hope stands in splendid isolation, well apart from other hills: a de-populated area that still carries the legacy of the Highland clearances. For almost everyone that means a long drive and an overnight stay.

Named by the Vikings for whom its conical shape was a navigational aid, Ben Hope means 'hill of the bay' from the Old Norse *hop*. When viewed from the north end of Loch Hope, the hill's appearance is symmetrical and pleasing. I have a small watercolour painted from there, a glorious reminder of a lovely hill.

Ben Hope lies east of the meandering Strathmore River, which flows into the southern end of Loch Hope. A steep, craggy escarpment runs almost the full length of the western side of the hill from the Moine Path in the north to beyond the broch, Dun Dornaigil, in the south. Only the southern slopes are gentle and easy and it is no surprise that they form the popular approach.

The A836 runs north from Lairg. On reaching Altnaharra take the single track road west, then north into Strath More. You may need a road map for the drive. For the hill you will need Ordnance Survey map 9 (Cape Wrath).

At map ref 462477 there is a small parking area on the east side of the road where a stream tumbles down from the escarpment that guards the west flank of Ben Hope. There is even a signpost, saying 'Ben Hope'.

Ben Hope is an easy day out ... once you get there. At 3041ft/927m it is not a particularly big hill (albeit with a start close to sea level) and with a distance of two miles to the top, the gradient on the popular route is easy. Bearing in mind the long journey, most hillwalkers – even on a poor day – simply go ahead and climb the hill regardless. The weather forecast for our day had been favourable. The actuality was somewhat different. We sat in the car for a while, then put on waterproofs as we muttered, "we've

The northern guardian of Ben Hope

No views, no dawdling at the trig point

come a long way, it is not a full day so let's get on with it". Jimbo had been keen to climb the much harder northern ridge, a route I had used on the previous visit. The ridge is a classic in coming out close to the top, but should be kept for a good day. Today it was to be the popular route.

Follow the worn Munro path by the side of the stream in a northeasterly direction, heading for the gap in the escarpment. This section is steep, eroded and boggy in places. Ironically however, erosion has removed some of the top-soil so that in places the sub-soil now provides a better path. Once through the escarpment at map ref 471483, the going is much easier on a gentler slope, grassy at first, then stony, on a well marked eroded path that keeps east of the escarpment.

Previous better chosen days have seen me dawdle on the top for more than an hour. Ben Hope is one of the finest viewpoints in Scotland, but you do need a good day. The view is enhanced by going a very short distance north from the cairn. Northwards lies the open sea with Orkney visible on a clear day. To the northwest is Cape

Wrath, not quite the most northerly point of mainland Britain. That title belongs not to John o' Groats, but to nearby Dunnet Head.

No views this time for us. We touched the cairn and headed downhill in the mist and rain, following the eroded path. On the way down you could remove some of the unsightly and quite unnecessary cairns that sprout there despite the efforts of myself and others. Bruce and I demolished quite a few; other wet hillwalkers were encouraged to participate.

On return to Ullapool – having spent more time in the car than on the hill – it was difficult to explain to Mary why the wet day had been so enjoyable. Cara just wanted to play football.

More Quality Books . . .

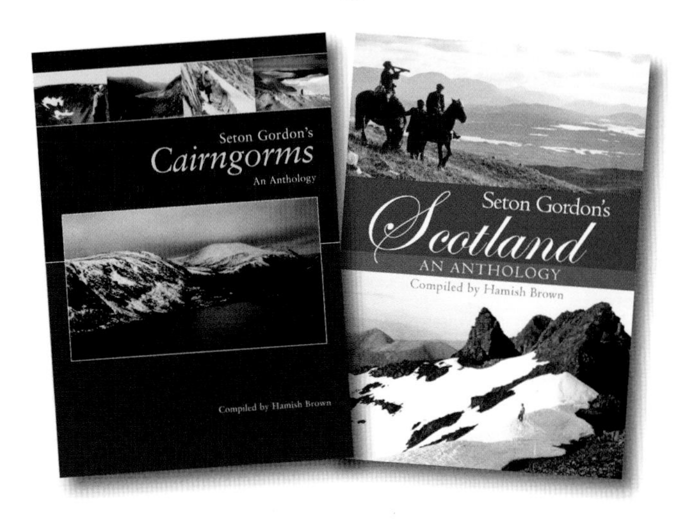